Modernization
and the Transformation
of International Relations

Perspectives on Modernization
Cyril E. Black, General Editor

Comparative Modernization: A Reader, Cyril E. Black

The Modernization of Japan and Russia,
Cyril E. Black, Marius B. Jansen, Herbert S. Levine,
Marion J. Levy, Jr., Henry Rosovsky, Gilbert Rozman,
Henry D. Smith, II, S. Frederick Starr

*Modernization and the Transformation of
International Relations,* Edward L. Morse

Modernization and the Transformation of International Relations

Edward L. Morse

THE FREE PRESS
A Division of Macmillan Publishing Co., Inc.
NEW YORK

Collier Macmillan Publishers
LONDON

The Free Press
A Division of Macmillan Publishing Co., Inc.
866 Third Avenue, New York, N.Y. 10022

Collier Macmillan Canada, Ltd.

Library of Congress Catalog Card Number: 75-32367

Printed in the United States of America

printing number

1 2 3 4 5 6 7 8 9 10

Library of Congress Cataloging in Publication Data

Morse, Edward L
    Modernization and the transformation of inter-
national relations.

    (Perspectives on modernization)
    Includes index.
    1. International relations. I. Title.
JX1391.M65   327   75-32367
ISBN 0-02-922200-1

For Linda

Contents

List of Illustrations

Acknowledgments

I am particularly indebted to Marion J. Levy, Jr. and Cyril E. Black of Princeton University who suggested that I write an extended essay on the effects of modernization on the international system, and to Susan and John Darley who proposed a perfect setting in which to draft the manuscript. Leon Gordenker, also of Princeton University, read through earlier versions of the manuscript with his characteristic diligence and care and made valuable suggestions for revision. Fouad Ajami, Miriam Camps, William Diebold, Ronald Goodman, Roger Hansen, Pierre Hassner, Jeanne Laux, Linda Morse, James Nathan, Harold and Margaret Sprout, Richard Ullman, and Richard Weisberg provided inciteful criticisms. Dorothy Dey, Barbara Healy, Wanda Prorock, and Laurie Sands typed the manuscript with diligence and care. Germaine Hoston and Jerome Kalmus, former research assistants, exercised invaluable critical judgments. I owe an enormous debt to all of them, and especially to my students whose critical reactions to arguments I made in lectures and seminars I greatly appreciate.

Chapters 4 and 5 contain revisions of arguments I put forward in Part I of *Foreign Policy and Interdependence in Gaullist France* (Princeton, N.J.: Princeton University Press, 1973). I am especially grateful to Pierre Hassner and Stanley Hoffmann, who provided helpful criticisms of that book and whose insights into international relations I have always found inspiring.

Introduction

Hitherto, all politics gambled on the *isolation of events*. History was made up of events that could be *localized*. Any disturbance had, at one point on the globe as it were, a boundless medium in which to reverberate; its effects were nil at a sufficient distance; everything went on in Tokyo as though Berlin were at infinity. It was therefore possible—it was even reasonable—to predict, to calculate, and to act. There was room in the world for one or several great policies well planned and carried out.

That time is coming to an end. Henceforward every action will be re-echoed by many unforeseen interests on all sides; it will produce a chain of immediate events—confused reverberations in a closed space.

Paul Valéry, *Regards sur le monde actuel* (1931).

Modernization represents nothing less than the complete transformation of international relations. A profound sense that the social order of the twenteith century is qualitatively different from anything that preceded it in human history has gained wide acceptance during the past seventy or eighty years. Moreover, this notion that international affairs no longer conform to implicit or explicit models of international behavior or to historical antecedents is by no means unique. It was frequently asserted by essayists, novelists, and even statesmen from the onset of the twentieth century. Paul Valéry, the prominent French poet, dramatist and essayist (1871–1945) quoted above (emphasis is his), was but one of many observers who, in witnessing the industrialization of Europe and World War I, was acutely sensitive to the unfolding of a new era in domestic and international relations. He had remarked on the end of the "era of free expansion" that was reached with the wave of European imperialism at the close of the nineteenth century and on the phenomenal growth of international interdependence that then ensued.[1] He had seen the transference of European habits and institutions to non-European regions of the world and predicted that the once great powers of his native continent would play a much diminished role in the world by the end of the twentieth century. Finally, Valéry pointed up the cause of this great transformation in human social life both domestically and internationally. It was science, he felt, which has transformed life and vastly increased the power of those who possess it. But by its very nature science is essentially transmissible; it is necessarily reducible to universal methods and formulas. The means it affords to some, all can acquire.[2]

This book is concerned with the central themes that Valéry and other writers sensed to be characteristic of modern international behavior. It represents an effort to describe and to explain what is unique and new about international relations in the contemporary world. It therefore will touch upon a wide variety of phenomena that I view to be central to an understanding of international affairs today. These include the norms and forms of modern statecraft, the ideal and actual behavior of foreign policy decision makers, the great upheavals that international society has witnessed in recent years, the expanded scope of diplomacy, the meaning and significance of the increase in international interdependence, and other phenomena that have resulted in the emergence of a transformed international system.

The argument presented in this essay rests on two suppositions. First, it presupposes that the development of the set of phenomena that have

---

[1] "An entirely new, excessive, and immediate interdependence between regions and events is the already perceptible consequence of this great fact [of the finite world]," he argued. "Henceforth we must see all political phenomena in the light of this new situation in the world; every one of them occurs either in obedience or in resistance to the effects of this definitive limitation and ever closer mutual dependence of human actions. The habits, ambitions, and loyalties formed in the course of earlier history do not cease to exist—but being insensibly transferred into quite differently constructed surroundings, they there lose their meaning and become causes of error and fruitless striving." *History and Politics* (New York: Bollingen Foundation, 1962 [1931]), pp. 15–16.

[2] Ibid., p. 17.

lately been labeled "modernization" have affected all the major dimensions of international politics in dramatic and transformational ways, and that they have served to undermine the stability upon which international politics previously relied. Second, it rests on the faith that these changes in statecraft can be understood through the application of the empirical method in human affairs, and that any hope for controlling the destabilizing effects of modernization depends upon the development of knowledge which is highly general and well tested.

As is evident from the title of this essay, it falls into one of two prevailing perspectives for intellectually coming to grips with contemporary international politics. One perspective assumes that the dynamics of international politics have been relatively fixed since the inception of the modern state system. Accordingly, a theory of international political behavior applicable to Europe in the seventeenth century would be appropriate for understanding global politics today. Different actors may have appeared on the world stage, new issues may have become the central concerns of diplomacy, but, in the terms of this school of thought, a set of basic "rules of the game" has been imposed upon international politics and can be derived from the prevailing conditions of the international system. If, as this view would maintain, there is no overarching structure of political authority, or no central government in the international system, then statesmen everywhere will be centrally concerned with maximizing the security of their political systems. Their actions, it is thought, are largely determined by the availability of resources and by the geopolitical setting, while their interactions are subjected to what Raymond Aron has called the "indeterminacy of diplomatic-strategic behavior."[3] In other words, once a theory or set of theories of international political behavior is developed, other factors may intervene by changing the conditions of the environment in which international politics takes place, but the theory itself would largely explain international behavior over time.

A second viewpoint, and the one represented here, focuses on the mutable aspects of statecraft. It is addressed to those conditions that the first perspective treats as environing factors, or to the context

---

[3] Raymond Aron, *Peace and War: A Theory of International Relations,* translated by Richard Howard and Annette Baker Fox (Garden City, N.Y.: Doubleday, 1966), p. 88.

in which international politics takes place. Proponents of this perspective would argue that as the result of conditions fostered by the advent of industrialization, the rise of high mass consumption societies, the emergence of mass politics and other concomitants of the processes of modernization, none of the traditional assumptions concerning the norms and structures of diplomatic behavior have gone untouched. Furthermore, they would maintain, the scale and scope of change in these environing factors have been so great that traditional statecraft has been and is continuously transformed. As a result, classical treatments of statecraft no longer serve to explain international political behavior. Traditional assumptions concerning alliances, the use of force, the role of economic diplomacy, the processes of foreign policy decision making, or the norms embodied in the international legal order are, as will be argued below, part of a paradigm of international affairs that is no longer adequate for explaining contemporary conditions. Rather, we seem to be in an era without a general concurrence on a paradigm that would serve to explain the changes that the international system has undergone.

This essay, then, is concerned with the reasons why the traditional paradigm for understanding international politics has become obsolete as well as with a description of some of the fundamental elements of the contemporary international system. It is for this reason that the emphasis is on the transformation of international relations. For my predilection throughout is to point out the novelties injected into contemporary statecraft by the processes of modernization. The framework into which this essay falls—the one that has a regard for the changing context of diplomacy—has become fashionable in recent years. Descriptions of changes in international politics in the twentieth century inevitably focus upon great transformations that have occurred in the international system and in the conduct of foreign policy. But no one to my knowledge has adduced an adequate explanation for them.[4] Advocates of a transformation which

---

[4]William T. R. Fox and Annette Baker Fox have described their view of these transformations as follows: "A list of these great transformations would include: (1) the expansion of the European state system into a world system, with the superpowers peripheral to Europe playing unprecedented roles in a bipolar system; (2) the diffusion outward from Europe to the Afro-Asian world of nationalism and of demands for rising living standards and the dignity of participation in the political process; (3) the democratization of the control of foreign relations at the same time that the widened sphere of state activity has made the conduct

would make the world a more decent place to inhabit usually base their position on an ideological sort of explanation whose importance resides in its reflection of the ways that rapid change has disrupted social relationships and has led men to seek utopian goals that, if achieved, would enable them to reintegrate themselves into their physical and social landscapes. We find such explanations in both Marxism and "dependence theories." But these explanations have little empirical validity, their scientific claims notwithstanding. Their importance resides in the way the norms they embody themselves reflect changes in values and orientations that are also part of the processes of the great transformations in international behavior.

What I hope to do here is to synthesize both the descriptive and normative viewpoints and to adduce the ways in which they stem from a perspective on international affairs that hypothesizes that the major ideal and actual structures of international politics have been transformed by the processes of modernization. In particular I hope to show that the structures of international society formed with the Westphalia system in the seventeenth century, have been submitted to accelerating change; that by the mid-twentieth century qualitative changes occurred in international society that were so great that it no longer conformed to the vocabulary traditionally used to described it; and that international society today is represented by a confusing set of overlapping structures that can be separated analytically for general discussion.

I am under no illusion that the analysis presented here represents a well-substantiated theoretical viewpoint. Nor am I convinced that I have actually demonstrated an entirely convincing linkage between the processes of modernization and changes in statecraft. The relationship between these processes and the transformations in international society are supported only by streams of indirect and often conflicting evidence. Although no one to my mind has yet made a strong or

---

of foreign relations ever more complex and difficult; (4) the sudden emergence of science and technology as great and semi-independent variables in the equations of world politics; (5) the drawing-together of the old states of Europe and the transoceanic states of European culture in varying forms of association, such as the European Coal and Steel Community, the British Commonwealth, and NATO; and (6) the new necessity, especially for the superpowers, to do things in peacetime which many states formerly did only in war—maintain a high level of defense mobilization, engage in coalition military planning, finance a massive foreign aid program, and develop a vigorous psychological strategy." *The American Study of International Relations* (Columbia: University of South Carolina, Institute of International Studies, 1967), pp. 16–17.

powerful theoretical link between the two, I feel strongly that efforts will be made in this direction in research during the coming years. Moreover, I feel that this theoretical task is an urgent one. International affairs today no longer conform to the theories of power politics that have been said to characterize an anarchic international system. Nor do they correspond to the utopias of world government depicting a single international society, although aspects of both are ubiquitous. Rather, foreign policy and international relations, are in a transitional position and assume mixed and, as I shall try to explain below, unstable forms. Conventional wisdom does not seem to me to be adequate for understanding or coping with changes that have occurred. Change has been so disordering to the world in which policy makers work that efforts to come to grips with it have become urgent political concerns. Yet policy, more than ever, must be based on sound theory. It must be predicated upon an understanding of the costs of manipulating different variables and of the relationships among these variables in the process of change. If change has accelerated, as many writers have argued, and if its effects have become more generalized than ever before, it must be brought under human control. Unless social scientists begin to formulate innovative explanations for the changes occurring during this century, such control will result only by accident, and we all might succumb to technologically engendered social upheaval more by reason of our stupidity than through the malice of some domestic or foreign enemy.

This book, then, represents what I consider to be a start at this sort of theoretical exegesis. It is still no more than a perspective. But I feel that the policy implications that follow from it are both obvious and significant. Officials who are responsible for formulating and implementing policies cannot postpone their actions until the day when the requisite theoretical knowledge is on hand. But they need not face situations of uncertainty in a complete theoretical void. Some of the knowledge of the effects of modernization on international affairs—especially on the growth of international interdependence—is already available and can serve them well. Such knowledge, however uncertain and weak, is real knowledge and can serve to sensitize officials to the additional range of political issues which have accompanied the new statecraft.

Modernization and the Transformation of International Relations

1
The Revolution of Modernization and the Interstate System

It has become part of conventional wisdom that the twentieth century has witnessed great transformations in the structure of international politics. At the beginning of the twentieth century the major decisions of foreign policy were taken by the great powers of Europe. With the exception of Germany and Italy, formed in the last half of the nineteenth century, these powers were the same ones that had dominated the interstate system since the consolidation of the modern European states in the sixteenth and seventeenth centuries. Diplomats were concerned largely with minimizing the probability that war would break out. They did this through conscious attempts to maintain what they felt to be an equilibrium among the major states—an equilibrium that was supported by shifting alignments among the powers. Although the balance had become more stabilized or polarized than it had been a century before, and although tribute was occasionally paid through the rhetoric of politicians to the desires of public opinion, diplomacy looked a great deal like it had always been. Indeed, the problems and vocabulary of statecraft had not changed significantly since the formal beginning of the modern state system at Westphalia in 1648.[1]

[1] The significance of the Westphalia model is discussed in more detail in the next chapter.

If one contrasts the structure of international society, the style of diplomacy, or the problems of statecraft today with those of fifty years ago, it quickly becomes apparent that more aspects of international affairs have changed in the past half century than in the previous two hundred fifty years, and that these changes have been qualitatively more momentous. The major states today are almost all extra-European for the first time since the emergence of the modern state system; the number of states in the system has increased threefold, and this has had the effect of changing the quality and complexity of diplomatic activity; there has been an expansion of the central issues of international politics beyond the focus upon state security and the use of force to the economic issues related to the scope and terms of trade; economic development has emerged as a major goal of the vast majority of states for the first time; domestic political considerations seem now to assume greater importance in foreign policy decision making than ever before; and, the norms of international behavior have expanded considerably beyond a focus on the use of force to questions of the most equitable distribution of welfare and the expansion of economic well-being.

These changes on the surface of international politics also reflect other trends that lurk behind them and that are not obviously linked to statecraft. Yet their importance for statecraft transcends the shifting locus of the axes of international relations. The expansion of the state system outside its original European center, for example, was directly related to the ability of the Europeans to transport goods, men, and weapons quickly and cheaply throughout the globe. Lower transportation costs and faster means of transportation became available to them relatively quickly, so that the great powers were able efficiently to colonize or otherwise dominate non-European societies. The emergence of new great powers outside the European framework reflected new requisites of power in terms of population size, scope of internal markets, and availability of resources, once these factors became determinate for economic growth. The depreciation of the utility of military force resulted paradoxically and dramatically from the accelerated development of more and more powerful weapons until the marginal benefits gained from increased firepower became disproportionately negative, since destructive capabilities were too great to be used. The expanded range of issues that have entered diplomacy, including economic issues related to expanded trade or the redistribution of the world's wealth, reflects not only conscious efforts to dismantle tariff barriers to trade but also, and perhaps more significantly, the dramatic increase in economic production that has occurred in the last one hundred years. Increased productivity not only has made it plausible for people to raise their expectations for material well-being but has become a self-fulfilling prophecy by inciting them to make demands on their governments that can be satisfied only through increased productivity coupled with higher levels of trade. Finally, changes in the normative aspects of international politics, including the rise of pacifism and demands on the part of poorer societies of the world for a redistribution of wealth, stem largely from the politicization of ever-increasing sectors of the population everywhere for a more adequate material basis for life.[2]

Perhaps the most momentous of all of the changes has to do with the question of the fate of the nation-state as the basic unit of international society. For several centuries the autonomous nation-state became increasingly the major political institution under which people organized their social relations. With the rise of nationalism in the nineteenth and twentieth centuries and the expansion of the state system from some fifty to some one hundred fifty individual states, the viability of the individual political communities seems to have been reinforced. Yet with the spread of industrialization and dramatic increases in the levels and scope of international interdependence the autonomy of these units in areas that seem requisite for their viability—in defense, in economic planning, or in conflict management—seems to have been undermined. This reduction in state autonomy, moreover, has occurred simultaneously with a marked expansion of the political goals that governments have everywhere adopted. As a result, new instabilities have been injected into international relations that are unique to the contemporary world. Effective decision making for *both* domestic and international affairs now requires centralization or collaboration between governments in increasing numbers of areas. But such collaboration requires the relinquishing of independent powers of decision-making that few, if any, governments are willing to lose.

All the basic transformations that have taken place in the international system, in short, are relatively easy to describe. Moreover, they seem to be linked directly to the high level of industrialization of a rather small part of the world and to the concomitant social and

[2]For a related description of changes in the international system, which is discussed in the context of the international configuration of forces that emerged after World War II, see Seyom Brown, *New Forces in World Politics* (Washington: Brookings, 1974).

political changes wrought by that process. But it is insufficient to identify this causative factor simply as the process by which economies have become industrialized, because increased productivity is apparently only one manifestation of a much larger syndrome. Rather, it seems to me that the underlying sources of the recent and dramatic changes in statecraft are better understood through the concept of "modernization," even at the risk of placing an empty label on a syndrome of phenomena, because its usage has been so diluted and is full of contradictions. The concept remains useful, after all, because it labels something that has brought novelty into all aspects of human affairs for the first time, perhaps, since the invention of agriculture and the domestication of animals nine thousand to ten thousand years ago. It represents one of the two or three revolutionary changes that mankind has undergone since human beings came into existence.

The dramatic and revolutionary effects of modernization have been noted and documented in the burgeoning literature on this subject.[3] Perhaps the most startling evidence of revolutionary change in human life is the size of the population level that available technology and energy resources have been able to support. Explosive and exponential population growth has accompanied each of these revolutions in human affairs. Paleolithic societies, which predominated for the approximately one million years that men inhabited the earth before the agrarian revolution, could not support populations in excess of 2.5 persons per square mile,[4] and for a variety of reasons, including the state of sanitation and ignorance of medical care, the populations of such societies were relatively stagnant. By the time the agrarian revolution occurred, human population was probably at a level of 7 to 10 million. Both the agricultural revolution and the industrial revolution resulted in explosions of human population that broke the equilibria

[3]Cyril E. Black, for example, claims that "the process of change in the modern era is of the same order of magnitude as that from pre-human to human life and from primitive to civilized societies; it is the most dynamic of the great revolutionary transformations in the conduct of human affairs." *The Dynamics of Modernization: A Study in Comparative History* (New York: Harper & Row, 1966), p. 4. Marion J. Levy, Jr., similarly believes "that there is something peculiar, something 'new under the sun,' about the structures of relatively modernized societies." *Modernization and the Structure of Societies: A Setting for International Affairs* (Princeton, N.J.: Princeton University Press, 1966), p. 14.

[4]See especially Carlo Cipolla, *The Economic History of World Population* (Baltimore: Penguin, 1962), pp. 73–106.

that had been previously established. "First of all," as Cipolla explains, "as they follow the diffusion of the Revolution, they become world wide. Secondly, they tend to be of exceptional intensity and magnitude."[5] Evidence of these revolutions, in short, can be found in a persistent and exponential population growth—a growth that gives evidences of an increased control over the physical environment by men. The scope and timing of these demographic explosions can be seen on Figure 1. As a result of the agrarian revolution, world population increased rather steadily so that it reached approximately 850 million people by the time the industrial revolution was under way. After that, the eruption of population was even more momentous, the exponential increase bearing witness to arguments that many observers now offer for controlling population growth. They claim that such control is one of the crucial problems of world affairs today—at the same degree of importance as minimizing the outbreak of war (about which, in fact, far more has been done).[6]

The exponential curves which describe the growth of the world's population since 1750 are highly generalizable and can be used to describe more than demographic change. Whether one looks at the destructive radius of weapons, changes in available transportation or communication rates, the use of energy, the number of technical journals printed in the world, the number of universities, university attendance, economic productivity, or a multitude of other phenomena since the late eighteenth or early nineteenth centuries, similar exponential tendencies obtain.[7] They provide graphic and empirical evidence of the dramatic and radical changes that have occurred in the world since the industrial revolution. They also lead to several questions that are of momentous importance for our understanding of international politics today. For example, are these trends the reflections of more generalized phenomena that would provide greater enlightenment for understanding contemporary global politics? Is the fact that they have each occurred within the same time span fortuitous? Can we ex-

[5] Ibid., pp. 84–85.

[6] See, for example, Richard A. Falk, *This Endangered Planet* (New York: Random House, 1971), pp. 132–159; and Bernard Brodie, "The Impact of Technological Change on the International System: Reflections on Prediction," *Journal of International Affairs*, XXV:2 (1971), pp. 209–223.

[7] For graphic descriptions of these, see Bruce M. Russett, *Trends in World Politics* (New York: Macmillan, 1965), pp. 7–14.

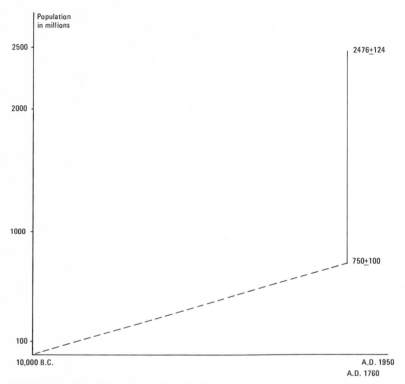

FIGURE 1. The Growth of World Human Population, 10,000 B.C. To A.D. 1950

From *The Economic History of World Population* by Carlo M. Cipolla, 6th ed., 1974, p. 114. Copyright © Carlo M. Cipolla, 1974. Reprinted by permission of Penguin Books, Ltd.

pect them to peak in the near future, or do they point up a set of indefinitely accelerating tendencies? Do they imply that changes today are qualitatively as well as quantitatively different from changes in previous eras? Can we find any relationships between scope and rate of change and problems which enter statecraft?

There are a number of compelling reasons to link together the exponential growth curves described above. In particular, they seem to be related to one of the defining characteristics of contemporary social relations—namely, that they are historically unique insofar as changes in them reflect the unprecedented and cumulative effects of increased knowledge that has grown out of the scientific revolution—[8] and in particular to what the economist Simon Kuznets refers to as "the extended application of science to problems of economic production."[9] The application of scientific, i.e., well-tested and reliable, knowledge with its technological implications to economic affairs, then, seems to be a major source of change in contemporary societies and will be a subject to which I shall refer throughout this essay.

It is clear that the application of scientific knowledge to economic affairs did not achieve continuous and self-sustained growth until sometime in the middle to late nineteenth century in England, the United States, and Western Europe.[10] Only by the mid-twentieth century could a group of states be clearly identified as having "high mass consumption" or highly modernized societies.[11] In defining these societies I will follow Levy, who "take[s] as the measure of modernization the ratio of inanimate to animate sources of power. The higher that ratio, the higher is the degree of modernization."[12] Although

---

[8] Black, for example, defines modernization as "the process by which historically evolved institutions are adapted to the rapidly changing functions that reflect the unprecedented increase in man's knowledge, permitting control over his environment, that accompanied the scientific revolution." *The Dynamics of Modernization*, p. 7.

[9] Simon Kuznets, *Modern Economic Growth: Rate, Structure, and Spread* (New Haven, Conn.: Yale University Press, 1966), p. 9.

[10] As Kuznets argues, "It was the *application* [of science] that was crucial, not merely for the economic growth that ensued but almost equally for its feedback effects upon the growth of science itself—a kind of self-stimulation of further economic growth." Ibid., p. 11.

[11] Russett and others have identified these as the Netherlands, West Germany, France, Denmark, Norway, the United Kingdom, Belgium, New Zealand, Australia, Sweden, Luxembourg, Switzerland, Canada, and the United States. See Bruce Russett and others, *World Handbook of Political and Social Indicators* (New Haven, Conn.: Yale University Press, 1964), p. 298. Their rankings were based on a composite index that included GNP per capita, percentage of population living in urban settings, literacy, and higher education characteristics of the population.

[12] Marion J. Levy, Jr., *Modernization: Latecomers and Survivors* (New York: Basic Books, 1972), p. 3. I agree in general with Levy that this is a convenient definition because it is fruitful for the formulation of hypotheses and because it avoids some of the pitfalls of other definitions. In particular I do not feel it necessarily leads to economic biases in analysis, and I think it avoids a weakness of Black's definition that is discussed below.

elements of modernity have virtually always existed in societies, the unique syndrome of characteristics associated with modernized societies (in terms of specialization of organized units, their self-sufficiency, level of centralization for decision making, etc.) emerges only in the nineteenth century, and it is only within the last seventy years or so that higher levels of modernization have occurred. What distinguishes modernized societies, then, from those which relatively are not modernized is "that comparatively small decreases of that ratio [of inanimate to animate sources of power] would have far-reaching effects—effects almost certain to be judged by the people involved as catastrophic."[13] The phenomena with which I am dealing, then, are extremely recent. And the special set of problems I am discussing can be said to be both novel and germane only to the contemporary international system.

If the use of inanimate sources of power and tools to multiply human efforts became highly generalized and increased with accelerating momentum only in the last one hundred to two hundred years, the scientific revolution upon which it is based has a longer pedigree. In fact, the scientific revolution is usually identified with Newtonian physics in the seventeenth century just as the origin of the modern state system is usually dated from that time. There are, however, important reasons for not identifying modernization either with the scientific revolution, as Black does, or with the rise of the nation-state, as Huntington and other theorists of modernization might prefer.[14]

---

[13]Ibid. Levy continues, "More simply put, I regard a society as modernized whenever small decreases in uses of inanimate sources of power could not be made up by increases in animate sources of power without far-reaching social changes. Not the least of such changes might be radical increases in death rates."

[14]Samuel Huntington, who is interested in explaining political modernization as a phenomenon independent of other aspects of social modernization, argues that political modernization has three characteristics: "First, it involves the rationalization of authority: the replacement of a large number of traditional, religious, familial, and ethnic political authorities by a single, secular, national political authority. . . . Secondly, political modernization involves the differentiation of new political functions and the development of specialized structures to perform those functions. Areas of peculiar competence—legal, military, administrative, scientific—become separated from the political realm, and autonomous, specialized, but subordinate, organs arise to discharge those tasks. . . . Thirdly, political modernization involves increased participation in politics by social groups throughout society and the development of new political institutions—such as political parties and interest associations—to organize this participation." "Political Modernization: America vs. Europe," *World Politics,* XVIII:3 (April 1966), p. 378.

In the first place, this identification may confuse modernization with important aspects of its political requisites. It has been argued that no relatively modernized society, i.e., one on this side of a line dividing relatively modernized from relatively nonmodernized societies, existed before the late nineteenth century. At the same time, aspects of modernity were obviously present, as in political institutions or in growing secularization. But what one seeks in defining a modernized society, while recognizing no end state in the process of modernization, is a set of criteria that would facilitate holistic accounts.

Second, the identifications made by Black or Huntington tend to confuse modernization with its historical origins. Obviously modernization has depended upon the scientific revolution and would not have occurred without it. But an identification of historical origins lends itself to the establishment of no criteria for determining a starting point. The seventeenth-century revolution in science has its determinants just as do the political changes that facilitated the unification of the modern political state. At best the historical definition of modernization would bring the cutoff point to an earlier date that would in my mind inhibit some of the important analytic distinctions I would like to make.

Third, and most important, this definition would equate the entire history of modern diplomacy with the modernization process. It thus would turn our focus away from the dramatic changes in statecraft that have occurred in the past one hundred to two hundred years, after several modernized societies emerged. And it would not give us the standards of comparison that are provided by the norms and operations of the state system that developed in seventeenth- and eighteenth-century Europe and that were transformed by the modernization process.

It is more convenient, then, to place emphasis on a later historical period, after the industrial revolution began to transform international affairs. Our interest is in what has occurred in the structure of the international system and the process of foreign policy making since highly modernized societies emerged.

The first structural change that accompanied modernization, and one of the most important, was the creation of high levels of *interdependence* in the relationships among most societies. The growth in interdependence, defined carefully in Chapter 5, is related, in the first place, to the cumulative effects of the application of scientific knowledge to human affairs. For the essence of cumulative knowledge is that it is inherently *transnational*. Once it is developed, it is exceedingly difficult, if not impossible, to create a national monopoly on it. "No matter where these technological and social innovations emerge," as Kuznets has argued, "the economic growth of any given nation depends upon their adoption. In that sense, whatever the national affiliation of resources used, any single nation's economic growth has its base somewhere outside its boundaries—with the single exception of the pioneering nation, and no nation remains the pioneer for long."[15]

The cumulative effects of knowledge and the consequent dependence of continuous modernization upon the development of institutions of higher education were largely a product of changes in the more modernized societies. As is indicated by the exponential growth curves examined above, the growth in the transnational stock of knowledge did not serve to affect international interdependence until after the industrial revolution enabled it to become a self-sustaining effort.

The most significant effect of the growth on international interdependence that has emerged is that it severely diminished the ability of governments to achieve national autonomy, the central goal that had been built into the traditional state system. This was perhaps first apparent in the goal of economic development, but it also affected traditional aspects of statecraft, including the classical goal of military security. And the upshot in both cases has been the questioning of the adequacy of the nation-state as a political unit capable of fulfilling goals that have emerged in virtually every national society.

The curves tracing the exponential growth of science and of economic productivity with which this discussion began point up a second characteristic of the contemporary international system—namely, that the structures of relations among the political systems in it, like the growth of science upon which they inevitably depend, are inherently *transitional*. Therefore, few of the structures are permanent and most are not likely to endure for long. The transitional nature of this system can be understood whether one accepts one or the other of the meanings that are usually associated with the term. For some people, social affairs are transitional because they are characterized by persistent change that has become the most fundamental and, paradoxically, most perma-

---

[15] Kuznets, *Modern Economic Growth*, p. 287.

nent feature of modern life.[16]   In looking at an exponential curve, where the order of magnitude of change accelerates, this implies that the quality of social life also continuously changes.

For others, international affairs are transitional because we live, as Zbigniew Brzezinski argues, in a transition "between two ages":[17] between the past age of the nation-state and some unknown future. The theoretical reasons for arguing this second view are strong, if not compelling. If, in fact, much of the change we have experienced is exponential, then the one thing of which we can be sure is that it cannot continue to accelerate at its current rates indefinitely. The growth of science and consequent growth in numbers of scientists, for example, cannot continue indefinitely (and indeed may have already reached a saturation point) because continued growth would mean that everyone on earth would have to become a scientist. Nor can the rates of population growth and of energy use continue, lest they exhaust the resources of the world. As one historian of science, Derek J. de Solla Price, argues, the transition through which human societies have been going seems to conform to a natural exponential growth cycle with some as yet unknown saturation point (see Figure 2):

> The normal expansion of science that we have grown up with is such that it demands each year a larger place in our lives and a larger share of our resources. Eventually that demand must reach a state where the civilization is saturated with science. This may be regarded as an ultimate end of the completed Industrial Revolution.[18]

We must expect, in short, that the curves on which we are riding will weaken sometime in the not too distant future and that the decline in the rate of change will have critical, if not catastrophic, implications for the way we live and are governed.[19] We must also note that the

[16]See, for example, Manfred Halpern, "The Revolution of Modernization in National and International Society," in Carl J. Friedrich, ed., *Revolution* (New York: Atherton, 1966), p. 195.

[17]See Zbigniew Brzezinski, *Between Two Ages* (New York: Viking, 1970).

[18]D. J. de Solla Price, *Science since Babylon* (New Haven, Conn.: Yale University Press, 1961), p. 113.

[19]Robert North and Nazli Choucri arrive at the same conclusion from a somewhat different perspective. See their essay "Population, Technology and Re-

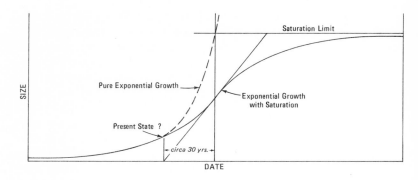

FIGURE 2. Curves of Exponential Growth, Pure and with Saturation.

From *Science since Babylon* by Derek J. de Solla Price, 1961, p. 116. Copyright © 1961 by Derek J. de Solla Price. Reprinted by permission of Yale University Press.

timing of this decline and its general effects are unknown, given the level of theoretical knowledge we now have.

The question of the end state of the contemporary transition leads to a variety of speculations. Does an inevitable decline in the growth of science imply a decline in wealth? Does it mean a shift in the basis of national power? Does it imply a dramatic shift in the level of global interdependence? If so, would it lead to greater political fragmentation in the international system or greater global political unity? We do know, for example, that in the past the natural decline of some modes of production has been compensated by the rise of new leading sectors, and that these shifts in production have benefited some states more than others. Kuznets argues, for example, that there has been a "continuous shift in the locus of growth from one area of knowledge to another, from one complex of basic application to another—so that the highest rates of technological and social innovations were in different areas of production and economic organization in successive periods."[20] And these shifts have resulted in the rise of new great

sources in the Future International System," *Journal of International Affairs,* XXV:2 (1971), pp. 224–237.

[20] *Modern Economic Growth,* p. 290.

powers, cresting on waves of new technological investment and superseding the older powers—the rise of Great Britain, for example, in the nineteenth century, and of Germany, Japan, and then the United States and Soviet Russia in the twentieth. Whether new growth rates in new areas will supersede older areas of technological growth in the future and allow the transitional period to continue, however, remains unanswerable.

In addition to the theoretical indicators that lead to this conclusion concerning transition, there is also an abundance of historical indicators. Perhaps the best historical statement of this point of view is that of Geoffrey Barraclough, who argues that the transition has in fact come to an end. For him the period between 1890 and 1960 delimits more or less "the great divide between two ages in the history of mankind"—[21] namely, the ages of "modern" and "contemporary" history. He also argues that the transformation derives from the scientific, technological, and industrial concomitants of modernization that have

> acted both as a solvent of the old order and as a catalyst of the new. They created urban and industrial society as we know it today; they were also the instruments by which industrial society subsequently expanded into the industrially undeveloped parts of the world.[22]

Barraclough's thesis is that a significant and revolutionary set of discontinuities marks off the contemporary world from all historical precedents. He includes in his catalogue of transformations the transcendence of a European-dominated world,[23] the rise of the United States and Soviet Russia, the creation and dissolution of the colonial empires of the European states, and the emergence of ideologies in the new leading centers of the world, each attempting to replace elements of the old diplomacy, including the balance of power, with a new system of relations. Such accounts, however, have by and large failed to specify what new structures of interrelationships have emerged in

---

[21] Geoffrey Barraclough, *An Introduction to Contemporary History* (New York: Basic Books, 1964), p. 2.

[22] Ibid., p. 43.

[23] A noteworthy and more traditionally historical account of this particular change can be found in Hajo Holborn, *The Political Collapse of Europe* (New York: Knopf, 1951).

the twentieth century.[24] In particular, they have failed either to specify the nature of new interdependences that have developed among the nations of the world or to suggest, from a dynamic and theoretical perspective, how they interact with one another or progress.

In summary, then, there are two significant ways in which modernization has affected the structure of the international system that can be derived directly as consequences of exponential growth: the emergence of certain forms of interdependence among a large set of states and the transitional nature of the international system. Theoretical knowledge concerning the effects of modernization on international and other social affairs, however, remains quite limited. Changes that have occurred and that are becoming more and more well known are easy to describe, but less easy to relate systematically to a set of underlying causes. It is useful, however, to catalogue some of these other changes, for they seem also to be effects of the process of modernization and are discussed throughout this essay.

A third rubric of effects that can be added to the first two discussed above has to do with the development of a global international system for the first time in human history.[25] Although the outward thrust of European states toward world conquest began in the fifteenth century, it was only after the industrial revolution that the universe of international politics became territorially closed, or finite. Changes in transportation technology that facilitated colonization and increases in

---

[24] One notable exception is George Modelski, "Agraria and Industria: Two Models of the International System," in Klaus Knorr and Sidney Verba, eds., *The International System; Theoretical Essays* (Princeton, N.J.: Princeton University Press, 1961), pp. 118–143. Modelski sketched out the structures of an emergent industrially based international system, but never carried his analysis very far.

[25] There have been numerous analyses of the effects of the spread of the European interstate system to the entire world. Although basically interested in problems of individual freedom in a world of industrialization, mass politics, and human alienation, Theodore H. von Laue lists a set of paradoxes resulting from what he calls "the global confluence." See his book *The Global City: Freedom, Power, and Necessity in the Age of World Revolutions* (Philadelphia: Lippincott, 1969). Z. Brzezinski, in his work cited above, draws some provocative insights from his analogy between the international system today and large metropolitan areas. He thus treats problems such as the incipient underworld (Third World) violence and regional problems affecting political control. The general notion concerning the "globalization" of politics and the consequent internalization of world politics or externalization of domestic politics is also treated in Stanley Hoffmann's *Gulliver's Troubles, or the Setting of American Foreign Policy* (New York: McGraw-Hill, 1968), especially pp. 26–33, 57–67.

world trade through the lowering of transportation costs, the decline of parochialism, and the institutional consolidation of political control in nation-states all contributed to this process. But not until the late nineteenth century were the changes that accompanied modernization in the last wave of European imperialism "extended to all other societies." The result was "worldwide transformation affecting all human relationships."[26]

This great transformation in global politics has become so familiar that we tend to ignore its novelty and to lose sight of the instabilities that accompanied its development. In this case instability (as well, paradoxically, as a good measure of stability, as explained in Chapter 5) apparently derives from the close interdependence that states historically did not experience. In the premodern international system peripheral areas helped relieve some of the pressures on violent international confrontation. But the global city of today has no safety valve at its periphery. It is integrated not only by a communications network that transmits information and ideas almost instantaneously but also by a set of strategic interaction patterns. These interaction patterns have become global by virtue of the development of nuclear weapons and ballistic missiles that have made global security indivisible, at least as far as nuclear war is concerned. And, as Raymond Aron has described it, for the first time in history

> The diplomatic universe is like an echo chamber: the noises of men and events are amplified and reverberated to infinity. The disturbance occurring at one point of the planet communicates itself, step by step, to the opposite side of the globe.[27]

A fourth effect imposed on international society by the revolution of modernization has to do with the paradox of change. Change involves not only persistent innovation and the creation of new social institutions, but a continual lingering, if not destruction, of outmoded structures as well. In some of these institutions, universal intergovernmental organizations such as the United Nations, history seems to validate the predictions of most theorists of modernization: universalism replaces particularism and parochialism and imbues institutions

[26] Black, *The Dynamics of Modernization*, p. 7.

[27] Raymond Aron, *Peace and War: A Theory of International Relations,* translated by Richard Howard and Annette Baker Fox (Garden City, N.Y.: Doubleday, 1966), p. 373.

with a basic transnationalism. Elsewhere the reverse is the case and, as with the proliferation of the nation-state in the process of decolonization, particularism replaces outworn or unviable universalist institutions. Thus international society over the past seventy to one hundred years has been characterized by both fragmentation and integration— by the collapse of the universal norms of European diplomacy and their replacement by the fragmented norms of modern nationalism; by the breakdown of empires and the multiplication of the nation-states; by the collapse of a universal economic standard of exchange (gold) and its replacement by a mixture of various standards of value. Simultaneously various kinds of transnational activities have grown, including the increased mobility of capital, of labor, of technology and goods and services, especially among the industrialized countries. Universal culture lives in a symbiotic relationship with fragmented countercultures. Such fragmentation and integration are the essence of the revolution of modernization in contemporary international society, and it is this feature that has made plausible the coexisting but contradictory interpretations of international history in the twentieth century, whether such interpretations stress linear and secular disintegration or stress increased interdependence.

A fifth effect of change on international political behavior in the twentieth century is the inevitable and increasingly destabilizing lag between perceptions of what the world is and external reality. In a world undergoing continuous and persistent change, no individuals, not even foreign policy decision makers, are capable of formulating policies or making decisions that foster a stable environment. In the absence of theory, decisions, like perceptions, are inevitably based on experience gained in the past and therefore in a context rather different from the present or the future. This lag between perceptions and reality may produce policies or decisions that are not only counterproductive but also potentially capable of resulting in violence.

Recent American foreign policy provides a conspicuous example of this. Decisions on American intervention in Vietnam have been repeatedly rationalized as analogous to past experience. The U.S. government waged a war in Indochina for over a decade convinced that conditions in Indochina resulted fundamentally from aggression perpetuated by a totalitarian Communist society against its neighbors. The Munich analogy, a lesson learned from the appeasement of German aggression in central Europe ("Never appease an aggressor"), coupled with the policy of containment designed for a European theater, was only remotely related to the revolutionary violence in Southeast Asia.

Given the increased complexities of the modern world, the increased interrelatedness of issues that arise in diplomacy, and the higher levels of interdependence of actions in different spheres, social engineering designed to order social change has become more and more urgent. Yet policy efforts to come to grips with the problem of ordering social change will inevitably have only a minimal chance for success in the absence of well-developed theories adduced to explain and predict the social and political consequences both of change and of various kinds of policy alternatives.

A sixth transformation in international society stemming from modernization has been the unprecedented growth of transnational activities. These activities involve "the movement of tangible or intangible items across state boundaries when at least one actor is not an agent of a government or an intergovernmental organization."[28] Whether one looks at movements of capital, of people, of technology and ideas, or of goods and services during the past century, one finds that the growth of transnational activities has been extremely great in absolute terms, even if their level relative to similar domestic activities is a source of controversy.[29] This growth has resulted from a combination of factors. In particular it has been made possible by technological innovations that have enabled people living in diverse societies to interact with one another—innovations such as those in transportation that have lowered the costs of transportation and increased its speed. But they could not have reached the levels they have now attained had no political authorities made decisions to remove barriers to trade and other forms of interchange between their populations. Transnational activities are therefore highly dependent upon the political relation-

[28] Joseph S. Nye, Jr., and Robert O. Keohane, "Transnational Relations and World Politics: An Introduction," *International Organization,* XXV:3 (Summer 1971), p. 332. This issue of *International Organization* is devoted to questions about the nature of transnational relations and is edited by Nye and Keohane. It is the most comprehensive effort to date to define and explain transnational activities.

[29] The ratio of transnational to national activities in such areas as flows of goods or capital movements has been used both by those who argue that world interdependence has decreased since the nineteenth century and by those who argue that it has increased. This controversy is discussed further in Chapter 5. For a detailed analysis of this debate, see my essay "Transnational Economic Processes," *International Organization,* XXV:3 (Summer 1971), pp. 373-397.

ships among those states where they have become significant[30]—namely, the highly industrialized states of the West. They obviously reflect the fact that they have emerged in what is essentially a security system among states that have renounced the use of force as a means of settling their disputes. This relationship between transnational activities, on the one hand, and security relations, on the other hand, is obviously crucial. But here too our knowledge is insufficient to enable us to generalize about the causal linkages between the two.

The growth of transnational activities has been uneven in the international system. It has occurred primarily in those sectors of the world where mobility of all human and nonhuman factors has been highest: in those that are the most highly modernized. It has not matched, in geographic terms, the limits of the globalized international system. What is has done is to exacerbate the problems associated with the gap between the highly developed and less developed sectors of the international system by making that gap seem even more insuperable. It too, therefore, presents a set of problems that are seemingly incapable of resolution without imaginative theoretical advances in our understanding of the dynamics of the international system.

A seventh effect of modernization has to do with the dramatic change in the geographic conceptualization of international politics. Concern with geography, more than perhaps with any other factor, distinguishes international politics from other social affairs. Statecraft has traditionally been based on calculations of distance regarded as important for the security of the state. Modern communications and technological innovations have revolutionized the concept of distance because they have tended to contradict the geopolitical allocation of political authority. As a result, it has become more meaningful to translate conceptualization of distance into the terms of dynamic processes based either on time or on costs. Thus in the delivery of missiles what matters is less the straight-line distance between enemy cities than the time it takes to deliver missiles or the costs of doing so.[31] We must

---

[30]Robert Gilpin would argue the extreme position that they are so dependent upon the political structure of the relations among the Western states that it is easy to imagine a virtual collapse of "transnational society" should the security linkages between the United States and the other industrialized states of the West break down. See his essay "The Politics of Transnational Economic Relations," *International Organization,* XXV:3 (Summer 1971), pp. 398-419.

[31]See Albert Wohlstetter, "Strength, Interest and New Technologies," in *The*

therefore think of cities such as London, New York, and Paris as much closer to one another than each of these cities is to outlying areas within its own society for such purposes as the mobility of capital. Similarly the physical distances between disparate cultures have been reduced, and simultaneously the probability of conflict among non-isolable areas has increased. Bottlenecks of transportation that exist wherever such modern linkages terminate also call for new instruments of social control to alleviate anxieties produced in the nonmodernized world when that world is confronted by phenomena completely alien to it.[32]

An eighth change brought about with the emergence of high levels of modernization has been the politicization of economic transactions, especially since World War II. Although, economic relations were eminently political in the age of mercantilism, for the century following the birth of liberalism, they were viewed as technical issues, which were to be divorced as far as possible from the intrusion of politics. However feasible this may have been when economic and political liberalism had its heyday, conditions associated with modernization have dramatically brought political and economic conditions together again in recent years. This has been the case because of the combination of factors present in the international situation after World War II. First, the policy-making elite of the superpowers became socialized into a world of nuclear weaponry and for practical purposes has by and large accepted the stalemate at the nuclear level. This has meant that plays for power and position, which once took place with intimations of the use of force, now more frequently occur when states adjust their economic positions to one another. Second, welfarist policy

---

Implications of Military Technology in the 1970s, Adelphi Papers, No. 46 (London: Institute for Strategic Studies, 1968), pp. 13 ff.

[32] There is a growing literature on the political aspects of the conceptualization of distance in temporal terms. See Marshall McLuhan and Quentin Fiore, *War and Peace in the Global Village* (New York: Bantam, 1968), for a brilliant if uneven essay on the political and social effects of "electric technology" and the revolution in communications. The most trenchant reflections on this matter can be found in several essays by Albert Wohlstetter. In addition to his essay cited above, see "Technology, Prediction, and Disorder," in *Toward a Theory of War Prevention,* Vol. I of Richard A. Falk and Saul H. Mendlovitz, eds., *The Strategy of World Order* (New York; World Law Fund, 1966), pp. 92-107; "Theory and Opposed Systems Design," in Morton Kaplan, ed., *New Approaches to International Relations* (New York: St. Martin's, 1968), pp. 19-53; and "Illusions of Distance," *Foreign Affairs,* Vol. 46, No. 2 (January 1968), pp. 242-255.

objectives have gained a more equal footing with the classical foreign policy goal of security. Thus attention to the politics of economic affairs has become increasingly important to the governments of virtually all states. Third, international economic affairs have become a substitute for high politics because they have presented the only area in which foreign policy action could be effective. Fourth and finally, economic relations have again become a focus of politics not only because of their recently acquired intrinsic political significance, but especially because of the forms of interdependence assumed in the relations among states. As will be argued below, as the advanced industrialized societies have become significantly interdependent with one another, the objectives of the various societies have become more and more incompatible, and this incompatibility has served to politicize economic relations as never before.

The upshot of the modernization process on contemporary international society has been a series of paradoxes and incompatibilities whose resolution is problematic. Modernization has been associated with growing secularism and materialism in the lives of people, with the emergence of egalitarian social norms, and with the hardening of the nation-state. It has also given rise to ideologies, has created high degrees of structural asymmetry between wealthy and poverty-stricken societies, and has produced problems that cannot be solved in the framework of the nation-state. These incompatibilities seem incapable of coordination; that is, things simply cannot remain as they are because the problems which ensue form them seem capable only of escalation, or worsening. It is to the analysis of the sources of these conflicts and incompatibilities that the rest of this book is devoted. We begin in Chapter 2 with the definition of the patterns of statecraft that emerged before the great transformations of the nineteenth and twentieth centuries occurred. This analysis is essential for two reasons. First, it provides an initial point with which we can contrast the changes of the past 150 years. Second, and equally important, it provides us with the basic vocabulary of statecraft—one that has more or less remained intact. In fact, one of the central problems that will be discussed is the growing incompatibility between this vocabulary, which has been developed to describe international politics, and the changes that have occurred in the international system. It is a vocabulary that was developed when the important political decisions were taken by dynastic ruling classes rather than through bureaucratic processes. Its referents, such as the balance of power, the sovereignty of the state, and power politics, are far removed from the realities of contemporary international life. This divergence between the norms of statecraft, built into its traditional vocabulary, and contemporary international politics is itself a source of conflict and dissension in the international system. It also tends to prohibit rather than to facilitate the resolution of international conflict. And here too one finds a need to return to the central theme of this analysis—the need to develop sound theory in order to inform policy analyses of the costs of manipulating different variables and the relationships among those variables in the processes of social change.

Subsequent chapters will trace the evolution of significant and isolable characteristics of the Westphalia system. In Chapter 3, three ideological responses to the modernization process will be examined in detail—liberalism, Marxism, and economic nationalism. Each has provided an explanation of the changes with which we are concerned, just as each has been a response to them. Since they have also influenced significantly the ways in which various governments ideally attempt to formulate their foreign policies, their inclusion in this essay is essential. The changes brought about in the actual behavior of governments in the field of foreign policy are outlined in Chapter 4, while changes in the structural relationships within international society are reviewed in Chapter 5. The evolution of international norms and of international law under the processes of modernization is the subject of Chapter 6, which relies heavily on all the analysis which precedes it. Finally, in Chapter 7, the various arguments put forward in this essay are brought together in a series of related paradoxes that characterize international relations in the contemporary world.

2

The Westphalia System and Classical Statecraft

Our ability to understand the political implications of changes in international affairs brought about by the process of modernization is extremely limited. The classical paradigm that once could have been invoked for understanding the dynamics of international politics has broken down, and we are now in an era without a paradigm to provide a framework for questions we ask about international politics or answers we expect to find sufficient as explanations. In this chapter we will review the traditional paradigm, which developed alongside the emergence of the modern state system and which was purported to explain it. This review will serve two central purposes. First, it will describe a historical situation that existed before the processes of modernization transformed interstate relations. If we are to describe these changes, it is important that we have some base period with which to compare the contemporary international system. In order to see where the system is going, what trends have emerged, and what aspects of international relations have broken down, it is, in short, essential to see where we have been. Second, this paradigm of analysis of the interstate system is one that has informed our intuitive understanding of international politics. It forms the basic vocabulary that scholars and statesmen alike have employed for describing and explaining international phenomena. This vocabulary was once congruent in both ideal and actual terms with what occurred in the international system, but it now serves only limited descriptive and explanatory purposes. If we are to understand the dilemmas that this disparity between international relations and our vocabulary for explaining them has brought to the practice of statecraft, it is essential that we take a brief look at its origins.

Although the traditional, classical framework for understanding state-craft consisted essentially of descriptive accounts of diplomatic history, these accounts were usually written in the context of a paradigm that patterned the questions asked about international phenomena. Few opportunities arose to challenge that paradigm until the social base underlying its assumptions had collapsed. These assumptions did not emerge in a coherent form until the early nineteenth century—with the writings of a new school of diplomatic history founded by Leopold von Ranke (1795-1886)—even though the origins of the system they were purported to explain were traced, for reasons I shall discuss later, to the middle of the seventeenth century.[1] The assumptions are based on an account of the ideal structures of the relationships among the great powers of Europe for which foreign policies were formulated and conducted. Since they were ideal structures, or accounts about how foreign policy "ought" to be conducted, they often conflicted with the actual practice of statesmen. But so long as the ideal structures were accepted by historians and by statesmen, contradictory practices were usually denounced rather than explained. This is one basis of the normative bias characteristic of traditional accounts.

Diplomatic histories usually begin with the rise of the modern state in Western Europe in the seventeenth century. In fact, diplomatic historians have often pinpointed a specific date for the origins of the modern state system, namely 1648, the year of the Peace of Westphalia, which brought an end to the Thirty Years' War. The system that emerged after

[1]These assumptions were, however, in the process of codification in the emerging structure of international law. Hugo Grotius was certainly instrumental in attempting to outline what the basis of international law ought to have been after the restoration of peace following the Thirty Years' War in his masterwork, *On the Law of War and Peace* (1624). But it was not until the Peace of Utrecht (1713) and the writings of Emmerich de Vattel (1714-1767) that one could speak of a codification of a system of international law. See Arthur Nussbaum, *A Concise History of the Law of Nations,* revised ed. (New York: Macmillan, 1954), Chaps. IV and V: and Charles de Visscher, *Theory and Reality in Public International Law,* translated by Percy E. Corbett (Princeton, N.J.: Princeton University Press, 1957), Chaps. 1 and 2.

that point has therefore become known as the Westphalia system and is frequently pointed to as the basis of international law and the modern state system.

The importance of Westphalia is partly symbolic and partly descriptive of a dicontinuity in diplomacy. The Congress of Westphalia marked the end of the Thirty Years' War in Europe, the last of the religious wars of the Middle Ages and Reformation, and also the first modern secular war. The Thirty Years' War was a period of political, social, and metaphysical upheaval in Europe. Its settlement marked the end of the notion of a universal Christian community as well as the beginning of the secularization of politics. It also marked the end of the metaphysical view that man had a defined place in a hierarchy of being, that he was fated to his social status, and that he could little affect the development of a political community through social engineering.[2] In this sense it marked, symbolically, a new period, that of "masterless man." This change was reflected in the literature of the period, which denoted it as one not only of political but also of cosmic upheaval—an upheaval that resulted in the philosophical and social separation or liberation of man from the organic unity of medieval Christendom and that was linked to the creation of secular society. The new man, or "masterless man," was no longer conceived as having a preordained place in a natural hierarchy of being. Masterless man was freed of the shackles of medieval society and had the power to shape the new societies as he willed. His new freedom included the freedom to order the political community.[3]

The symbolic importance of Westphalia in marking off a new age in diplomacy thus has to do with the secularization of political matters and their demarcation from transcendent and other worldly affairs associated with the Christian community.[4] This can be seen symbolically in the way diplomacy was conducted at Westphalia.

The restoration of peace was divided in two parts and in two separate

[2] See E. M. W. Tillyard, *The Elizabethan World Picture: A Study of the Idea of Order in the Age of Shakespeare, Donne and Milton* (London: Chatto, 1943), for an analysis of the medieval cosmology.

[3] For a case study of this change in the metaphysical views of European thinkers based on the radical politics of English Puritanism, see Michael Walzer, *The Revolution of the Saints: A Study in the Origins of Radical Politics* (Cambridge, Mass.: Harvard University Press, 1965).

[4] For a detailed and scholarly analysis of the peace, see Cicely V. Wedgwood, *The Thirty Years' War* (New Haven, Conn.: Yale University Press, 1939).

congresses, one in Osnabrück and the other in Münster. This division of a peace had no precedent and has never been repeated in diplomatic affairs. Although several complicating factors having to do with the allies in dispute and the fact that warfare was still being waged dictated this bifurcation of a peace conference, other reasons for the two separate parts of the Westphalia Congress were intimately connected with the birth of the diplomatic system. The two-town conference was used as an empirical solution to a problem of diplomatic precedence that arose from the fact that the shifting coalitions in the Thirty Years' War had been based on both religious factors and secularized political conceptions of national interest. The Holy Roman Emperor, God's supposed earthly vicar, had to deal with both Catholic and non-Catholic rulers at the same time. The two-town conference allowed the emperor to deal with both Catholics and those non-Catholics who did not recognize his otherworldly role so that the postwar European order could be reorganized on a stable basis.

The Holy Roman Emperor had claims over the sovereignty of all other rulers. These claims stemmed from religious and ideological assumptions based on the theory that as the head of the empire he was also the secular head of Christian society. The claims derived from a conception of European society that had been predominant for approximately a thousand years. International society was supposed to be both monolithic and hierarchical. The problem of the organization of the Peace of Westphalia was to reconcile this outmoded view with a new vision of international society. The new view recognized that the members of international society—the sovereign rulers of the various states—were not equal in terms of their power. Yet the ideal view of a lasting and stable international order was one predicted on the reciprocal and equal treatment of the rights of sovereigns who, in their exercise of authority over domestic groups, were independent of one another.

The Peace of Westphalia, then, is taken as the basis of the modern international system for several reasons. First, it codified the recognition that politics was based on secular rather than otherworldly claims. Second, it recognized the notion of political sovereignty as a basis of international law.[5] Third, it was the first time that a general European

---

[5] The development of the notion of sovereignty and of international law is critically linked to the Westphalian compromise, and especially to the social context in which the Peace of Westphalia took place. This was a period of nation building, when rulers were attempting to demonstrate their supremacy in domes-

congress was created in order to bring about the settlement of international conflict. As one historian has argued, "from that time to our own the diplomatic history of Europe has stridden along from one congress to another."[6]

Although the emperor did not immediately renounce his pretensions after Westphalia, the two sets of treaties that marked out a new European diplomatic system "reduced him to a position little higher than that of the first among the German princes";[7] and the principle of the equality of sovereigns was embodied in a settlement, even though it was not formally accepted by the emperor.

The major assumptions of the traditional framework for analyzing international statecraft thus derived from the political situations of the monarchs who together ran the interstate system. One of these assumptions was that the highest political good is political order, which could be found only in political society, that is, in the state.[8] Outside the state reigned anarchy or a state of nature that knew no law save "natural law." Since the highest political good was found inside political society and since individual political societies coexisted with others in a prepolitical condition of anarchy, the supreme obligation was conceived to be the maintenance of the security of the political community. This was the basic task of the monarch, in whose care the state was placed by God or contract.

This contrast between order in political society and anarchy in international society was coupled with another assumption that was basic

---

tic affairs and to do away with rival domestic groups. They attempted to implement a monopoly on road building and the issuance of currency, for example, in order to overcome domestic particularism. From this social and political problem, which was predominant in virtually all European states in the seventeenth century, one can find a direct link to the concept of sovereignty, which codified the right of the prince of a state to rule in his internal realm unchallenged by external or domestic opposition. The reciprocity of recognition of sovereign rights as a basis of international law can thus be understood from the domestic political situations at this time. By securing external recognition of his domestic monopoly on the use of force, a ruler was able to reinforce his internal authority.

[6] Sir George Clark, *The Seventeenth Century,* 2d ed. (New York: Oxford University Press, 1947), p. 135.

[7] Jacques Boulenger, *The Seventeenth Century in France* (New York: Capricorn Books, 1963), p. 149.

[8] This is the Hobbesian assumption, which underlies classical statecraft. See Kenneth N. Waltz, *Man, the State and War: A Theoretical Analysis* (New York: Columbia University Press, 1954), pp. 166 ff.

to the practice and to the historiography of diplomacy and that was also sanctified by the Peace of Westphalia. This is the notion of "masterless man" discussed above. The apotheosis of this concept was the person of the divine-right king who was the artisan of the modern state. It was no accident that the philosophical notion of masterless man reached its apogee in the state of Louis XIV in the period following the three decades of social chaos that characterized the Thirty Years' War. In fact, the development of this social and philosophical concept was a condition requisite for the creation of the secular state as defined by Westphalia. Both developments are articulately summarized in Carl Friedrich's study of the baroque era. Friedrich argues that there is an underlying common core to political and economic thought and institutions in this period:

> This core is the new sense of power, the power of man to shape his own society, his own destiny. This sense of power was, in some of the key thinkers and actors of the age, Promethean in its limitless striving. Who is to say whether the modern state emerged in this period because some of its most striking representatives were filled with this sense of power, or whether they were filled with sense of power because the modern state emerged? In any case it is clear that the two developments were closely linked and that they molded the climate of opinion, the *Weltegefühl* and *Weltanschauung,* the fundamental outlook and feeling of man in the seventeenth century.[9]

The framework of traditional statecraft that emerged from the Westphalia system provided the paradigm of thought used for analyzing international behavior until very recently. In order to understand changes that occurred in this framework and that were brought about by the processes of modernization, I shall analyze five central aspects of traditional statecraft. These will be re-examined separately in later chapters in terms of the changes that have occurred in them as a result of modernization. They can be summarized as follows:

1. The underlying political and economic system that described traditional statecraft pertained to the assumptions of *mercantilism.*

---

[9] Carl J. Friedrich, *The Age of the Baroque, 1610-1660* (New York: Harper, 1952), pp. 36–37.

The mercantilist order that developed alongside the Westphalian system has informed our vocabulary with norms and rhetoric that have lasted to this day. At the same time, the social conditions that supported mercantilism have changed drastically, so that international affairs conform to it only in such terms of political currency as "balance of trade" and "balance of power."

2. The notion that states are formally and ideally *equal and sovereign* likewise formed a fundamental part of the classical framework of statecraft. The equality of the sovereign rulers of the European state system was an integral part of the secularization of politics. As a result of this secularization, at least in ideal terms, the obligations of sovereigns to a Christian community that transcended the state system were reduced and sovereigns secured a reciprocally recognized equality in terms of their rights to rule internally and in terms of their obligations and responsibilities under the emerging system of international law.

3. The principal of the *primacy of foreign policy* over domestic affairs was a norm of statecraft that served to free the sovereign rulers of Europe to act in foreign policy autonomously of domestic interests. It therefore was related to the assumption that foreign and domestic affairs belonged to different realms and could be treated with different sorts of instruments.

4. The *heroic framework* of diplomacy was a direct result of the structure of the ruling dynasties in Europe in the seventeenth century. This framework gave the impression that political leaders were the only ones who counted in making foreign policy and was also picked up by analysts who discussed the operations of the interstate system. It represents a genre of analysis that followed from the assumption of masterless man discussed above and has only recently been challenged in writings on international politics with the growing recognition of the bureaucratic and organizational constraints that have become characteristic of foreign policy decision making today.

5. *The balance of power* was the principal notion that was invoked to describe the structure of the international system. Invented shortly after the Peace of Westphalia as a structural norm to be implemented in international society because it assured the continued existence of the member states, it has been preserved in the language of diplomacy until this today, even though contemporary structures of international relations show no clear-cut balance and in fact have been enriched by a series of overlapping interdependences of various sorts.

MERCANTILIST ASSUMPTIONS ABOUT
INTERSTATE BEHAVIOR

Classical statecraft cannot be understood outside the social context in which it developed. The states in Europe during the seventeenth century were primarily concerned with nation building, or the formation of a unified and centralized economic and political system. The assumptions about foreign policy and international politics that characterized classical statecraft can be derived almost completely from this central social context. In this sense, the domestic situations confronted by the leaders of the great powers of Western Europe were the primary determinants of their foreign policies.

One of the most noteworthy aspects of nation building in the Westphalia system was the tight relationship between economics and politics. They were not, as was later the case under liberalism, thought to belong to separate spheres. Rather, they were seen as part of the same phenomenon of state building. The power of the ruling princes was enhanced by the creation of a centralized economy but also by differentiating it from the economies of other societies. As one economic historian has argued,

> One of the chief tasks of mercantilist policy was to eliminate [tolls on highways and rivers] and to create a free internal trade. Mercantilism is often associated with protectionism. This is accurate so far as *inter*national trade is concerned, but it should be emphasized that mercantilism stood for free *intra*national trade.[10]

The inseparability of economic and political factors built into the domestic economy under mercantilism also characterized foreign policy. In both spheres the principal aim of mercantilist doctrine was the augmentation of the power of the sovereign, and in this respect the wealth of the sovereign was like other elements of power. As Jacob Viner has characterized the relationship between wealth and power in mercantilism,

---

[10] Dudley D. Dillard, *Economic Development of the North Atlantic Community: Historical Introduction to Modern Economics* (Englewood Cliffs, N.J.: Prentice-Hall, 1967), p. 165.

(1) wealth is an absolutely essential means to power, whether for security or for aggression; (2) power is essential or valuable as a means to the acquisition or retention of wealth; (3) wealth and power are each proper ultimate ends of national policy; (4) there is a long-run harmony between these ends, although in particular circumstances it may be necessary for a time to make economic sacrifices in the interest of military security and therefore also of long-run prosperity.[11]

A second characteristic of mercantilist thought has to do with the extent of global wealth and power. For mercantilism, both are finite: there exists a fixed and limited amount of each in the world. Two implications of this are of moment for statecraft. Since it was assumed that there was a finite amount of global wealth (usually measured in gold stocks) and power, an increase in the wealth or power of one sovereign meant an inevitable decrease in that of another. International behavior was therefore conceived to be zero-sum. Second, this meant that there was a built-in bellicosity in interstate relations. If each sovereign sought the same goal (an increase in power or wealth) and if that goal could only be achieved at the expense of another sovereign, trade wars and armed conflict were integral parts of mercantilism. There was a conflict of interest between buyers and sellers trading with one another across borders just as there was a conflict of interest in vying for prestige, territory, and other concomitants of power. Trade, like war, had an offensive role, and each sovereign sought simultaneously a "favorable" balance of trade and a "favorable" balance of power. As one student of mercantilism has argued,

Translated into common language, mercantilist policy signified: prohibitions, reprisals, export subsidies, prescriptions, continual commercial wars and incessant armed conflicts. It led fatally to war because it meant a desire to impose on others unacceptable obligations devoid of any reciprocity.[12]

Policies of autarky and of autonomy (or complete self-sufficiency of the national economy) constitute a third fundamental feature of mercantilist doctrine. Such policies should be understood in the social and political context of the European societies in the seventeenth

[11] Jacob Viner, "Power versus Plenty as Objectives of Foreign Policy in the Seventeenth and Eighteenth Centuries," *World Politics*, I:1 (October 1948), p. 10.

[12] Edmund Silberner, *La Guerre et la paix dans l'histoire des doctrines économiques* (Paris: Sirey, 1957), p. xli. The translation is mine.

century. Secularized monarchs were trying to establish their authority within their national realms. These princes equated their own interests with those of the societies over which they ruled. In order to consolidate their authority, they had to create centralized political institutions that could serve both domestic and foreign ends. On the one hand, they sought to destroy localized authority exercised by lesser feudal princes who were potential rivals to them. They therefore created free trade areas within their realms. By breaking down the feudal tax structures that were the source of wealth and power of local barons, they could simultaneously establish nationally based economies and reinforce their own authority. On the other hand, the goal of autonomy also served to differentiate the prince's realm from other sovereign jurisdictions and impede the development of any dependence upon other rulers. "The aim of mercantilism," as one student of politics has noted, "both in its domestic and in its external policies, was not to promote the welfare of the community and its members, but to augment the power of the state, of which the sovereign was the embodiment."[13]

The quest for power in all its manifestations was, then, a fourth component of mercantilism. Power served the glory of the prince and was embodied in the magnitude and density of the population over which he ruled, in the size and wealth of the territory of his domain, and in the gold stock at his disposal.[14] Ideally, his power was to be absolute so that he could properly carry out his responsibilities. He therefore had to avoid any dependence upon others and was preoccupied by the need to maintain and, whenever possible, increase his power. In the domestic sphere this meant that the government would by necessity be interventionary. It would counter the growth of any domestic interests that might compete with the ruler, and it would promote industries whose output would increase the state's wealth. This meant, in effect, industries whose products could be exported to support a favorable trade balance and those that manufactured munitions. In the international sphere it meant the need to seize any opportunity to foster the king's glory and thereby increase the stature of his realm. The need to increase the king's power through foreign undertakings was made urgent by the

[13] Edward Hallett Carr, *Nationalism and After* (London: Macmillan, 1968), p. 5.
[14] See, for example, Andrew Lossky, "The Nature of Political Power According to Louis XIV," in Leonard Krieger and Fritz Stern, eds., *The Responsibility of Power: Historical Essays in Honor of Hajo Holborn,* (Garden City, N.Y.: Doubleday, 1967), pp. 107–122.

belief noted above that the total amount of power in the world was finite and that accretions of power on the part of other rulers would
diminish that of the king. This need was coupled with a fifth assumption of mercantilism: that all humans are egoists pursuing their own
interests and that as a result there were inherent conflicts of interest
among princes.

The notion that there were conflicting interests among rulers and,
therefore, among states was perfectly congruent with the fundamentally bellicose nature of the international system in the mercantilist world.
Commerce and other aspects of international interaction were predicated on this belief that the goals of the various monarchs were inevitably conflictual. If a sovereign was not vigilant in seeking greater
power, he could be certain that another would take advantage of any
situation that could redound to his detriment. Moreover, the princes
had reason to perpetuate the view that conflict was inherent in social
life. Since each was concerned with building and preserving his own
domestic authority, he found it useful to exaggerate the dangers to his
kingdom presented by foreign rulers. As the sixteenth-century political
philosopher Jean Bodin had argued, "the best means of perserving a
state, to prevent rebellion, sedition and civil war, and to maintain the
good will of subjects, is to have an enemy. . . ."[15]

The pattern of interactions and the prescriptions and beliefs associated with mercantilism frequently diverged from the model outlined
above. But the many varieties of mercantilism that appeared resulted
from the peculiarities of the context in which the doctrine was formulated and the idiosyncracies of the princes of Europe. These diverse
patterns of the doctrine shared a fundamental common feature: they
represented the policies of modern states in the early stages of state
building. They were, in short, determined by the need to create authority in a world whose social foundations were undergoing rapid
and radical change.

THE CONCEPT OF SOVEREIGNTY

The theory of sovereignty was developed along with the Westphalia
system and the doctrine of mercantilism, although it was first articu-

---

[15] Jean Bodin, *Les six livres de la république* (Paris, ed. 1580), p. 760.

lated by Jean Bodin almost a century before the end of the Thirty Years' War. Bodin and his successors defined sovereignty as the capacity to make laws that inheres in the power of a ruler. As a lawmaker, a sovereign could not himself be bound by the laws he made, but also could not simply rule arbitrarily.[16] What was new about this concept was that it made the ruler a legislator, or inventor of rules of behavior for his society, and not simply an interpreter of what under an earlier tradition was felt to be a permanent body of divine law. The concept, therefore, stems from a prescriptive theory of politics that established a predominantly secular view of authority.

The concept of sovereignty is thus intimately tied to the process of building the modern state.[17] Emerging with the breakdown of the Christian community, it served two essential functions. On the one hand, it provided a rationale for creating and preserving domestic order by making the ruler a legislator whose duty it was to enact laws that would preserve society. On the other hand, it provided a motivation for the defense of the political community against external attack. In both cases, it stressed the need to provide for the security of the ruler and the survival of his domain rather than the improvement of the welfare of his subjects, as could be expected when the emerging states were under the constant threat of domestic upheaval or external aggression.

Although Bodin and the other early theorists of sovereignty were careful to define the limits of sovereign actions lest they be arbitrary, the concept became associated with the notion that states are above the law. J. L. Brierly, a noted British legal scholar, has asserted that

> there have been two main developments which have brought about this astonishing reversal of its original effect. One is that sovereignty came later to be identified with absolute power above the law, and the other is that what was originally an attribute of a personal ruler inside the state came to be regarded as an attribute of the state itself in its relations to other states.[18]

The reversal of Bodin's original and limited concept of sovereignty is

[16] Bodin argued that sovereigns are bound by divine law, by laws of nature, and by the fundamental or constitutional laws of the political communities in which they rule.

[17] For a history of the concept of sovereignty, with a concise bibliography, see Francis Harry Hinsley, *Sovereignty* (London: Watts, 1966).

[18] J. L. Brierly, *The Law of Nations*, 6th ed. (New York: Oxford University Press, 1963), p. 11.

tied to the political exigencies of the post-Westphalia period. Since the rulers of the various states were trying to impose a new secular order to replace the crumbling edifice of the Christian community, they found it necessary to recognize their mutual and equal sovereign rights over their own domestic realms. The sovereigns were equal in the sense that each had the power to order the affairs of his own society. Sovereign equality implied a reciprocal recognition of the right of each to legislate in order to preserve order within his own state. Recognition of the equal rights of sovereigns, then, served to bolster the authority of the ruler within his own society. But such recognition had important international effects, since it provided the basis for the development of positive international law.

THE PRIMACY OF FOREIGN POLICY

The concept of sovereignty implied an ontological as well as a normative divorce between the conduct of domestic affairs and the pursuit of foreign policy. That distinction rested on the assumption that foreign policy was more important than domestic policy, since its principal concern was the survival of the political community itself—a concern that was logically primary in a period when the security of the newly formed state was constantly threatened.

Although the distinction between foreign and domestic affairs was implicit in the theory of political sovereignty, it found its most famous formulation in the writings of Leopold von Ranke (1795-1886) in the nineteenth century. It is summarized in Ranke's principle of the primacy of foreign policy:

> The world, as we know, has been parcelled out. To be somebody, you have to rise by your efforts. You must achieve genuine independence. Your rights will not be voluntarily ceded to you. You must girth for them. . . . With independence a foundation has been laid, a community achieved. But should it rise to universal significance, it needs moral energy above all else. Only through this can the rivals, the enemies in world competition, be overcome.
> . . . The position of a state in the world depends on the degree of independence it has attained. It is obliged, therefore, to organize

all its internal resources for the purpose of self-preservation. This is the supreme law of the state.[19]

Thus the fundamental assumption that explains the separation of foreign policy from domestic policy is that foreign policy has special significance that other policies do not have in that it concerns the existence and security of a society. Foreign policy is a requisite of statehood that is derived from the soi-disant Hobbesian or anarchic state of international society. The most rudimentary element of "national interest," it serves also as a guide for "reason of state."

Under the traditional framework foreign policy was thought to differ from domestic policies in three respects. The ends of foreign policy were ideally thought to embody the national interests of the whole society as defined by the state's geographic position and national customs, while those of domestic policies pertained to particular interests within the society. Even more important was the distinction with regard to political means, or policy instruments. In foreign affairs any means could be invoked, including the resort to the use of force, or violent means, while in domestic affairs the political leadership could legitimately invoke only those means permitted by the society's political "constitution," or traditions. Finally, the targets of foreign and domestic policies were thought also to differ fundamentally. Foreign policies were thought to be directed toward a decentralized, anarchic milieu over which any individual state maintained very little control. Domestic policies, on the other hand, were ideally centralized arenas in which the government had a monopoly over the instruments of social control.

The assumption of the primacy of foreign over domestic policies had normative as well as intellectual consequences. When the exigencies of domestic political life impinged upon the conduct of foreign policy or contradicted the principle of primacy, they were denounced for undermining "national interests" or for preventing the implementation of policy according to reason of state.[20] The traditional distinction be-

[19]Leopold von Ranke, "A Dialogue on Politics," in Theodore H. von Laue, *Leopold Ranke: The Formative Years* (Princeton, N.J.: Princeton University Press, 1950), pp. 167–168.

[20]In contemporary writings, this normative bias is characteristic of the heirs of the traditional framework who have been associated with the doctrine of political realism. George Kennan, one proponent of political realism, notes, for example: "I must confess that the professional diplomatist is often possessed by a congenital aversion to the phenomenon of domestic political competition. He sees it,

tween foreign and domestic policies, in short, was based on normative grounds that had a strong empirical foundation in terms of which statesmen actually behaved. Levels of interdependence among states were generally so low that governments could take independent actions in domestic and foreign arenas with relatively little likelihood that spillover would exist at significant enough levels to affect the other. The instruments used to implement either domestic or foreign policies did not significantly alter existing policies in the other sphere. In other words, the external aspects of domestic policies and the domestic aspects of foreign policies did not, as a rule, alter significantly other courses of action. This is not to say that domestic factors did not significantly affect foreign policy or that the general international setting did not affect the substance of policies. What it does suggest is that the distinction made in ideal terms between foreign and domestic activities was relatively well matched by actual conditions. The degree to which they did not actually coincide led to debates on ways to improve the efficacy of foreign policies or domestic policies, or on the basic goals of either type of policy. But the degree of divergence was not so severe as to call the distinction entirely into question.

THE HEROIC FRAMEWORK

The Westphalia system emerged in a period of political heroism that idealized the capacities of "master builders" of the new political order.[21] Even as the significance of political leadership diminished with the consolidation of nation-states, a heroic cast remained one of the characteristics of the ideal conduct of diplomacy. This tendency derives from the assumptions that were discussed in the introductory remarks in this chapter. On the one hand, reason of state, stemming from the anarchic nature of the international system, required that the control of foreign policy be concentrated in the hands of a small po-

---

everywhere, as a seething cauldron on which there rises to the surface, by the law of averages, a certain mutation of the human species." "History and Diplomacy as Viewed by a Diplomatist," in Stephen D. Kertesz and M. A. Fitzsimmons, eds., *Diplomacy in a Changing World* (Notre Dame, Ind.: University of Notre Dame Press, 1959), p. 104.

[21] See Friedrich, *The Age of the Baroque,* Chaps. 1–3.

litical leadership for reasons of efficiency, continuity, and unity. On the other hand, the realist assumption of masterless man, capable of creating order from his environment, results in an emphasis on the ways individual leaders systematize their environment in their particular "art" of statecraft. By virtue of the monarchic tradition, the interests of the state were identified with the interests of the ruler. No distinction was made between public and private goods as concerned a monarch. They were the same as far as a ruler was concerned. Thus, by "divine right," "social contract," or "natural law" theory, the individual monarch became identified with the state at whose helm he was situated. And to speak of Louis XIV or Frederick the Great was to speak of the France or Prussia of his time. The monarch and his state were not only grammatically synonymous; they were also thought to be equivalent.

The assumption concerning the heroic style of diplomatic activity has intellectual consequences for the analysis of statecraft. It directs attention to the activities of individuals who are assumed to have the capacity to direct external events as they will. What remain questionable, then, are the personal motivations, values, and goals of particular statesmen, rather than the means they possess to implement them. Their policies may be analyzed in terms of perseverance, efficiency, unity, and continuity, but rarely in terms of capacity. Capacity enters analysis only as a crude measure to differentiate great powers from lesser powers. Great powers are assumed to have the capacity to do their will.

There is a further consequence of the heroic framework for the intellectual operations associated with traditional writings on diplomacy. This is the idiosyncratic cast into which they are molded. Since the assumption of heroic style directs attention toward the individual statesman, foreign policy is related only to the psychological variables that determine the reactions of individual policy makers. As a result, scholarly writings in the heroic cast have been noncumulative, for comparisons are made at best at the individual level and rarely at the analytic level of whole political institutions or societies.

The normative consequence of the heroic framework follows directly from the intellectual operations associated with it. Policies are evaluated as a function of the degree of insulation of the foreign policy process from domestic institutions, and also as a function of the degree they are conducted by individual statesmen who are said to understand the time-tested and immutable principles of diplomacy. This results in a philosophy by which a policy that is successful is viewed as well formulated, while one that is a failure is poor. It also results in a selective interpretation of diplomacy stemming from an unwillingness to understand the foreign policies of individual statesmen in terms of their societies. Evidence is usually sought to explain the success or failure of the individual in terms of the values of the writer. This explains the fluctuations in the reputations of the great statesmen of the past, such as Metternich, Bismarck, or Wilson.

THE BALANCE OF POWER

Perhaps the most enduring of all the concepts that were developed along with the Westphalia system to describe and to explain international behavior is that of the balance of power. Like the balance of trade, a core concept of mercantilism, the balance of power was viewed as a permanent feature of international life that rulers were interminably attempting to tilt in their own favor. But unlike the concept of balance of trade, that of balance of power was never rigorously and specifically defined. It has remained an ambiguous notion with conflicting descriptive, explanatory, and prescriptive meanings.[22] Because of its ambiguity, many analysts have rejected it as a useful concept. Yet it has recurrently appeared as a fundamental description of international political life.

The term "balance of power" did not enter the vocabulary of statecraft until more than a half century following the Westphalia settlement. It was a concept associated with the Enlightenment in Europe and a derivative of the eighteenth-century paradigm of order. But its origin is tightly linked to the political problem that emerged with the collapse of the metaphysical basis of medieval life. It will be recalled that the fundamental political problem confronted in the Westphalia settlement was the establishment of a new and secular vision of po-

---

[22] For analyses of these various meanings, see Ernst B. Haas, "The Balance of Power, Prescription, Concept, or Propaganda," *World Politics,* V (1953), pp. 442–477; Inis L. Claude, *Power and International Relations* (New York: Random House, 1962), pp. 11–93; and the excellent historical and analytic essay by Martin Wight, "The Balance of Power," in Herbert Butterfield and Martin Wight, eds., *Diplomatic Investigations* (London: Allen & Unwin, 1966), pp. 149-175.

litical society. The ideal hierarchical cosmology of the Middle Ages ordained by divine will had collapsed. The rulers of the emerging nation-states had to find a new set of notions to justify and legitimate their rule. At first it had been argued that the creation of political order was an act mimetic of divine will. The statesman was viewed as an artist whose task was the creation of political order out of social chaos. Unlike the domestic political order, the international arena was thought to be in a state of nature. For some this anarchy was evil, for others benevolent; in either case it was without order. "Balance of power" emerged as a descriptive and explanatory concept of a new order that seemed, in fact, to characterize the international arena and that replaced the notion that international politics was inherently anarchic and disordered. Although writers have found more than twenty different meanings associated with the term, only three of these are important for present purposes. These see the balance of power as (1) an automatic mechanism, (2) a system of relationships among nation-states, and (3) a type of foreign policy.[23]

When the balance of power was invoked as an automatic mechanism for creating equilibrium in international society, it was thought to be a natural law that governed the relationships among states.[24] It was mechanistic, thought to be a means for providing automatic self-adjustment to disorders in international politics and for preventing mankind from slipping into an anarchic Augustinian universe. It implied equilibrium among the states in the international system. Briefly, according to this law, whenever a center of power existed in international affairs, one or more additional power centers would arise to preserve an equilibrium. This natural law was based upon many of the assumptions of mercantilism, but especially the assumption that each state in existence was eternally trying to maximize the power at its disposal. As a result of the mutual attempt of each state to maximize its power, there was a tendency for the whole system to remain in equilibrium, preventing thereby the predominance of any single state. This equilibrium assured stability in the international system and preserved the security and autonomy of each state.

---

[23] This discussion follows closely the argument of Edward Vose Gulick, *Europe's Classical Balance of Power* (Ithaca, N.Y.: Cornell University Press, 1955).

[24] See especially David Hume's essay, "Of the Balance of Power," in *Essays: Moral, Political and Literary,* edited by T. H. Green and T. H. Grose (London: Longmans, Green, 1898), Vol. 1, pp. 348-354.

When the balance of power was used to describe a system of relations among societies, it stressed conditions that historically existed in a specific historical arena. It invoked no natural law of politics. This is the way the concept is usually used when it describes what has been called the "classical balance of power" that emerged after the Westphalia settlement, especially in the eighteenth and nineteenth centuries. The assumptions about that classical system bear upon our treatment of the traditional framework of statecraft. The historian Edward Vose Gulick has noted four central assumptions.[25] These are the existence of the state system; its limited framework; its relative homogeneity; and the rational basis for estimating power associated with it.

The political system in which the balance of power classically operated was one in which nation-states were the only units of international life. Each had a leader who could act relatively autonomous of constraints imposed from below, so that he could pursue a flexible and supple policy. The one decision rule that was primary in his pursuit of power was the slogan "No permanent ties, only permanent interests." Each of the five great powers in the classical network—Britain, Austria, Prussia, Russia, and France—was capable of exercising predominant influence beyond its borders through the use of force. The interaction of their conflicting wills in pursuit of conflicting goals and objectives resulted in a dynamism that was assumed to have a meaning independent of the individual units. This is to say, the state system, including the balance of power that operated within its confines, was thought to represent a phenomenon that was greater than the sum of its parts and that could not be understood through an examination of the actions of the individual states that composed it. Rather, it represented a new force, with its own internal dynamics.

At the same time, the state system was limited. Its particular geographic and spatial limits within the continent of Europe enabled the system to work smoothly by providing it with a built-in flexibility. The system was flexible because the states that composed it were by and large noncontiguous. Rather, they were separated from one another by the fragmented principalities of central Europe that became the pawns in the battles for power that the major powers continually fought.[26] The system was limited also in the sense that the great

---

[25] See Gulick, *Europe's Classical Balance of Power*, pp. 3–29.

[26] The emergence of two unified states in the center of this checkerboard, Germany and Italy, toward the end of the nineteenth century was a significant factor

powers were relatively equal in size and had relatively equal disposable power. Where they were not equal, flexibility was assured by the safety valve provided by the vacuum between the states and by areas beyond the shores of Europe that provided room for territorial expansion. Flexibility also existed in this sytem because of the factor of time. It took a relatively long period of time for any state to mobilize its forces for war. This provided the states with a period for "cooling off" and for diplomatic maneuvers in periods of great stress. Finally, the number of states—some four or five great powers and two dozen lesser units—provided flexibility by making available a large pool of potential allies so that balance could usually be maintained.

The relative homogeneity of the states in the system was another factor essential to its smooth operation. The states shared a common cultural base and had relatively similar political structures. Moreover, their rulers shared the common aim of preserving a balance of power in order to assure their own survival and autonomy. Whenever any one power might attempt to create a hegemony and disrupt the balance, a sufficient number could form a coalition to preserve it.[27]

Finally, the system was based upon the belief that power, consisting of disposable resources, could be estimated on a rational basis. As we saw in the discussion of mercantilism above, power was thought to be commensurable and consisted of such factors as population, territory, gold stocks, numbers of ships, and size of armed forces. There thus existed a rational basis for determining one's own power as well as that of potential enemies or allies.

A third meaning of the concept of balance of power was that of a category of foreign policy behavior. A policy of balance of power sought to preserve balance in the system, thereby assuring that no single power could predominate and endanger the security and autonomy of one's own state.[28] It was thus a predominantly conservative policy, oriented to the maintenance of the status quo and designed to prevent change in the international system. The principal instrument of this

---

in the creation of inflexibility in the classical balance of power and was central to the breakdown of the system.

[27]Harold Nicolson makes much of this point in *The Congress of Vienna: A Study in Allied Unity, 1812-1822* (New York: Harcourt, Brace, 1946).

[28]One of the principal ambiguities associated with this kind of policy had to do with whether the balance to be preserved was "favorable" to the state pursuing the policy, thereby enhancing its own power by impinging upon the autonomy of other states, or was "neutral."

sort of policy was the creation of alliances. Thus the classical system of diplomacy was one of constant flux in the alignments of states.

THE EVOLUTION OF THE WESTPHALIA SYSTEM

The framework of assumptions about international politics associated with the Westphalia System provided a system of norms that emerged with the creation of the modern nation-state. These norms and assumptions also spread as the nation-state system grew from its original European basis to include virtually the entire populated world. The framework seemed to be a permanent part of the interstate system that had to exist so long as international society was composed of discrete and semiautonomous units. As the forces associated with modernization emerged and spread, however, the standards provided by the Westphalia system became progressively challenged.

I have examined this sytem as a base for contrasts and as a starting point against which changes can be measured and evaluated. It is a fundamental argument of this essay that the ideal structures of international society formed with the Westphalia System have been transformed by the processes of modernization so that international society no longer conforms to those structures. Rather, it represents a confusing set of overlapping structures that can only be separated out analytically.

This viewpoint is by no means universally accepted. There are some, for example, who would argue that the techniques of foreign policy, the structures of international society, and the nature of international politics have remained essentially unchanged since the nation-state first emerged in the seventeenth century.[29] Others would argue that international society today is essentially different from some periods of the past but not from all of them.[30] Each group would be able to marshal a fair amount of empirical data to reinforce its arguments.

---

[29] In the United States, this position has long been associated with Hans J. Morgenthau and his influential textbook, *Politics among Nations,* 4th ed. (New York: Knopf, 1967). Morgenthau does recognize, however, that nuclear weapons have in fact served to dislocate many traditional concepts.

[30] This is a position argued implicitly by E. H. Carr (*Nationalism and After*) and explicitly by Stanley Hoffmann. See Hoffmann's *Contemporary Theory in Inter-*

Those who argue that international society today is not very different from what it was in other periods since Westphalia base their analysis on the undisputed fact that the international arena has remained decentralized. New political units may have risen to prominence and others may have declined; thus the United States, the Soviet Union, Japan, and China have moved to the center of international politics. But, these people would argue, the new powers also compete for influence and attempt to play one side off against another. Moreover, they would claim, the development of nuclear weapons has, if anything, reinforced the fundamental features of the Westphalia system. These weapons have hardened the territorial bounds of the nation-state and have enabled even small powers with nuclear capacity to "equalize" the power of the giant superstates. That argument, associated mainly with certain European military strategists[31] and with former French President Charles de Gaulle, is a powerful one indeed. But it ignores not only some of the other trends in international society but also, as we shall see in later chapters, some of the peculiar characteristics of nuclear diplomacy.

Others who argue the position that interstate politics are governed by laws derived from the decentralized milieu in which they take place encounter normative difficulties in their analyses. When they see situations that do not conform to traditional *realpolitik,* they usually plea for changes in foreign policy on the basis of prudential wisdom. An extreme form of this argument can be found in the widely used text of Professor Hans J. Morgenthau.[32] Morgenthau assumes that in any international system in which there is no overarching political structure having a monopoly over the instruments of violence, states must conform to rules of political realism in order to survive. That is to say, the rules of political behavior in international affairs are imposed from the outside, by the nature of the international system and the exigencies of survival. But very few statesmen seem to follow to precepts of political realism, and their societies have persevered.

---

national Relations (Englewood Cliffs, N.J.: Prentice-Hall, 1960), Part III, and his essay, "International Systems and International Law," in Klaus Knorr and Sidney Verba, eds., *The International System: Theoretical Essays* (Princeton, N.J.: Princeton University Press, 1961), pp. 205–237.

[31] See in particular the analysis of French General Pierre Gallois, *The Balance of Terror: Strategy for the Nuclear Age,* translated by Richard Howard (Boston: Houghton Mifflin, 1961).

[32] See *Politics among Nations,* pp. 3–35.

Some other writers argue that international politics do not always conform to the same rules, but that certain types of relationships tend to repeat themselves historically. Thus Henry Kissinger has argued that in periods of political upheaval recurrent dilemmas of conservative statecraft appear.[33] This enables a statesman to draw upon "lessons of the past" to guide his actions.

None of these alternatives seem to explain adequately the transformations that international society has undergone in the course of the past century. The world simply does not conform to the patterns established in the Westphalia framework, and lessons drawn from the past can be applied only with extreme modesty. This will be argued at greater length in the chapters that follow. Briefly, I shall now outline the changes that have occurred in terms of the framework elaborated in this chapter.

The mercantilist assumptions of classical diplomacy have been replaced on the ideal level by three alternative systems of ideas. Economic and political liberalism began as an attack on each of the fundamental premises of mercantilism and has become the prevailing ideology in the industrialized West. Marxist philosophy criticized both mercantilism and classical liberalism and offered another system of political and economic ideas that has gained acceptance throughout the Communist and less developed world. Economic and political nationalism, which was more derivative of mercantilism than was either liberalism or Marxism, combined modern and more traditional ideals and once flourished in the ideology of fascism. It appears again to be taking hold in certain nonmodernized societies. While it may be that new theorizing now associated with a group known as ultra-Keynesians will develop a new pattern of thought that subsumes mercantilism, neoclassical liberalism, and Marxism, for the time being the basic concepts of mercantilism have found no advocates in the modernized world. At the same time, the vocabulary of statecraft is riddled with mercantilist terms that seem to bear less and less resemblance to the international interactions that have been taking place.

The idea that the interstate system should be composed of equal and sovereign political units has retained its place at the core of positive international law. Yet it has been so undermined by changes in the international system that its utility has been significantly reduced.

[33]See in particular his essay "The Nature of Statesmanship," Chap. 17 of *A World Restored* (Boston: Houghton Mifflin, 1957).

The emergence of some 150 political units with distinct differences in levels of economic development or military potential has made the ideal of equality a fiction. Moreover, the political units have lost their place as the unique subjects of international law as the rights of national groups and individual citizens have been increasingly recognized. The development of significantly higher levels of internationl interdependence than ever imagined by the statesmen of the classical period has so reduced the autonomy of all states that the concept of sovereignty has also lost its hold. The development of transnational activities has contributed to this. Presumed rights of intervention in the domestic affairs of other states on moral grounds, as in the case of repressed minority groups in South Africa, have been established. The obligation of wealthy societies to redistribute their wealth to poorer countries has also become a new principle of international welfare. The upshot has been the emergence of new patterns of norms governing the relations among societies. These new patterns overlap with the older classical patterns in a confusing hodgepodge of principles and law.

In no society of the modernized world can foreign and domestic affairs be separated from one another. It therefore has become impossible for any but short-term purposes for a government to maintain a primacy of foreign over domestic policies. In fact, the major ideologies of the contemporary world, liberalism and Marxism, are based on the primacy of domestic over foreign affairs. Moreover, the exigencies of political life in any modernized society, whether it has a pluralistic or command structure, require the subservience of foreign policies to domestic ends.

The heroic framework that characterized classical diplomacy was at first undermined by the growth of nationalism in the nineteenth century. But the vocabulary of statecraft easily adapted to this change by equating the interests and rights of the prince of the early nation-state with those of the nation as a whole. The result was the personification of the nation-state that has confused more than it has informed diplomatic rhetoric. More significant has been the emergence of bureaucratic politics and interest group politics in most highly developed societies. Policy has become increasingly the outcome of clashes among competing groups within national governments that have more interest in advancing their own careers than in achieving policy goals. Policy has thus lost its rationality and continuity—the virtues associated with monarchic statecraft—even for short-term periods.

Finally, the balance of power has ceased to be useful as a description of the international system, except perhaps at a level so general that it has lost its force. The growth of regionalism in the international system, as that system spread beyond Europe to virtually all of the societies of the world, and the development of several types of cross-cutting interdependences have become far more significant aspects of interstate relationships than the balance of power. It certainly is no longer viewed as a "law of politics" by most observers of international affairs. It is also difficult to find more than a few states that have actually pursued what was once called a balance-of-power policy.[34] Not only has nuclear deterrence superseded the balance of power, but non-military aspects of diplomacy have assumed a political importance that may be unique to the contemporary world. Moreover, the number and types of political units have grown so in number and diversity that the assumptions of the classical balance-of-power system have become completely antiquated. And many analysts have argued that the major instrument of balance-of-power diplomacy, the alliance, has lost its utility.

It is far easier to describe the changes that have occurred in the traditional framework of international politics than to explain these changes satisfactorily. But each of the changes that has occurred seems linked to the others as well as to the logic of the process of industrialization and modernization. By looking at these changes in greater detail and by linking them to the process described in Chapter 1, we ought to be able to develop a coherent perspective on the effects of modernization on the fundamental dimensions of international relations.

[34]Some observers have argued that the Nixon-Kissinger foreign policy represented a rebirth of balance-of-power diplomacy. See in particular James Chace, *A World Elsewhere* (New York: Scribner, 1973). Others have argued that in spite of these efforts such a policy could not work. See, for example, Zbigniew Brzezinski, "The Balance of Power Delusion," and Stanley Hoffmann, "Will the Balance Balance at Home?" *Foreign Policy*, No. 7 (1972), pp. 54-59; and 60-87.

3

Ideological Alternatives to Classical Statecraft

The classical framework of statecraft, outlined in the last chapter, has had so powerful a hold over our fundamental conceptualization of diplomatic behavior that it still forms the core of ideas that informs analyses of international relations. Yet, ironically, this system of descriptive terms and normative concepts has been under attack for almost two centuries. The assault against classicism has been twofold. On the one hand, classical statecraft has provided inadequate and unsatisfactory explanations of the actual processes of interstate relations. On the other hand, it has been viewed as a rationalization that legitimizes the authority of ruling elites and perpetuates a system of continual conflict and that thus prevents the realization of the "true interests" of those who are ruled.

It is no accident that the empirical and normative critique of classical statecraft begins with the industrialization of England and France in the eighteenth century, the phenomenal spread of the market economy and the emergence of bourgeois classes who perceived their own interests as antithetic to those of the landed aristocracy in the old regimes. This critique originates, in short, with breakdowns in the system of governance at both the national and international level that accompanied the modernization process. Political and economic liberalism, in particular, marks the first systematic alternative that was given to the classical norms characteristic of the Westphalia system.

Nor is it an accident that under Marxism and nationalism the liberal alternative was regarded as unsatisfactory on normative and empirical grounds. While liberalism and its focus on internationalism may have provided a useful critique of the diplomacy of the old regimes, it too could be viewed as the rationalization of the power of the bourgeoisie, which frustrated the working classes by holding them in perpetual poverty, and the nation as a whole by perverting the unfolding of its inherent *telos,* or spirit.

These alternative frameworks for understanding international politics can be viewed, then, as a response at the level of ideas to the challenge to classical statecraft of industrialization and the process of modernization. I shall refer to them as ideological alternatives, in spite of the multiple meanings of the term "ideology."[1] Ideology will be understood for our purposes as a doctrinal or intellectualized response to the modernization process that serves to rationalize and explain the breakdown in the relations not only among societies but within them as well, and that also acts as a guide to political action and as a means of reintegrating societies as they undergo modernization.

It is important to note that these ideological responses to industrialization and the breakdown in the classical system precede by about a century that point delimited in the first chapter where modernization so affected interstate behavior that it can be said that international relations underwent a major transformation. That is to say, the ideologies associated with modernization arose in advance of the major breakdown and change in the international system that one also associates with modernization.

Several explanations can be adduced for this apparent discrepancy. The most important of these seems to be that the older patterns were highly resilient and lasted for over a century following their first challenge. Modernization, after all, did not proceed in quantum leaps. It was an accelerating and cumulative process that did not cause the old system to break down at once. Indeed, the former framework still served to explain a large portion of international affairs and to guide diplomacy. It is natural for old procedures to linger as they are amended by new ones. The result is the existence of a set of overlapping and contradictory structures that describe international affairs today.

[1]For a succinct historical and analytic treatment of these manifold meanings of "ideology," see George Lichtheim, "The Concept of Ideology," *History and Theory,* IV (1965), pp. 164–195.

In addition, there is a distinction that must be made between ideal and actual patterns of behavior. Ideal patterns are those that describe the way people ought to behave as opposed to the ways that statesmen actually conduct their affairs. Ideologies combine normative values with descriptive and explanatory propositions.[2] The ideological systems that we are concerned with, as alternatives to the classical framework, are hortatory and normative. It should not be surprising, therefore, that they emerged in a period of change and preceded the major transformations with which we are by and large concerned.

For our purposes we shall follow Stanley Hoffmann's description of an ideology as "a body of ideas, emotions and symbols that aim at presenting a systematic and global vision of the world and its history, that serve as a commitment to, a guide for and a legitimization of action, and that are institutionalized in an organizational political movement."[3] Our interest, however, focused on the ideas embodied in the three ideologies to be examined and the global visions of the world they present than in their institutionalization or the operations of the political movements that have adopted them. But it is important to emphasize that these three systems of ideas have been selected precisely because they have been institutionalized in political movements and regimes and have therefore served on a normative level as the major alternatives to classicism.[4]

Two of these ideologies, liberalism and Marxism, share significant features. They are both modernist in that the ideal orders they wish to institute are novel and have never existed in human history. These orders are based upon the realization of the full potential of mankind

----

[2] As Gustav Bergmann has argued, an "ideological statement" is "a value judgment disguised as, or mistaken for, a statement of fact." The illusion provided by formulating value judgments as statements of fact serves hortatory purposes: "The motive power of a value judgment," Bergmann posits, "is often greatly increased when it appears within the rationale of those who hold it not under its proper logical flag as a value judgment but in the disguise of a statement of fact." "Ideology," in May Brodbeck, ed., *Readings in the Philosophy of the Social Sciences,* (New York: Macmillan, 1968), p. 129.

[3] "The American Style: Our Past and Our Principles," *Foreign Affairs,* Vol. 46 (1968), p. 369.

[4] Thus we are not looking at ideologies as Napoleon did, as armed ideas whose function is similar to that of terror in imprisoning the minds of masses. Nor are we examining their function in the sociology of knowledge, as rationalizing the interests of ruling groups. While both of these perspectives on ideology are important, the present purpose is to examine alternative ideas for explaining and describing the dynamics of international society.

to achieve material and psychological satisfaction. They therefore depend upon a relatively high level of industrialization for their achievement. Moreover, both ideologies are universalistic in that they hope to transcend particular interests that impede the fulfillment of man's potential.

Both ideologies also call for a "new diplomacy," which is really no diplomacy at all in that within the new systems they would create, individuals and societies would transcend political divisions that impede the achievement of a fundamental harmony of interests among them. They both aim, therefore, at similar long-term goals: they wish to create a world that is devoid of politics, a world of material abundance where political divisions can be eliminated.

The third system of thought, nationalism and associated national economics, represents a combination of modern and premodern ideals. While liberalism and Marxism are specifically internationalist philosophies, nationalism is self-consciously anti-internationalist. It seeks to preserve and to foster the values of national societies as did the system of norms of classical statecraft. But the fulfillment of national values is to be achieved through the marshaling of industrial forces and of other processes associated with the modernized world. Nationalism thus forms a natural dialectic with the two internationalist ideologies.

POLITICAL AND ECONOMIC LIBERALISM

We have seen that one principal objective of mercantilist philosophy was the creation of free trade within national markets. The creation of internal markets served to bolster the power of ruling dynasties against rival claimants for political authority within their realms and to provide them military and economic potential against rival sovereigns abroad. But the development of these internal markets in the evolution of the modern nation-state also created potential rivals to the authority of traditional ruling monarchies by fostering newcomers to power and influence whose livelihoods were dependent upon the functioning of the newly created markets. It is among members of the bourgeoisie, therefore, that we can find the articulation of a new doctrine that threatened the position of authority of the traditional ruling classes. These groups began to see that the political philosophy underlying the monarchic system and the economic theory underlying mercantilism inhibited the realization of their own objectives as determined by their attachment to the market system. The critique that they developed represented a revolutionary onslaught on the entire political philosophy that we associate with the Westphalia system, both in terms of its norms for international statecraft and its preferred domestic institutional arrangements. We can perhaps best understand their critique and its revolutionary impact in terms of the paradigm described in the last chapter.

The liberal critique of the old system was predominantly normative. The old system, it was felt, perverted the interests of middle-class society by preventing the development of individual liberty. In political terms, liberal philosophers like John Locke attacked the notion that political order and freedom were incompatible and argued that within the structure of a society where government preserved order, individuals ought to be given the freedom to preserve and perpetuate their own rights as distinct from those of the monarchy. The economic analysis of liberalism, like the political argument, was based on natural-law precepts about the individual and his rights. As Adam Smith argued, the system of individual liberty in a free market would enable the society as a whole to achieve a higher level of material benefit than could be achieved under the system of mercantilism. In both political and economic terms, this emerging philosophy of liberalism, in contrast to that of the old order, assumed that egoistic individualism could be harnessed to the mutual benefit of all members of society. This new philosophy, therefore, attacked the fundamental assumptions of the old order.

We have seen that one of the core presumptions in the Westphalia system was the tight relationship between—if not the equation of— economic and political goods. This notion was viewed by liberal philosophy as fundamentally wrong. In liberal doctrine, in fact, the equation of the two was regarded as an instrument of monarchic groups for achieving their own interests, as opposed to those of society as a whole, and prevented the realization of the political goals of the individuals in a society as well as the development of the wealth of the nation. This can be seen in the liberal critique of traditional power politics. The power politics of the monarchic dynasties were regarded as preventing the realization of the basic harmony of interests among people and among societies. In economic terms, as Viner has argued, the mercantilists "grossly misunderstood the true means to and nature of plenty. What they were lacking in was not economic motivation but economic understanding."[5] In short, the development of individual liberty for the individual and the development of individual and social wealth rested upon the *separation of economic and political factors.*

Political liberalism, then, was based upon an attack on the balance-of-power system and on power politics in general. It saw in the old diplomacy a system that perpetuated war because war was a principal instrument of political action that served the interests of the ruling groups. This rejection of old-regime diplomacy really meant a rejection of diplomacy altogether, since it served the interests of ruling groups against those of the population as a whole. The goal of the liberals was therefore to reform the entire system of diplomacy.

The separation of economic and political factors upon which the new diplomacy of liberalism rested was built institutionally into the treaty system that was emerging in the eighteenth century. The Peace of Utrecht (1713) not only was the first official document in which the balance of power was specifically mentioned as a goal of political settlement, but also gave rise to the first set of treaties that dealt separately with trade and political arrangements. As Felix Gilbert has shown in his extraordinary essay on the origins of the new diplomacy, the new pattern only slowly gained acceptability.[6] By the time the newly independent American government began to debate the sorts of treaty arrangements appropriate to it, the view that alliance arrangements could be made independent of trade arrangements was gaining acceptability and more and more coming to characterize the diplomacy of democratic regimes.

One consequence of the separation of political from economic factors was a new view of the nature of power and plenty.[7] In contrast to the mercantilist system, in the new liberal system neither wealth nor power was viewed as fixed. This was especially the case with regard to economic goods. The new liberal system of economics was in fact based

---

[5] Jacob Viner, "Power versus Plenty as Objectives of Foreign Policy in the Seventeenth and Eighteenth Centuries," *World Politics,* I:1 (October 1948), p. 10.

[6] Felix Gilbert, *To the Farewell Address* (Princeton, N.J.: Princeton University Press, 1961), Chap. 3.

[7] The new view depended upon an analytic separation of economic and political factors that itself was a requisite to the development of economic theory.

on the presumption that wealth could be increased. This could occur through the process of creating free markets that enabled men to use economic resources more efficiently and through economic growth. While growth had occurred under the mercantilist system, wealth nonetheless had been viewed in the end as finite and fixed.

The liberal system attacked two core mercantilist assumptions: (1) the presumed zero-sum quality of international relations and (2) their inherent bellicosity. On the one hand, if wealth and power were not fixed, then international relationships were inherently non-zero-sum in the liberal system. Both political and economic liberals felt that if artifically erected boundaries among societies were broken down, individuals would be enabled to increase their own happiness and welfare. The new liberal system of diplomacy therefore called for an increased number of transactions (of a nonpolitical nature) among people in various societies. All parties could gain from transactions and all could be better off, it was argued. This was in marked contrast to a world where wealth and power were fixed and where a gain for one party meant a loss for another.

On the other hand, the antibellicose nature of liberal doctrine stemmed from the belief that the interests of diverse societies were common. Among these shared values was an interest against the alliance and warfare politics of the dynastic regimes. If the dynastic regimes could be overcome, it was felt, a natural harmony of interests could develop among people in different societies. In practical terms, freedom of transactions among people meant that there ought to be freedom to trade. This was, after all, what the bourgeois groups sought in creating a new system of politics. The desire for commercial freedom, associated with the rise of modern democracies, is also what has given a heavy economic emphasis to American diplomacy. As Gilbert has articulately argued,

> This feeling that one civilization now encompassed the whole world was reinforced by the astounding growth of economic interdependence. In the centers of European civilization, people could rely on having a regular supply of goods from all over the world. . . . The barriers that existed seemed artificial and ephemeral in comparison with the fine net by which the merchants tied the individuals of the different nations together like "threads of silk." As Sédaine says in his famous comedy *Le philosophe sans le savoir,* the merchants—whether they are English, Dutch, Russian, or Chinese—

do not serve a single nation; they serve everyone and are citizens of the whole world. Commerce was believed to bind the nations together and to create not only a community of interests but also a distribution of labor among them—a new comprehensive principle placing the isolated sovereign nations in a higher political unit. In this eighteenth century, writers were likely to say that the various nations belonged to "one society"; it was stated that all states together formed a "family of nations," and the whole globe a "general and unbreakable confederation."[8]

The new system of diplomacy was also a consequence of the rise of political liberalism and the ideal of creating the new domestic democratic order. Internationalism associated with a democratic regime had a function to play in democratic politics. If all societies were to evolve into democracies, it was felt, a peaceful order would replace the bellicose order of the old diplomacy, and this new order would enable the democratic regimes to concentrate on perfecting themselves. There was a double consequence to the new domestic order for international affairs. In the beginning, as in the origins of American diplomacy, the emergence of democratic regimes would have a revolutionary effect on international society. Even if only a single society fostered the new diplomacy, it was felt, that society would have the effect of breeding the seeds of destruction of monarchic regimes by providing bourgeois classes with both the wherewithal and the inspiration to revolutionize their societies. But the new domestic order was also to have a built-in capacity to wage war and carry out foreign adventures. Thus, in the long run, democratic societies had to be prevented by their own constitutional arrangements from carrying out the old diplomacy. They would be aided in this by constraints as well as by an inevitable *primacy of domestic politics* over foreign policy in liberal regimes.

Liberalism therefore attacked what had been felt to be the virtues of monarchic diplomacy: unity, continuity, secrecy, freedom of action, and coherence. These "virtues" of monarchic society were, under democratic regimes, viewed as impediments to the realization of the true interests of people and the source of the "rotten state of politics" in the balance-of-power system in Europe. Democracies implied the very reverse virtues in the conduct of foreign affairs. They rested on the

[8]Gilbert, *To the Farewell Address*, p. 57. (Footnotes in original.)

reign of public opinion and implied anything that would weaken the continuity and coherence of old-regime foreign policy.[9]

In practice, it was of course impossible to create a constitution that could embody completely this vision. This was seen especially in the first important written constitution, that of the United States, which recognized that it was important to grant government the power to go to war in order to protect itself from aggression from outside. The constitutional compromise was the provision of a mechanism to provide security for the population and at the same time to make it difficult for the government to go to war or to use the traditional instruments of diplomacy that would pervert the interests of society. The major philosophical problem, of course, was that of reconciling a democratic government with the need to have a foreign policy, since democratic political arrangements imply the legislative control of governmental affairs, including warfare. At the same time, foreign policy requires secrecy, finesse, threats to use force, and flexible responses, all of which necessitate a degree of executive control. Such executive action necessarily impinges upon domestic life and especially upon its economic organization. Moreover, it was also recognized that under existing international law the full sovereign power of the state in executing foreign policies inhered in the executive.

The philosophical question of whether democracies could be reconciled with the need to conduct foreign affairs, at least so that they could provide a minimal degree of security for their members, was confronted by the eighteenth-century philosopher John Locke, who argued that a federative power inhered in civil society:

There is . . . [a] power in every commonwealth which one may call natural, because it is that which answers to the power every man naturally had before he entered into society. For though in a commonwealth, the members of it are distinct persons, still in reference to one another, and as such are governed by the laws of the society; yet in reference to the rest of mankind, they make one body, which is, as every member of it before was, still in the state of nature with the rest of mankind, hence it is, that the controversies that happen between any man of the society with those that

[9] For an analysis of the virtues and vices of monarchic and democratic diplomacy, see Joseph Barthélemy, *Démocratie et politique étrangère* (Paris: Librairie Félix Alcan, 1917).

are out of it, are managed by the public; and an injury done to a member of their body engages the whole in the reparation of it. So that, under this consideration, the whole community is one body in the state of Nature, in respect of all other states or persons out of its community.

This therefore contains the power of war and peace, leagues and alliances, and all the transactions, with all persons and communities without the commonwealth; and may be called federative, if any one pleases. . . .

These two powers, executive and federative, though they be really distinct in themselves, yet one comprehending the execution of the municipal laws of the society within itself upon all that are parts of it; the other the management of the security and interest of the public without, with all those that it may receive benefit or damage from; yet they are always almost united. And though this federative power in the well or ill management of it be of great moment to the commonwealth, yet it is much less capable to be directed by antecedent, standing, positive laws than the executive; and so must necessarily be left to the prudence and wisdom of those whose hands it is in, to be managed for the public good. For the laws that concern subjects one amongst another, being to direct their actions, may well enough precede them. But what is to be done in reference to foreigners, depending much upon their actions and the variation of designs and interests, must be left in great part to the prudence of those who have this power committed to them, to be managed by the best of their skill for the advantage of the commonwealth.[10]

What Locke argued, in short, was that in democracies the executive authority was bounded by the laws enacted by the legislature and by constitutional restraints. In foreign affairs, however, two functions are in practice fused and liberated from these constraints. Here the executive wields a prerogative to act beyond specified legal prescriptions.

In practice, this philosophical marriage between executive and federative power does not resolve the dilemma confronting democracies in the pursuit of foreign goals, but leads instead to an interminable constitutional debate that, as in the case of the American war in Vietnam, can become frequently acute. Most written constitutions now provide for the sharing of power to conduct external relations between execu-

[10] *An Essay Concerning the True Original, Extent and End of Civil Government (Second Treatise of Government)* (1690), paragraphs 145–147.

tive and legislative bodies, which depends upon a separation of powers to enact and to implement law. Yet even this cannot resolve completely the basic dilemma. Thus, as one student of constitutions has put it,

> The process of foreign policy-making, in a historical perspective, undoubtedly displays an increasing participation of the parliament, commonly called the "democratization" of foreign policy. The main present-day problems of the executive-parliamentary relationship seem to be the preservation of a unified and coherent foreign policy, based on a coordinated and cooperative making of it between the two principal policy-making organs as well as within them.[11]

Even if democratic regimes faced a practical problem of security that impinged upon the primacy of domestic life over foreign affairs, they nonetheless were sufficiently different from the monarchic regimes with which they were contrasted to be viewed as posing a revolutionary danger to the old order. We have already seen the distinction between monarchic or mercantilist foreign policy and democratic ideals in the presumed relationship between political and economic goods, in the notion of the expandable or fixed nature of power and wealth, in the question of the primacy of domestic or foreign policy, and in the ideal views on the use of force. This distinction also applied to the other dimensions of the classical system: the heroic framework, policies of autarky, and the ideal of the balance of power.

The heroic framework of classical international relations rested upon the monarch's exclusive right to conduct foreign affairs. We have already seen that liberal doctrine viewed that monopoly as leading to the perversion of the true interests of the majority of the members of society. The virtues of democracy were precisely its presumed ability to break down that monopoly and to permit the natural evolution of social relations among members of different national groupings. The rule of the majority was thus logically and tightly linked to the goals of liberalism of replacing policies of national autarky with free international trade and of transcending balance-of-power diplomacy. Economic liberals thought that they had proved that free trade and the development of an international division of labor based on natural comparative

[11] F. A. M. Alting von Geusau, *European Organizations and Foreign Relations of States: A Comparative Analysis of Decision-Making* (Leyden: A. W. Sythoff, 1964), p. 62.

advantage would provide a more efficient economic order and greater well-being for all people. But to assure that, they needed to replace the regime of war, or the balance of power, with a regime of peace; and the overcoming of balance-of-power diplomacy depended upon the spread of liberal regimes throughout the world. Gilbert describes this revolt against old regime diplomacy as follows:

> The existing methods of diplomacy were so much geared towards power politics and war that they could never serve the opposite purpose—the preservation of peace. The main target of the philosophies was the assumption that the only possibility and guarantee for peace lay in the maintenance of a balance of power among the states. . . . In contrast to the ostensible aim of promoting peace, balance of power had, it was said, always done harm to a system of lasting peace and was opposed to it. . . . With the overthrow of this central concept of eighteenth-century diplomacy, the other concerns of the traditional diplomacy were also re-evaluated and shown up in their futility and dangerousness.[12]

This new diplomacy of liberalism, then, was bound up with the notion that mankind could evolve and continuously improve itself, as opposed to the more static notions of the interminable drama of balance-of-power politics. As reason and rationality, associated with the rise of industrial manufactures, spread through the world, so would the new order of peace. This growth in reason had paradoxical short-term consequences insofar as democratic regimes could become revolutionary and, as in the case of the French Revolutionary adventures, embark upon wars of revolutionary change in order to assure their own survival and to bring about the new era of peace. It also meant that democracies were likely to vacillate between periods of extreme extroversion and introversion. What is more significant for our purposes is the new rhetoric and set of norms brought into statecraft by the emergence of liberal doctrine. All aspects of power politics were severely depreciated as remnants of the immoral behavior of authoritarian leaders. Alliances, secret diplomacy, and threats to use force were to be replaced as instruments of diplomacy by open relations among people. "Power to the people," and direct "people to people" relations were the operative keys to a new era of peace. These new norms not only spread rapidly in diplomatic rhetoric but created the illusion that all

[12]Gilbert, *To the Farewell Address*, p. 60.

aspects of classical diplomacy either no longer existed or could be entirely overcome. The new doctrine appealed widely, especially because it provided a coherent and specific attack on traditional diplomacy and only an amorphous and vague notion of what the new order would be like. As we shall see, it was not the only new doctrine to do so.

MARXISM AND LENINISM

The second set of doctrinal principles with which we are concerned, Marxism-Leninism, shares much in common with the first. Like liberalism, it seeks to create a world in which political divisions are transcended and to replace the state system with a universal stateless society. It also is based on the progressive improvement of human conditions in society through increased productivity, which can liberate workers from the shackles of the soil or industrial life and provide them the wherewithal for their development. Like liberalism, it was originally based on a moral revulsion against the political conditions in the societies in which it emerged as a doctrine. But the target of the Marxist attack was not the dynastic order of the old regime. Rather, it was bourgeois society, which, while it was as viewed a stage in man's evolutionary development, was seen as the principle cause of war.

Classical marxism had its origins in the socialist philosophies that emerged in mid-nineteenth-century Europe. What all forms of socialism had in common was an outcry against the excesses of industrialization in Europe, an emphasis upon the uneven distribution of wealth as a cause of domestic and international conflict, and the belief that industrialization provided the basis of a new age of abundance, which, if equally distributed among members of the population, could also herald a new age of justice.[13]

---

[13]Socialism was one of three major new currents of intellectual and social thought that prevailed in the nineteenth century. A second was social Darwinism, which in many ways was derivative of the monarchic framework analyzed in the last chapter. Like that paradigm, social Darwinism stressed the inherently conflictual nature of social relationships; and like the biological Darwinism upon which it was based, it stressed the "survival of the fittest" or most powerful nation-state in a world of bellicosity. While its most outstanding spokesman was the British philosopher Herbert Spencer (1820-1903), Darwinism eventually

My emphasis here is on the Marxist analysis of international relations, rather than on other currents of socialism, not simply because of the enormous and distinct impact it has had but also because of the coherent intelllectual framework in which it is cast. In my examination of the thoughts of Marx and Engels, and later of Lenin, as they bear on international politics, some necessary oversimplification and selectivity will necessarily be involved, given the richness of their writings and my omission of an examination of the historical context in which Marxism emerged. Just as liberalism represented a revolutionary onslaught against the mercantilism and monarchic system of statecraft analyzed in Chapter 2, Marxism contained an equally revolutionary attack on the practices of liberal regimes as well as on the ideal norms they sought to implement. As in my analysis of liberal ideology, I shall examine Marxist views of international politics in terms of the same basic issues that I outlined in analyzing the Westphalia system.

While Marxism, like liberalism, provided a fundamentally normative view of how social relations both within and among societies ought to develop, it also had claims of being scientific as a total theory of human relationships. Unlike liberalism, however, Marxism and other variants of socialism held that the basic units of society were not individuals, but rather were social classes. In the Marxist view, capitalist or liberal-bourgeois regimes (as Marx labeled them) did result in the achievement of industrial growth and abundance. But this growth benefited one class in society (the capitalist class) at the expense of the progressive impoverishment of workers. The implementation of liberalism therefore perverted the interests of the majority of the population by withholding from it the fruits of its labor and in so doing also perverted the interests of all of society by providing a much lower level of economic growth than could be attained through the creation of a so-

---

grew to have its greatest impact in the United States (where it developed under the philosophy of individualism) and in newly unified Germany. Although Darwinism had an impact on a few significant statesmen, including Theodore Roosevelt, it never emerged as an ideological movement (save perhaps as it was embodied in some forms of fascism) and therefore wll not be examined directly in this chapter. A third school of thought that emerged in the nineteenth century was positivism, which had a direct heritage in the eighteenth-century Enlightenment. The French philosopher Auguste Comte (1798-1857) and other positivists were among the first "social scientists" who recognized that industrialization would have an enormous impact on the nature of international relationships. Some significant strands of positivism wll be examined in greater detail in the next chapter.

cialist order. The sources of this perversion were such middle-class institutions as property, the state, and the bourgeois family structure, which supported the class-based society. Marxism, therefore, attacked the liberal-capitalist regime of the nineteenth century in terms of the progressive division of classes within society. Class conflict, the inevitable result of class division, also lay at the heart of the Marxist interpretation of the motor force and evolution of international society. As Marx and Engels expressed it in "The Communist Manifesto" (1848),

> The history of all hitherto existing society is the history of class struggles.
>
> Freeman and slave, patrician and plebian, lord and serf, guild-master and journeyman, in a word, oppressor and oppressed, stood in constant opposition to one another. . . .
>
> The modern bourgeois society that has sprouted from the ruins of feudal society has not done away with class antagonisms. It has but established new classes, new conditions of oppression, new forms of struggle in place of the old ones.[14]

The goal of Marxism was a world of material abundance and egalitarian distribution which would terminate class division, replace class-based social institutions with those of classless society, and by thus eliminating all causes of grievance also result in a system of peace. No system of perpetual peace could be based on bourgeois society, since, as a predominantly class-based society, it perpetuated the exploitation of workers. The only way a viable system of peace could be instituted was by rooting out class divisions through the revolution of the proletariat. I shall return to this analysis below when I analyze in greater detail the evolution of the doctrines of Marxism-Leninism in the context of the role of conflict within and among societies and the notions of the historical evolution of the international system contained in them.

The achievement of a regime of world peace in Marxism, just as in liberalism and in classical statecraft, depended upon a fundamental relationship between economic and political variables. Unlike the classical order but like liberalism, Marxism postulated that political and

---

[14] "Manifesto of the Communist Party," in Karl Marx and Friedrich Engels, *Selected Works In Two Volumes* (Moscow: Foreign Languages Publishing House, 1962), Vol. 1, p. 34.

economic variables were separable. Here, however, the two types of variables were said to relate to one another in such a way that political variables were dependent upon key and independent economic variables. Class divisions, the source of all social conflict, were themselves dependent upon the technological and economic bases upon which society was built. As Marx argued in his "Preface to *The Critique of Political Economy*,"

> In the social production of their life, men enter into definite relations that are indispensable and independent of their will, relations of production which correspond to a definite stage of development of their material productive forces. The sum total of these relations of production constitutes the economic structure of society, the real foundation, on which rises a legal and political superstructure to which correspond definite forms of social consciousness. . . . At a certain stage of development, the material productive forces of society come in conflict with the existing relations of production, or—what is but a legal expression for the same thing—with the property relations within which they have been at work hitherto. From forms of development of the productive forces the relations turn into fetters. Then begins an epoch of social revolution.[15]

Thus Marx's criticism of the mercantilist regime agreed with the liberal view that it embodied a misunderstanding of the relationship between power and plenty. But Marx went further and argued that the entire motivation of mercantilist society was economic, and that foreign policy was pursued for the special advantage of mercantile classes. In his own study of eighteenth-century diplomacy Marx argued;

> As to their [British] *foreign policy*, they wanted to give it the appearance at least of being regulated by the mercantile interest, an appearance the most easily to be produced, as the exclusive interests of one or the other small fraction of that class would, of course, be always identified with this or that Ministerial measure. The interested fraction then raised the commerce and navigation cry, which the nation stupidly re-echoed.[16]

[15] Marx and Engels, *Selected Works*, Vol. 1, pp. 362–363.
[16] Karl Marx, *Secret Diplomatic History of the Eighteenth Century*, edited by Eleanor Marx Aveling (London, 1899), pp. 55–56, as cited in Jacob Viner, "Power versus Plenty as Objectives of Foreign Policy in the Seventeenth and Eighteenth Centuries," *World Politics*, I:1 (October 1948), pp. 28–29.

Marxism's conception of the relationship between foreign and domestic policies was closely tied to its formulation of the linkages between political and economic variables. Again we find a view that is related to that of liberalism yet also distinct. In liberal thought, the goals of separating foreign from domestic policy and of placing priority on foreign policy under classical statecraft was criticized for perverting the interests of most members of society. The institutionalization of a democratic-liberal order with an emphasis on the primacy of welfare goals and domestic policy would assure peace, since the true interests of society were against aggression. The Marxist view was (and remains) that foreign policy is always a function of the structure of the domestic order. If, as Engels noted in *Anti-Duhring,* "force is only the means, and ... the aim is economic advantage"[17] for the ruling class, then foreign policy always developed from the interests of that class; and as Lenin warned, "the most profound roots of both the home and foreign policy of our state are determined by the economic interests, the economic position of the ruling classes of our state."[18]

The nature of the state system was thus inevitably a function of the nature of the various domestic orders. A system in which warfare and thus the use of force prevailed was not a function of the political fragmentation of international society, as under classical statecraft. Nor would it disappear under a liberal-capitalist order. Indeed, under the latter, since class divisions were exacerbated and since the technology of armaments would have progressed, warfare would be more bitter, fierce, and widespread than ever before in history.

Wars were fought for a set of reasons tied to the nature of the economic basis of society in different historical epochs and the domestic or international divisions of classes. Thus in the search for economic advantage (the securing of resources or additional markets) war was a vital instrument of diplomacy for mercantile and bourgeois classes. A second motivation for warfare in any system of classes was the functional need to perpetuate class divisions by raising the national banner to mobilize those who were repressed at home. A third motivation for warfare, one stressed more by Lenin than by Marx and Engels, had to do

[17]F. Engels, *Herr Eugen Duhring's Revolution in Science (Anti-Duhring)* (New York: International Publishers, 1939), p. 178.

[18]V. I. Lenin, "The Soviet Foreign Policy," in *Collected Works,* Vol. 23 (New York: International Publishers, 1945), p. 15.

with the international division of classes. Here bourgeois states could ally with one another against the downtrodden abroad or against any socialist revolutionary regime, which were supposed to challenge their dominance.

Although war was generally condemned under classical Marxism as an instrument of the bourgeois ruling elite to perpetuate class divisions, the classical Marxists themselves viewed war ambivalently. If war was largely an epiphenomenon which reflected the need and desire of the ruling elite to accumulate economic and material advantage, it was also somewhat of an independent force which, as it reinforced internal contradictions, helped to spur on the proletarian revolution. Whether one ought to be for or against particular wars, therefore, depended upon an examination of the concrete situation. Thus we find Marx himself a proponent of the wars of German unification before 1870. The creation of a large German market would help create a large industrial base and therefore the conditions for proletarian revolution. After the Franco-Prussian War, however, Marx assumed a rather conservative posture, since he felt that future wars might have a detrimental effect on proletarian solidarity in Germany. For similar reasons, he was against German annexation of Alsace-Lorraine lest it provoke revisionist claims by France and future war, which would also be detrimental to worker solidarity.[19] In the long run, of course, the proletarian revolution would have to take place, regardless of short-term impediments to it. Yet, here as a primary tactical issue based on the theoretical examination of concrete instances, determinations could be made on the desirability of war or peace.

The Marxist analysis of international relations nonetheless remained rather rudimentary and was more of an offshoot of the analysis of capitalism than an independent line of inquiry until Lenin's classical analysis of late-nineteenth-century European imperialism. It was Lenin's account which was to become highly influential in the course of the twentieth century as leaders of various nationalist movements in less developed countries learned it in studying at universities in their former metropoles. Lenin's argument was as much a justification of his own political program as it was a balanced analysis of European expansion. It relied heavily on the accounts of the Austrian economist Hilferding and the British economist Hobson and also involved a cri-

---

[19]See Hélène Carrère d'Encausse, "Communisme et nationalisme," *Revue française de science politique*, XV:3 (June 1965), pp. 466–498.

tique of Kautsky and the social democrats in infighting in the international movement. Nevertheless, the line of argument provides a succinct theoretical analysis, which has coherence and immediate relevance to our survey.

Lenin noted several changes in the development of capitalist societies not taken into account in classical Marxism. From his observations he built an elegant and simple argument, which may be summarized as follows:[20] (1) As capitalism develops, the means of production and centers of capital become highly concentrated and organized around monopolies, which play an increasing role in economic organization and activity. (2) Industrial capital and bank capital eventually merge, thus creating a new form of financial oligarchy, which is the basis of finance capital. (3) A surplus of capital develops as domestic markets achieve the limits of viable expansion under the capitalist regime; trade barriers are raised to prevent other capitalist states from penetrating protected home markets; and, as a result, the exportation of capital gains an increased importance and eventually surpasses (in significance) the export of commodities. (4) International capitalist monopolies develop and divide world markets among themselves. (5) Since capitalist states are run by the new financial oligarchy, the capitalist powers territorially divide the whole world. (6) In this new industrial-financial imperialism, the capitalist states will eventually conflict with one another, in the ashes of global confrontation will spark the proletarian revolution, and the new regime of international proletarianism will rise.

It is not my objective to analyze the logical or empirical basis of Lenin's theory. Nor shall I trace the evolution of this theory under various programs of the Communist Party of the Soviet Union as they have taken into account such newer developments as the creation of nuclear weapons.[21] The important point is that the Marxist account places its emphasis on the evolution and eventual transcendence of class conflict by the elimination of the state as an instrument of social repression. As Kenneth Waltz has argued,

The importance of Marx and Engels in this respect lies not in the thought that the end of states is the end of war but instead lies

[20]See V. I. Lenin, *Imperialism, the Highest Stage of Capitalism* (New York: International Publishers, 1939 [1916]).

[21]For an excellent survey and critique see George Lichtheim, *Imperialism* (New York: Praeger, 1971), pp. 134–152.

precisely in the fact that Marxist theory subordinates the problem of war and peace to the triumph of the revolutionary world proletariat, at which point men live no longer in states but are united in a nonpolitical free association.[22]

The upshot of Marxism, in short, is the creation of a new order of proletarian internationalism. The bourgeois state, which was to be denounced as an instrument of class superiority, had major and necessary achievements. It not only brought about a new era of abundance through industrialization but also was responsible for the creation of the working class as a new actor in world politics, whose eventual victory would herald a new era in the transformation of relations between peoples and societies. It is not clear whether the emergence of a new global regime of international proletarianism represents the transcendence of diplomacy or the institutionalization of a transformed system of diplomatic relations. What is clear is that (for Marxism) the ideal international order is inherently non-zero-sum. The zero-sum nature of the system of classical statecraft, like the disguised bellicosity of the liberal regime, stemmed from domestic and international class conflict rather than from national divisions. With the elimination of classes and instruments of class oppression, including that of the state, generalized conflict would also be terminated.

The end of Marxist society is, then, rather akin to the end of the liberal order: the transcendence of politics and all forms of political conflict and the apotheosis of a natural harmony of interests among all. Proletarian internationalism would reflect a real communality of class interests, and with the elimination of oppression would come the elimination of alienation not simply of workers but of all of society. The question of how to achieve abundance was not problematic in industrial society. What was problematic was how to achieve a new democratic order, defined in terms of a just and egalitarian distribution of social wealth and classless society. With the achievement of classless society, national and international frictions alike would be eliminated.

Marxist analysis thus places an emphasis on certain qualities of the ideal international order. If the basis of this order was somewhat ambiguous and lacking in concreteness, what was clear was that the mono-

---

[22]Kenneth Waltz, *Man, the State and War* (New York: Columbia University Press, 1954), p. 127.

causal nature of conflict under this analysis predicted that the new society would necessarily be one of perpetual peace. The Marxist account of liberalism had argued that the liberal norm of a natural harmony of interests among democratic-liberal states formed part of the superstructure of capitalist society which allowed states like Britain in the nineteenth century to pursue a policy of disguised (and eventually overt) imperialism. The Marxist ideal might well reflect a similar sort of ideological bias. If the new order of proletarian internationalism was stateless yet one in which national self-development could occur, how, for example, could conflicting aims of the different nationalities be reconciled? This rejection of diplomacy and of other alternative theories of conflict under Marxism did not go unrecognized by other political movements and was one of the primary issues raised by the third school of thought that we will now examine.

THE ECONOMIC REVIVAL OF NATIONALISM

The two ideologies we have just reviewed, liberalism and Marxism, together contrast starkly with the third. Both ideologies are fundamentally cosmopolitan and reflect the interconnections among societies that developed along with the process of modernization and industrialization. The processes of industrialization served progressively to knit together the world in a variety of ways. The spread of markets for industrial goods, the search for sources of raw materials to feed industrialization, the development of an international division of labor through specialization, and technological breakthroughs in transportation and communication went hand in hand with the increasing rapidity with which ideas and habits spread throughout the world. Both ideologies tried to come to terms with this new global society in order to explain it and to lend it moral and normative dimensions. They also tried to justify the hope that industrialization would bring about the conditions of perpetual peace.

Another significant and common feature of liberalism and Marxism was their depreciation of politics. Both ideologies pointed toward a world that could transcend conflict in domestic and international affairs. Universal society would in each case eventually dissolve the particularism of national distinctions and create the basis of the development of a commonality of interests among people on a global scale. Both ideologies thus pointed to "the end of history." Mankind would enter a state of "satisfaction," with the elimination of the seeds of all conflict. For liberalism this would be accomplished by the institutionalization of democratic regimes throughout the world and the lowering of barriers to movements of goods and services or to movements of the mobile factors of production (capital, labor, and technology). A network of interdependent relationships would thereby develop, and market mechanisms would eventually create a just and egalitarian distribution of wealth, and each being compensated according to his contribution to economic production. Marxism, which began with criticisms of the excesses of capitalist industrialization and the failure of liberalism to live up to its normative claims, argued that the road to world peace was via the elimination of those excesses and the revolutionary institutionalization of a socialist regime which could eliminate classes and class conflict and thereby permit the progressive establishment of an international community of interests, known as proletarian internationalism.

It would be a mistake, however, to argue that liberalism and Marxism reflect the basic and underlying tendency of modernization to create a world either of global cosmopolitanism or of peace. As argued in Chapter 1, modernization not only has a tendency to dissolve old bonds and old forms of particularism, like the nationalism of the eighteenth century. Along with this universalist aspect of modernization there is established a new set of social bonds and particularisms that contradict and counterbalance universalist tendencies. Nowhere can this be better seen than in the emergence of modern nationalism, which, while it does not embody as coherent a set of notions as either liberalism or Marxism, has had an equal influence in the political rhetoric of the contemporary world as an ideological explanation of events that also can serve as a guide to action.

Since no state in the contemporary international system is devoid of elements of what might be called this new nationalism—not even a predominantly liberal state like the United States or one, like the Soviet Union, whose political beliefs are derivative of classical Marxism—it is perhaps best to look at the origins of political and economic nationalism in a context in which neither liberalism nor Marxism played a major role. For our purpose, which is the exposition of ideas rather than of historical detail, we will look at some of the notions of Friedrich List and other "protectionists" of the nineteenth century, whose ideas have a frequently unacknowledged presence in the ways contemporary governments tend to behave. This is no less true, I shall argue in the next chapter, of cosmopolitan regimes in the northern hemisphere than it is among "newer" states of the economically less developed world, where economic nationalism is now fostered with unabashed pride.

The proponents of economic nationalism began their analyses with the same set of observations as those of liberalism or Marxism, yet they also formed strong dissents from the normative and empirical conclusions of both.[23] For this school of thought industrialism did represent a new phenomenon in international affairs. But the novelty of industrialization lay not in its transformatory character. For economic nationalists neither the ideal patterns of international society nor the fundamental motivations of statecraft were changed by industrialization and modernization. The novelty of industrialization was that it had become a new stake in the perpetual battle of international relations.

Economic nationalists admitted, and indeed based their arguments on, the view that what industrialization created was the opportunity to provide for a progressively better standard of living for the members of society and, of equal importance, for the ability of new states to compete for the stakes of global power. They thus confirmed the assumptions that were prevalent both in mercantilism and in classical statecraft. They tended to view liberalism through what paradoxically might be called Marxian lenses. It was no accident for them that Manchester liberalism and free trade made up the dominant ideology of British diplomacy. Nor did the seminal writers in this school, like the German economist Friedrich List (1789-1846), deny that free trade served to maximize global wealth. Their objection to liberalism, however, was different from that of the Marxists, who had argued that liberalism was the ideology of capitalist classes that enabled them to preserve for a time their control over the instruments of the state just as they exacerbated class divisions. Rather, their objection was dual and focused on liberalism as a national rather than class-based ideology.

---

[23] For an excellent and comprehensive but brief survey, see J. B. Condliffe, *The Commerce of Nations* (London: Allen & Unwin, 1951), Chap. 9. Condliffe includes socialism and Marxism in his survey of "The Dissenters," because his primary focus is liberal thought. He does not pose the distinction between universalist and particularist doctrines upon which this chapter is partially based.

The economic nationalists argued, in the first place, that liberalism was an appropriate political strategem for Britain, which, as the first and largest industrialized society, gained a great deal from free trade. In their eyes, however, liberalism was nothing less than a form of disguised imperialism. While all Britain's trading partners might well gain from free trade, they argued, Britain gained more than the others. Liberalism, in short, was visibly non-zero-sum in its effect but in the end had an undeniably zero-sum aspect in that the world was asymmetrical, and in such a world the largest trader gains more than others. More important, however, was the argument that free trade had negative consequences for relatively nonindustrialized societies. It gave to Britain undeniably comparative advantage in the production of industrial products, which British producers could sell at low prices, thus impeding other states from developing their own industries so long as they engaged in free trade with Britain (given the high start-up costs of industrial production).

This second objection to the liberal system reflects the economic nationalists' views of international society as well as the basis of their argument for protectionism. It demonstrates also why industrialization became a global stake under this philosophy. Liberalism could not, in the end, eliminate international conflict through the implementation of a regime of free trade, just as Marxism could not achieve peace even with the elimination of class conflict. This was because, for economic nationalists, the basic and unchanging unit of international affairs had to remain the nation-state. It was an unexamined assumption of economic nationalists that the nation was the appropriate and permanent focus of social organizations. List made this perfectly clear when he argued,

> I would indicate, as the distinguishing characteristic of my system, NATIONALITY. On the nature of *nationality,* as the intermediate interest between those of *individualism* and of *entire humanity,* my whole structure is based.[24]

Since the nation-state could not be transcended and since it would always be the "natural" unit of human organization, the acceptance by a relatively nonindustrialized society of a regime of free trade was

[24]Friedrich List, *The National System of Political Economy,* translated by Sampson S. Lloyd, revised ed. (London, 1922), as cited in J. B. Condliffe, *The Commerce of Nations* (London: Allen & Unwin, 1951), p. 277.

tantamount to relinquishing its autonomous ability to govern itself. This was irresponsible for any government to countenance, given an additional assumption of economic nationalism which stemmed from classical statecraft.[25] This was that the world was and would always be essentially zero-sum, or conflictual. One nation's gain would always be another's loss, and this, as we have seen, was aggravated by the ability of Britain to disguise its position through liberal economics. Neither industrialization nor democraticization, even on a global scale, could transcend a world of conflict, because conflict was an inherent part of the human condition. In a world in which the major objectives of government are the maintenance of individual governmental autonomy and the pursuit of domestic economic growth, history would continue to be a continual manifestation of struggles among nations for power and grandeur.[26]

The proper attitude for any government desirous of preserving its autonomy and increasing domestic wealth was thus one that accepted the inherently conflictual nature of global politics. Two general types of policy instruments were required for use by any government which, not yet industrialized, sought to become so. On the one hand, economic protectionism was both necessary and desirable. Here we find a generalized acceptance on the part of protectionists of views that had earlier been propounded in the United States by Alexander Hamilton in his *Report on the Subject of Manufactures* of December 1791. In that report Hamilton had laid out all the basic arguments in favor of protectionism, including the infant-industry argument, the need to encourage the development of an internal market, and the need to foster economic growth and autonomy in a world of perpetual conflict among nations. In short, economic nationalists argued that in spite of the liberal critique of mercantilist protectionism, under proper conditions protectionism worked to achieve real economic and political gains that could not be achieved under free trade. Here protectionism was oriented toward the flow of goods and services from abroad. It

---

[25] For a history of the continuity of this assumption in European and especially German thought, see Friedrich Meinecke, *Machiavellism: The Doctrine of Raison d'Etat and Its Place in Modern History,* translated by Douglas Scott (New Haven, Conn.: Yale University Press, 1957).

[26] The views of a variety of protectionists concerning the inherent bellicosity of global politics are found in Edmund Silberner, *La Guerre et la paix dans l'histoire des doctrines économiques* (Paris: Sirey, 1957), pp. 104–168.

was interested in keeping out these goods so that indigenous industry could develop in an increasingly large internal market. It was not oriented to the erection of impediments to the flow of capital and technology from abroad, which could enhance the development of internal industry. Nor would it necessarily be oriented toward the erection of barriers to the flow of labor, if critical labor shortages existed in the internal market (as they have in the United States throughout most of American history).

The second policy instrument that economic nationalists propounded was the use of force. Here they sharply disagreed with the liberal view that wars never paid. Not only did they argue that wars could not be eliminated, due to the inherent bellicosity of a world of nation-states, but they also argued that war, like other forms of the use of force, could result in real rather than illusory gains. It was never clear, as liberals had argued, that wars always brought costs to all sides. The economic nationalists argued that it all depended upon concrete circumstances. At a minimum, a victor in war could achieve two sorts of permanent gains that could be achieved less well by other means. On the one hand, wars spurred on the industrialization process within the economy, especially, though not only, by strengthening the armaments and arms-related industries and also increasing the national income. On the other hand, the material fruits of war, including territory and natural resources as well as perhaps increased deference from foreign governments, could also place a society in a superior position for the achievement of its economic goals.

We have thus far focused upon the views of economic nationalists concerning some of the fundamental features of international society. Their views on other aspects of international relations that we have examined under classical statecraft, liberalism, and Marxism should by now be obvious. Unlike classical statecraft and like the other two ideologies, economic nationalism stressed the indissoluble bonds between domestic and foreign policy. Although in each case the nature of this bond is different, it is a significant observation and normative posture of all modern ideologies that foreign and domestic policies ought not to be separated from one another. This has not meant, however, that the specific analysis of this bond is the same in all cases. In fact, given the acceptability of conflict in economic nationalism and its stigmatic quality in the other ideologies, we ought not to expect this. For all three the bond is and ought to be tight insofar as recognization of the linkage is fundamental to the achievement of some state of "satisfaction" for society as a whole. But in the case of the economic nationalists, the linkage is focused upon an economic growth that results in real gains for the society at the expense of others (as for instance in the separation of the national market from the global market). Protectionists in this school would also, unlike liberals or Marxists, justify militarism and military expenditures in economic terms, and have spent a good deal of their analyses focusing upon the economic utility of military preparations and permanent standing armies and navies, as well as trying to prove the economic nonsense of disarmament.[27]

The relationship between economic and political affairs in economic nationalism is obviously as tight as it was under mercantilism. It is no accident that the focus on domestic economic growth in all contemporary societies, whether or not one accepts the view that global politics is essentially conflictual, has been called neomercantilist. Economic growth and power are different faces of the same phenomenon. In an era in which economic growth is a fundamental goal of virtually all governments, the liberal or Marxist view that one can separate it from its political aspects must be illusory.

Similarly, economic nationalists place a premium on both the growth in the power of the state and the importance of statist intervention in economic life. The planned economy owes as much in its origins to economic nationalism as it does to the socialist desire to provide for a more egalitarian distribution of social wealth. The state is a natural human phenomenon and the most appropriate institutional form of human organization. Its power is important in a world of bellicosity where a nation's autonomy is a value to be preserved regardless of cost and where only state intervention can assure a society that it can achieve an equitable share of international wealth.

Economic nationalists obviously did not accept the heroic framework of classical statecraft any more than did the liberals or Marxists. Nationalism had by the mid-nineteenth century superseded the identification of a ruling class with a national realm. Nationalism came to be equated with the rights of individual cultures, sharing a common cultural and political heritage, language, and frequently religion, to self-determination or self-fulfillment.[28] The value of national traits was

---

[27]See ibid., pp. 116–120.

[28]See Alfred Cobban, *The Nation-State and National Self-Determination* (London: Oxford University Press, 1945), ch. 3.

thus an inherent part of economic nationalism and perhaps the basic motivation in its stress on protectionism and gains from the use of force. But while it differs in this respect from classical statecraft, it did not differ in terms of the desirability of maintaining the balance of power as the ideal form of international organization.

International balance was viewed by economic nationalists as the only appropriate means of organizing international life, given the permanence of the nation state and the desirability of all to preserve autonomy. Here too economic nationalism, at least in the nineteenth century, accepted the division within classical state-craft between great powers and others. It was primarily the great powers for which protectionism and the resort to force were requisite instruments of state policy. It was their autonomy which had to be preserved, and their economic growth that was best fostered in terms of some form of national encapsulation. For them autonomy could be preserved if a number of great powers coexisted, reconciling their conflictual goals with one another and preventing any one from gaining dominance, as Britain did when it ascended to industrial primacy and global power in the nineteenth century. Other nations, not well endowed in territory, population, or natural resources, would be too small to achieve economic growth and national power through protectionism. For them the use of force was perhaps too risky. The best strategy for a lesser power desirous of achieving economic growth was association with a natural ally in a more open economic relationship. In its case autonomy would not likely serve it well.

CONCLUSIONS

In this chapter we have traced and compared the fundamental ideas of three major normative interpretations of the process of industrialization and its effect on statecraft. These three ideological responses to the process of modernization preceded by perhaps a century the time when"objective observation" could perhaps have more decisively indicated that significant aspects of international politics had changed. Yet they reflected contemporary observations that industrialization had in fact had momentous effects upon domestic and international politics. Their significance also lies in the tremendous impact that

these sets of ideas have had in both explaining and guiding state behavior in the nineteenth and twentieth centuries.

If the three ideologies we have traced in this chapter share a common
effort to come to grips with modernization, they also contrast greatly
within one another in significant respects. Liberalism looked to industrialization and the implementation of a global regime as the means
of developing a network of global interdependence that was to assure
the progressive enfolding of an epoch of permanent peace. Industrialization and democratization would inevitably pacify society.
Marxism argued that there was not simply one kind of industrial society, but rather there were two, one of which was bellicose and the
other pacific.[29] Free trade was for Marxism the agency for creating
international interdependence. It also was the means of enhanced
competition among bourgeois regimes, exacerbation of the class struggle, and the institutionalization of peace via the proletarian revolution,
which would transcend class conflict by providing for the common
ownership of all the means of production. Both liberalism and Marxism also called for the transcendence not only of balance-of-power
diplomacy, but of politics itself. For liberalism this would occur
through the replacement of the monarchic state by the limited "night
watchman" state. For Marxism, after the proletarian revolution an administration would perform necessary functions for society but the
state as an instrument of social oppression would be eliminated. Liberalism and Marxism also both called for a just and equitable distribution of social resources; the former argued that this could come about
through an automatic global process of redistribution that accompanied
free trade; the latter argued that it would require revolution.

Economic nationalism differed with both on the question of whether
industrialization would pacify international society. Economic growth
which accompanied industrialization had become a new stake for
diplomacy, but one which could have no consequence for questions of
war or peace, since conflict was built permanently into the human condition. The economic nationalists and protectionists thus disagreed with
Marxism's observation that there were both peaceful and conflictual
industrial societies; all would necessarily compete with one another.
They did agree with the Marxists in arguing that free trade was the

[29]This contrast is spelled out in detail in Raymond Aron, *War and Industrial
Society* (London: Oxford University Press, 1958).

ideology of the dominant industrial society and a means of maintaining its dominance. The answer to this was not, however, proletarian revolution, but rather the erection of economic barriers to trade in order to right the international balance. Correcting and maintaining the balance of power also called for the growth of state power, rather than its elimination. Only the state among social organizations could perform the functions required of industrialized society.

All modern ideologies have had a tendency to be practiced in excess. The French Revolution resulted in the effort of an imperialist France to revolutionize the world with egalitarian and universalist principles just as the Bolshevik Revolution did with respect to collectivist principles in twentieth-century Russia. Liberal America has likewise been attacked for trying to impose on the world a regime of free trade that would benefit it alone and that was similar to the system of free trade imposed by Britain in the nineteenth century.[30] And economic nationalism was embodied in its most extreme form in twentieth-century fascism, especially in Germany.

None of the three ideological systems that have come to predominate in the rhetoric of twentieth-century diplomacy can seriously be said to offer a coherent explanation of the effects of industrialization on international politics. They are each more normatively than empirically based. Yet together they offer significant hints concerning the general effects of modernization on diplomacy. In particular, the stress that each has placed upon technological change and economic instruments of diplomacy points up major innovations in the ways that governments behave and attempt to reconcile their mutually conflicting goals. In the next two chapters we will look more closely at changes within societies that result from modernization and try to offer a more empirical and less normative explanation of the effects of these changes on statecraft.

---

[30] This has been the central theme of revisionist interpretations of twentieth-century American diplomacy. See in particular the seminal work of William Appleman Williams, *The Tragedy of American Diplomacy* (New York: World Publishing, 1959).

4

The Transformation of
Foreign Policies

The notion that foreign policy is transformed once a society becomes industrialized has been debated ever since the physiocrats and liberal economists of the late eighteenth century attacked the conflict-prone old regimes of Europe. Most of this debate, as we have seen, has centered upon the questions of whether industrialized societies are inherently bellicose or pacific and whether industrialization promotes peaceful international intercourse among nations or exacerbates conflicts of interest, thereby increasing the likelihood of war.

As in the last chapter, it will be argued that the development of conditions that held out promises of an age of abundance had a fundamental and transformatory effect on statecraft. But the emphasis will be somewhat different. The ideological view of industrial society as bellicose or pacific, conflictual or cooperative, opens up far too many questions and provides few answers concerning the nature of this transformation. In this examination of several principal aspects of the conduct of foreign policies in highly modernized societies, we will inevitably touch upon several of the fundamental questions concerning the inherent bellicosity or pacifism of industrial societies. The aim, however, will be to cast a wider net. Our major interest is the ways the major aspects of foreign policies—their goals and substantive orientations, the procedures associated with their formulation, and their effectiveness—are transformed once societies become highly modernized.

The general argument that societies and the diplomacy of their governments are transformed under industrialization is not, of course, a new one. Modern social science originates with this proposition. Not only do liberal, Marxist, and nationalist arguments stem from this observation, but positivism, the major intellectual school of nineteenth-century France which is frequently viewed as the basis of modern sociology, also began with a set of observations concerning the effects of industrialization on the conduct of war. In particular, the writings of Auguste Comte (1798–1857) reflect a more widespread nineteenth-century notion that warfare was condemned by the natural evolution of societies.[1]

The arguments put forward by Comte and other early sociologists were based on detailed observation and embodied rigorous logic. They also had an apparent theoretical elegance. As Comte argued,

It is certainly the industrial quality of modern societies which offers their first great contrast with those of antiquity. . . . After the emancipation of the primitive labourers, the most advanced societies were mainly distinguished by the gradual preponderance of the industrial over the military way of life. . . .[2]

Comte continued his argument by observing that industrial societies have a natural tendency to foster antimilitaristic feelings. He felt that the development of military conscription, for example, demonstrated the difficulties governments encountered in attracting manpower for military purposes. An additional proof which Comte offered was somewhat more involuted. He observed that the industrial capabilities of Britain and France could have supported weapons systems far more destructive than those that had actually been produced. What seemed to Comte to be the declining role of defense expenditures in an expanding economy was additional evidence of the progressive pacification of society that resulted from industrialization. This trend, together with the stakes of industrial society in peace in order to maintain stable

[1] See Raymond Aron, *Main Currents in Sociological Thought,* Vol. 1, translated by Richard Howard and Helen Weaver (New York: Basic Books, 1965), Chap. 2.

[2] *The Positive Philosophy of Auguste Comte,* Vol. 3 translated by Harriet Martineau (London: George Bell, 1896, p. 204.

conditions for economic growth, meant that warfare would be inherently inconsistent with the bases of modernization.[3]

Equally influential were the predictions of Comte's teacher, Henri de Saint-Simon (1760–1825), concerning the evolution of industrial Europe.[4] He saw an evolution in the governance of industrial society, where an administrative elite would eventually emerge and replace older political elites. The complexity of industrial societies meant that they had to be led by officials who had expertise in the increasingly complex functions of society. What industrial society required, in short, was government by what later social scientists called functional elite groups. An expanding division of international labor and the spillover of administrative functions from one field to another led Saint-Simon to predict that at least in industrial Europe some form of supranational institutions would emerge and be administered by an administrative class which owed allegiance to no member nation. This would herald an age of international cooperation, integration, and the transcendence of national political divisions.

Comte's own conclusion that industrialization meant the end of the state of war in international society may have been premature, but his analysis did focus upon some significant aspects in the evolution of societies and foreign policies. If Comte was correct in his observation that antimilitarism either accompanied industrialization or resulted from it, he also failed to see an inherent contradiction in highly modernized societies which rests upon a set of contrasting trends in such societies. For example, we find in them an impetus to cooperate internationally in order to maintain an expanding level of economic growth—what Comte would have considered the emergence of rationalism with industrialization. We also find, however, that the bonds of the nation-state become strengthened and impede the growth of international cooperation. In short he failed to note that at least in highly modernized societies there was an affirmation of universalism as well as national particularism, of empirical economic goals but also of older transcendental political goals. Moreover, if the marginal costs of the

---

[3]Comte's ideas are developed in more detail and subjected to rigorous criticism in Raymond Aron, *War and Industrial Society* (London: Oxford University Press, 1958).

[4]See his essay "The Reorganization of the European Community," in *Social Organization, The Science of Man, and Other Writings,* translated by Felix Markham (New York: Harper & Row, 1964), pp. 28–68.

use of force have increased in highly modernized societies, as Comte argued they would, these costs also appear to result less from the advance of economic or administrative rationality than they do from the development of nuclear weapons. While the latter development is certainly based upon economic growth and new technological capacities, it also represents a phenomenon with which Comte could hardly have concerned himself in the mid-nineteenth century.

Our argument begins with a set of observations and generalizations which are similar to those originally set forth by Saint-Simon and Comte but which also take into account ambiguities and contradictory trends that they wrongly thought would disappear. Foreign policy has apparently been transformed radically by the revolutionary processes of modernization wherever high levels of modernization exist, and this is so regardless of whether the government in a highly modernized society is totalitarian or pluralistic, socialist or based on a free enterprise economy, a great power in the international arena or a relatively small-scale power. Moreover, the foreign policies conducted by the governments of such societies are, it will be argued, necessarily more similar to each other along certain specified dimensions than they are to the policies associated with nonmodernized societies.

Modernization has affected both the domestic settings in which foreign policies are formulated and the international arenas toward which they are oriented. The centralization of governmental institutions and decision-making processes and the predominance of domestic over external goals are among the most significant internal aspects of modernization, which also contradict some of its international or external aspects. There, modernization is accompanied by increased levels and types of interdependences among societies, which require but do not necessarily or always obtain a high level of international cooperation.

Three fundamental conditions have developed in the foreign policies of highly modernized societies as a result of these changes. First, the distinction between foreign and domestic affairs that was basic to classical statecraft has broken down, just as the ideologies we examined in Chapter 3 indicated it would. At the same time, however, the myths associated with sovereignty and the state not only have been transcended but have been reaffirmed. Second, the classical distinction between "high politics" (associated primarily with the continued existence and security of the state) and "low politics" (pertaining to task-oriented goals specific to industrialized societies) has been transformed. Not only are the two traded off for one another with increasing frequency, but for most modernized societies low politics have become high politics or as the economist Richard N. Cooper has argued, "trade policy is foreign policy."[5] Finally, while modernization has increased the ability of governments to control events in their environments by fostering state centralization, the actual ability of governments to control events either internal or external to them has decreased and is likely to continue to do so. This decrease in control has affected the efficacy of governmental policy in all industrialized societies, thus creating a crisis in governmental authority and legitimacy which is fundamental to current debates concerning the future not simply of the nation-state, but of industrialized societies themselves.

It is important to note that these generalizations pertain to highly modernized societies alone. We have not at all concerned ourselves with the behavior of governments in various phases of any presumptive natural evolution toward such a state. Indeed, we have by and large set aside the complex behavior of societies undergoing industrialization, since modernization begins in a wide variety of societies having an equally wide-ranging set of political institutions and organizations. Such phenomena as arms races, the new imperialism of the late nineteenth century, and "economic warfare" can all be traced in some measure to the processes of modernization. Both because of the complexities involved and the lack of a verified theory which would relate modernization to foreign policy, we will restrict ourselves to generalizations concerning highly modernized societies themselves. Nor, therefore, will we be concerned at present with the conduct of foreign policy in contemporary and relatively nonmodernized societies, although they will be analyzed to some degree later.

We are, thus, concerned here with those few highly modernized societies which attained this level during the nineteenth and twentieth centuries, including those fourteen identified by Russett and others as "high mass consumption" societies.[6] It is important to reiterate that while Russett's group is composed exclusively of modern democracies,

[5] Richard N. Cooper, "Trade Policy Is Foreign Policy," *Foreign Policy*, No. 9 (Winter 1972–73), pp. 18–36.

[6] Bruce M. Russett and others, *World Handbook of Political and Social Indicators* (New Haven, Conn.: Yale University Press, 1964), p. 298. These are the Netherlands, West Germany, France, Denmark, Norway, the United Kingdom, Belgium, New Zealand, Australia, Sweden, Luxembourg, Switzerland, Canada, and the United States.

there is no good logical or empirical reason to disassociate from our generalization the foreign policies of nondemocratic modernized societies.

FOREIGN VERSUS DOMESTIC POLICIES

The fundamental distinction made between foreign and domestic policies in classical statecraft and under notions of political realism breaks down in manifold ways under modernization. We have noted that the distinction breaks down in ideal terms under each of the modern ideologies we examined, but it also breaks down in other ways. This distinction is far more prominent both ideally and actually in nonmodernized societies than in modernized states. In the latter, the growth of both predominantly political and nonpolitical interactions across societies and the development of such transnational phenomena as labor movements and multinational corporations make it extremely difficult to maintain the two on separate tracks. Indeed, the activities and processes associated with modernization so blur this distinction that it is frequently impossible to say that a policy is predominantly domestic or foreign and frequently equal weight must be given to the two. For example, when Richard M. Nixon made his historic trips to China and the Soviet Union during 1972, it was clear that his re-election was as much at stake as the pursuit of international stability. Or, when Chairman Brezhnev led the movement in the Soviet Union for détente with the United States, he was as much concerned with the allocation of resources within Russia and the power of various domestic interest groups as he was with curtailing international tensions.

Foreign policies can still be distinguished analytically or definitionally from domestic policies. For our purposes, foreign policies will be considered those that are, at a minimum, manifestly oriented to some actual or potential sphere external to a political system (i.e., outside the jurisdiction or control of the polity). They are contrasted with domestic policies, which are oriented to some sphere within the jurisdiction and control of government. Thus while foreign policies may be oriented principally to a particular domestic interest group, so long as they bear a minimal intention and recognition of external orientation, they are foreign policies.

The Rankean distinction between the two sorts of policies, examined in Chapter 2, assumed that there is an ontological divorce between foreign and domestic affairs, since the former aim at national rather than particular interests, utilize any means to achieve the goal of security including instruments of violence rather than only those considered "legitimate" under a constitution, and are oriented toward a decentralized, anarchic milieu as opposed to the centralized domestic order, where a state monopolizes the instruments of violence. That distinction seemed, in fact, to have a strong empirical foundation under classical statecraft, since levels of interdependence among societies were extremely low and governments could act in the domestic or foreign sphere without affecting their goals in the other sphere. Foreign policy was, of course, affected by domestic factors as well as by characteristics of the international setting, but generally the inherently normative distinction between foreign and domestic policies was well matched by existing conditions.

The distinction breaks down in empirical terms once societies become highly modernized, and any effort to maintain it over extended periods of time is bound to create difficulties for a government. The sacrificing of foreign policy goals for domestic political reasons can both jeopardize a state's security and impair its economic growth. If domestic policy is forced to take second place to external goals, demands put upon governments by a population may well be unsatisfied, thereby undermining domestic confidence in the government. The upshot is a dilemma confronted by all modernized governments, which are more often than not unable simultaneously to achieve both domestic and foreign policy goals.

The interrelationships between foreign and domestic policies do not imply that "foreign and domestic policy in developed Western systems constitutes today a seamless web," as Carl Friedrich has argued.[7] Analytic and definitional distinctions still obtain. Moreover, governments continue to formulate their policies with a predominant orientation to external or internal conditions. But in modernized societies foreign and domestic policies appear to affect one another in new ways that derive from interdependences between societies or from the expanded

---

[7]Carl J. Friedrich, "International Politics and Foreign Policy in Developed (Western) Societies," in R. Barry Farrell, ed., *Approaches to Comparative and International Politics* (Evanston, Ill.: Northwestern University Press, 1966), p. 97.

range of governmental interventions. Before modernization, for example, governmental expenditures were devoted to three major activities: the costs of defense (preparation for future wars), the costs of servicing the national debt (paying for past wars), and the costs of governmental administration.[8] As the government's role in the economic and social life of a society increases, concern for foreign policy must decrease relative to the concern for domestic affairs. Moreover, with the growth in international interdependence the external consequences of domestic policies become more significant, just as the domestic effects of foreign policies become more pronounced. And unintentional policy consequences also must increase, since the interconnectedness of different policy realms increases. Thus undesirable policy consequences also increase.

The growth in the ties between domestic and foreign policy forms the basic characteristic of the breakdown in the separation of domestic and foreign affairs under modernization. This breakdown is far more complex than this brief analysis implies, as will become obvious later in this chapter. The analysis nontheless suggests some of the ways in which foreign policies are transformed by the process of modernization and the creation with it of high levels of interdependence among societies. This breakdown apparently obtains wherever modernization takes place and regardless of the type of political institutions in which foreign policies are formulated. Having looked at the breakdown in this general context, we will now turn to an examination of the transformation of the basic dimensions of foreign policy under modernization.

FOREIGN POLICIES IN MODERNIZED SOCIETIES

The effects of modernization on the conduct of foreign policy can be analyzed in terms of policy *content,* the *processes* by which policy is formulated, and policy effectiveness, or *outcomes.* My general argument can be summarized as follows:

[8] See Walt Whitman Rostow, *Politics and the Stages of Growth* (London: Cambridge University Press, 1971), pp. 26–53.

In terms of policy *content,* the ideal pattern of foreign policy, with its emphasis on high policy functions related to the maintenance of the integrity of the state (security and territorial defense) or to the enhancement of some attribute of the state (population, territory, fulfillment of national ideals), has been widened into—and frequently replaced by—a new pattern. For those states, like the United States and the Soviet Union in particular, with a large territorial and economic base, there is a broadening of the spectrum of policy goals, so that goals of wealth and welfare become as important as those of power and international position associated with high policy. For most other states, these older ideal patterns tend to be almost completely overshadowed by the growth in significance of low policies.[9]

What is apparently distinctive and new about these policies is that they seem to be primarily nonconflictual. At least the general framework of international relations has been reversed to a large degree because of the exigency of international cooperation for the attainment of basic domestic policy goals. If in an earlier period cooperation took place in a primarily conflictual context, now, under the impetus of modernization, conflicts among states tend to take place increasingly in a context that is primarily cooperative. Moreover, like the relations of which they are a part, some of these policies are merely fleeting and casual; others are explicitly cooperative and involve the production and distribution of collective goods at the international level[10] and require compatible efforts on the part of officials and other elite groups in different societies.

An additional distinctive quality in foreign policies of highly modernized societies is that the goods that are produced and that involve

[9] Some scholars, like Stanley Hoffmann, offer another argument concerning low policies and high policies. In his essay "Obstinate or Obsolete? The Fate of the Nation-State and the Case of Western Europe," *Daedalus,* XCV (Summer 1966), pp. 862–915. Hoffmann argues that nuclear deterrence has served to reinforce the attributes of the nation-state by stabilizing the structure of postwar international society. Low policies do not generate the spillover expected of them by prophets of international integration.

[10] Definitions of public goods generally place emphasis on one society rather than on a group of societies. The focus is then on nonexclusivity or the incapacity of a single organization or government to prevent any individual members from receiving its benefits. See Mancur Olson, Jr., *The Logic of Collective Action and the Theory of Groups* (Cambridge, Mass.: Harvard University Press, 1965). It is also true, however, that incentives exist for cooperation with a group, based on the attraction of greater benefits.

cooperative behavior *are seen as* economic goods, even though they may be essentially political. They arise from such phenomena as the growth in international trade and the need to regulate trade imbalances, to produce new liquidity to finance trade, and to maintain the whole set of regulatory devices required to govern economic behavior. Although many such goods are measurable primarily in economic terms, they are largely political and relate to one of the central features of politics under modernized conditions, where the politics of wealth and welfare have overshadowed the politics of power and position. The latter tend to be played out in economic terms, especially though not only among modernized societies. The high costs of the use of force, among other things, have made trade rounds in the General Agreement on Tariffs and Trade (GATT) and reform measures in the International Monetary Fund (IMF) the essence of international politics today for the more highly modernized societies in their relations with one another. Less modernized societies too, especially in their relations with wealthier, more highly industrialized societies, place an emphasis on the distribution of primarily economic goods and sometimes attempt to gain other policy goals by the manipulation of market conditions, as has been the case especially with exporters of resources in recent years.

Before modernization foreign policy goals tended to be transcendental, by which we mean that they were never completely reducible to empirical states of affairs. Goals like "security," "grandeur," or "power" are characteristic transcendental goals of foreign policy.[11] In the case of highly modernized societies an additional spectrum of goals develops, which tend to be predominantly empirical ones, or at least almost completely transferable to empirical ones, and which generally refer to qualities associated with the pursuit of wealth and welfare. Paradoxically, however, a new set of transcendental policies also arises out of modernized societies. As I shall argue below, these new transcendental policies result less from the inherent value of grandeur or power, as in premodern societies, than from the difficulties that modernized governments have in providing effectively the wealth and welfare goals that they are expected to pursue.

With respect to the second set of policy conditions, the *processes* by

[11] For a discussion of the transfer of referents of social action from transcendental to empirical ones, see Marion J. Levy, Jr., "Rapid Social Change and Some Implications for Modernization," in *International Conference on the Problems of Modernization in Asia, June 28–July 7, 1965* (Seoul, 1965), pp. 657–658.

which policy is formulated, it is modernization rather than democratization that seems to have transformed foreign policy decision making. Before modernization reached high levels, cabinet-style, closed-arena decision-making processes prevailed both domestically and in international negotiations. Now, while the locus of decision making has remained fundamentally administrative, the scale of modern administration has changed so greatly that decision making has become far more complex and increasingly open, if only because those involved in the policy process appeal to groups outside the official decision-making structure for support. Moreover, the infusion into foreign policy of ideologies that tend to deal with intersocietal rather than intergovernmental relations, together with enhanced international networks of communication, has made governments appeal increasingly to the populations and not simply the governments of other societies as a means of achieving their foreign policy goals.

Finally, with respect to the third set of foreign policy issues—those dealing with the problems of implementing and controlling foreign policy—conditions have also been transformed under modernization. In one sense, the problem of controlling events external to the state is the major problem of foreign policy regardless of the type of society involved. This is the case because political systems exist in an international arena whose fundamental feature is the absence of any overarching structures of political authority. At one time great powers could be differentiated from others by the degree to which they could control their external environments. But the growth in international interdependence has made the issue of control problematic for all societies, and, as I shall argue in Chapter 5, all modernized societies have witnessed a loss of control not only over their international environments but also over domestic conditions. As a result of the complexity of the problem of control under conditions of interdependence, no state can be regarded as a great power in the old sense of the term. What is special, then, about foreign policies conducted under modernized conditions is the scale of the problem of control. I shall argue that the loss of control both domestically and in the external environment will prove to be the central problem of international politics in the coming years. This problem has significant implications, including several that concern the future of the nation-state and the nature of functional equivalents to it that can be devised in areas where governments have lost their effectiveness.

We will now investigate each of these components of foreign policy in somewhat greater detail.

The Transformation of Policy Objectives

In recent years scholars concerned with international relations have become increasingly aware of the degree to which economic and other affairs associated with low policies have become central to foreign policy. For a long time, preoccupation with high policies and with traditional foreign policy objectives and instruments drew their attention away from the changes in policy goals that have accompanied modernization, and especially from the increased salience of low policies and the merging of goals of power and of plenty.[12] General discussions of foreign policy goals still focus on high policies, which analysts often thought of as ultimate, transcendental ends. Arnold Wolfers, for example, defined the classical goals of statecraft as "self-extention" or "self-preservation."[13] These were transcendental goals, as were imperialism, security, prestige, and the ideal position or role that a government might postulate for itself in international affairs. For example, a transcendental security goal might be identified with stature in the international system, or with a certain set of role premises, like "mediator" or "balancer."

Earlier I suggested that just as the classical goals of power and security have been expanded or superseded by goals of wealth and welfare, there has also been a change in the empirical referents used to identify transcendental goals. Transcendental goals always have some reference to empirical conditions, but they are only partially identified with them. Power and prestige, for example, have been associated in the past with such empirical issues as increased population and accretions of the territorial domain of the state. What is of interest to us is

[12] John J. Weltman, "On the Obsolescence of War: An Essay in Policy and Theory," *International Studies Quarterly,* 18:4 (December 1974), pp. 395–416.

[13] Arnold Wolfers, *Discord and Collaboration: Essays on International Politics* (Baltimore: Johns Hopkins Press, 1962), pp. 91–102. Wolfers has a third category, "self-abnegation," which is a logical possibility with virtually no empirical example.

that empirical referents of transcendental goals "change; new ones are created; old ones pass out of existence; and their relations . . . are shuffled."[14]

Under modernization, the former identification of power and security with territory and population has been changed to an identification of welfare with economic growth and a just or equitable distribution of resources. As Klaus Knorr has argued, "Territorial conquest by force of arms has lost the perennial attraction it possessed throughout mankind's violent history."[15] Unlike the goals of power and prestige, the new goals of growth and the distribution of the fruits of abundance appear to be almost wholly commensurable. It would thus seem that foreign policy goals under modernized conditions are no longer as transcendental as they were under the old regime. This would especially be the case if it were true that modernization also brings with it "the end of ideology."[16] It might well have been that if governments had been able to control growth and distribution equitably, their populations would have been so satisfied that transcendental policy objectives would have been eliminated. However, modern governments seem to be highly restricted in their ability to implement their policies, especially their domestic reform programs. One result has been the re-emergence of transcendental foreign policies, especially but not only in Europe. These policies are focused less on tangible than on elusive objectives (building a new European identity, carrying out a new Eastern policy, etc.) and are designed to create the illusion in the minds of the population that the governments have been engaged in significant and novel activities. Unlike the transcendental politics of the past, when the monarchs of Europe sought genuinely after power and glory, the new transcendental politics is one of activity for its own sake, even when the activity is uninformed by either grand designs or short-term empirical goals. But in spite of the re-emergence of transcendentalism in foreign policy, there has been a radical change in the substance of policy goals. Two general transformations associated with high levels of modernization appear to be responsible for the change. One has to

[14]Levy, "Rapid Social Change," p. 657.

[15]Klaus Knorr, *On the Uses of Military Power in the Nuclear Age* (Princeton, N.J.: Princeton University Press, 1966), p. 21.

[16]For a set of essays concerned with debates over the end of an age of ideology, see Chaim I. Waxman, ed., *The End of Ideology Debate* (New York: Funk & Wagnalls, 1968).

do with the classical instruments of policy—armaments—and the changes brought about in external goals by the development of nuclear weapons and their delivery systems. The other relates to a more general transformation in domestic society under modernization.

The development of nuclear weapons has had so profound an impact on the conduct of foreign policy that it ought to receive a separate examination. I shall recapitulate here some of the major effects that have been noted as results of these weapons' emergence in global politics.[17] At a minimum, the developments of weapons of massive destruction, of delivery systems capable of launching them on target virtually instantaneously, and of international deterrence have been cross-cutting. On the one hand, these developments have made the territorial state incapable of providing security through defense, not simply because they are based on offensive weapons systems but also because they have created the first truly global system, unified by the possibility of generating unacceptable levels of human destruction that no state can potentially escape. On the other hand, nuclear weapons have paradoxically reaffirmed the viability of the nation-state as a political unit, by making the costs of expansion prohibitive.[18]

Nuclear weapons have other paradoxical effects, for nuclear and non-nulcear powers alike.[19] As Knorr has argued, the revolutionary impact of nuclear weapons stems from their uniqueness in terms of (1) the scale of their destructive capability; (2) the superiority they render to offensive over defensive forces and postures; (3) the uncertainty they create in judging both the power and actions of other governments, thus making rational calculation extremely difficult; (4) their apparently unlimited range, which depreciates the effectiveness of geographic barriers; and (5) the high speed of their delivery, which eliminates any

[17]See, for example, Bernard Brodie, *Strategy in the Missile Age* (Princeton, N.J.: Princeton University Press, 1959); and Robert E. Osgood and Robert W. Tucker, *Force, Order, and Justice* (Baltimore: Johns Hopkins Press, 1967).

[18]For an analysis of the set of cross-cutting effects of nuclear weapons on the state, see Pierre Hassner, "The Nation-State in the Nuclear Age," *Survey*, LXVII (April 1968), pp. 3–27. Also see the two essays by John Herz, "The Rise and Demise of the Territorial State," *World Politics*, IX (1957), pp. 473–493; and "The Territorial State Revisited," *Polity*, I (1968), pp. 12–34.

[19]This discussion is based on the following sources: Pierre Hassner, "On ne badine pas avec la force," *Revue Française de Science Politique*, XXI (1971), pp. 1207–1233; Knorr, *On the Uses of Military Power;* and Hans J. Morgenthau, "The Four Paradoxes of Nuclear Strategy," *The American Political Science Review*, LVIII:1 (March 1964), pp. 23 ff.

meaningful attempt to permit a time for reaction to their deployment and consequently also creates a virtual certainty of retaliation by the target state in the event of attack. This last point also provides, paradoxically, for stability in the relations among nuclear powers.[20]

Nuclear weapons, the most massively destructive ones ever created, have helped bring about, not total war, but rather the rebirth of strategy in an era of total war because of the fear of the consequences of their use. They have imposed a rationality on policy and almost forced states—especially the superpowers—to avoid ideological conflict and focus upon mutual interests. They also have provided for stability among nuclear powers. But, given the costs of using them, they have paradoxically enhanced the freedom of action both of less developed societies and of allies of the superpowers. They thus have created a seemingly permanent tension between the major nuclear powers, which have a stake in the international status quo, and the others, which may tend to have a stake in changing the status quo in order to enhance their own autonomy and perhaps lower their dependence on the superpowers.

One key, then, to the obsolescence of territorial goals that accompanied the development of nuclear weapons has been the increased cost of territorial accretion. No modernized society can afford it. It should not be surprising, therefore, that major territorial disputes have virtually disappeared from relations among the highly modernized states. They occur either when there is no danger that nuclear weapons will be used, thus accompanying nation-building efforts in the nonmodernized world, or where little industrial infrastructure has been created that could significantly be destroyed in a territorial dispute (also only in the nonmodernized world). Modernized societies may be involved in major territorial disputes, but generally in cases which also involve some nonmodernized society, as in the border dispute between the Soviet Union and China. The decline in the significance of territoriality has also affected defensive strategies and alliances. American security, for example, once required territorial bases encircling the Soviet bloc, thus giving the U.S. a stake in alliance with Japan and Western Europe. With the development of ICBMs (intercontinental ballistic missiles) and SLBMs (submarine-launched ballistic missiles), territorial bases abroad are no longer as necessary for the territorial defense of the

[20] See Knorr, *On the Uses of Military Power in the Nuclear Age*, pp. 80-87.

United States, and as a result, some of the necessity of maintaining military alliances abroad is now open to dispute.

While the transformation of policy goals that accompanies modernization is rather striking with reference to the identification of power with size of national territory or population, it is more subtle with respect to the identification of power and wealth. As noted in Chapter 2, the pursuit of both power and wealth was thought to involve zero-sum conditions in classical statecraft. Both were thought to be constant, so that one state's gain was another's loss. This notion has been altered significantly as a result of domestic economic growth, the development of international interdependence, and the politicization of large groups within modernized societies, which make a wide variety of demands upon their governments.

Domestic economic growth, whose level and rate of change is one of the prime indices of modernization, has a profound effect on the relative priority of domestic and foreign policy goals as well as on their contents. Once economic growth reaches high levels and sets in as a continuous dynamic process increasing the real wealth of most members of society, the value of additions to national territory and population decreases and the "domestic savings and investment and advancement of education, science, and technology are [seen as] the most profitable means and the most secure avenues to the attainment of wealth and welfare."[21] One consequence of high levels of economic growth, then, is the turning of minds away from those foreign policy goals pursued by the ruling elites of monarchic Europe and toward the further development of domestic wealth through domestic means and under peaceful conditions.[22]

Economic growth and the costs of pursuing activist foreign policy in a nuclear world offer only partial explanations of how foreign policy goals are transformed. The development of transnational structures and a set of interdependences among highly modernized societies also helps to explain the increased significance of low policies and the emergence of cooperative strategies in foreign policy. As will be argued in greater detail in Chapter 5, the interactions of citizens across boun-

[21] Knorr, *On the Uses of Military Power*, p. 22.

[22] The "introversive" tendencies of highly industrialized societies are examined in greater detail in Karl W. Deutsch, *The Analysis of International Relations* (Englewood Cliffs, N.J.: Prentice-Hall, 1968), pp. 111 ff.

daries and actions by governments either to foster the interests of their citizens or as responses to private group behavior also help foster the pursuit of low policies. One paradox is that the goals of low policies are themselves undermined by the growing scope of nongovernmental, private interactions across boundaries.

Like that of nuclear weapons, the emergence of low policies both reflects and fosters cross-cutting effects. One aspect of them reflects a motivation of governments to cooperate with others and to build new transnational structures, not simply to foster foreign policy goals but, more importantly, for the achievement of domestic goals. Of apparently equal significance is the way they foster domestic social goals at the expense of foreign governments, or permit the re-emergence of conflictual behavior in economic affairs in a form now known as neomercantilism.

The incentives for cooperative behavior and the construction of new international organizations may be seen in the creation of the customs union in Europe (European Economic Community). One of the motivations for the fostering of the Common Market was the increased wealth such as an enlarged market brings to the citizens of each member state as a result of increased levels of trade. The fostering of domestic goals through international behavior creates that principal characteristic of foreign policies under modernized conditions that reflects more the pole of cooperation than the pole of conflict. Conflictual or political activities, therefore, take place within the context of predominantly cooperative arrangements. Attempts to gain power or position at the expense of others in relations among the modernized states occur in the predominantly positive-sum worlds of the international monetary system or NATO rather than in predominantly conflictual and anarchic arenas.

It would be wrong, however, to overestimate the degree to which governments have transcended a world of conflictual behavior. There are in fact several elements of conflict in the economic goals that the industrialized market-based economies have been pursuing and that make the international coordination of policies highly desirable but also extremely difficult. Some of these stem from confusion that has accompanied the rapid shifts in economic power which began to take place after the late 1960s. Others, labeled "neomercantilism" in recent discussions of foreign economic policy, stem from the various reasons that impel governments to pursue policies aimed at the achievement of a current account surplus in their balance of payments.[23] Such policies are inevitably conflictual, since it is impossible for all to achieve a surplus simultaneously—at least one must be in deficit if the others are to achieve that goal. While neoclassical economists point out that such policies may be economically irrational since a surplus in exports over imports means that real goods and services are being sent to foreigners, there are political and also economic reasons why governments continue to pursue them nonetheless.

One of the primary motivations for seeking a current account surplus relates to the size of the market for an economy's products and its effects on domestic employment and industrial structures. Governments aim to assure full employment, and production for a large international market with visible exports fosters full employment and, of equal political importance, demonstrates that effect to labor unions. Acceptance of a current account deficit allows unions to argue that the government has "exported jobs" to areas where production of the imported goods takes place. Textile workers in the United States were able to gain great political capital with such arguments after 1968, even though objectively their claims concerning the export of jobs of American textile workers may not have been justifiable. Additionally, with a large market for exports, governments can assure that certain basic industries can be maintained and grow, especially those for which the research and development costs of high technology are very great and can only be returned with large markets. Since in most modernized societies governments do not want to risk being blamed for relinquishing control over the society's destiny to foreigners, keeping up with technological change to assure control over the nation's fate has also become a powerful incentive for the pursuit of trade surpluses. Finally, these surpluses are sought for market reasons simply as a political means of warding off domestic sentiment for protectionism. Protectionist groups gain in power when an economy submits to prolonged

[23]This discussion is based on analyses found in Harald Malmgren, *International Economic Peacekeeping in Phase II,* revised ed. (New York: Quadrangle, 1972), Chaps. 1 and 2; Ernest H. Preeg, *Economic Blocs and U.S. Foreign Policy* (Washington: National Planning Association, 1974), Chap. 10; Joan Robinson, *The New Mercantilism* (London: Cambridge University Press, 1966); and, especially, Hans O. Schmitt, "The International Monetary System: Three Options for Reform," *International Affairs* (London), 50:2 (April 1974), pp. 200–205.

trading deficits. So long as the government can maintain exports, it is also better able to maintain relatively liberal trading policies. While it is doubtful that some left-wing economists are correct in arguing that full employment policies in market economies inevitably involve neomercantilist policies, it is clear that this is the case for some.

Policies related to advanced technology provide a second and closely related source of neomercantilism, especially for governments whose domestic markets alone cannot provide adequate returns on investments or economies of scale. Governments find it desirable to develop productive capacities based on advanced technology for purposes which include *inter alia* national defense (e.g., aircraft or computer industry), or fear that to do otherwise would severely restrict national autonomy. In order to facilitate the economic feasibility of such investments, producers must rely upon foreign markets, which will enable them to maximize production and to reduce costs. Thus in areas of advanced technology one finds an additional incentive to achieve trade surpluses.

Current account surpluses are also pursued by governments because of their relationship to capital flows abroad. This third argument for surpluses stems from the fact that economies which export more than they import gain capital that can be used for direct investment abroad. The long tradition of American current account surpluses was, for example, largely responsible for the ability of American firms to penetrate foreign markets through direct investment abroad. The larger the level of such foreign direct investment, the greater the assurance companies have that rivals will not develop abroad that could affect their markets.

A fourth motivation for pursuing current account surpluses relates to the desire of governments to finance other foreign activities. A surplus allows them, for example, to carry out programs of foreign aid and assistance in the less developed world. If a government pursues a policy of foreign aid in order to foster its own national cultural traits abroad or in order to marshal support from a particular set of less developed countries, it will need some continuity of trade surpluses in order to gain the wherewithal to do so. The same motivation underlies attempts by a government to maintain a military presence abroad. The maintenance of American foreign bases or the ability to fight foreign wars, as in Vietnam, depends on the ability of the government to finance its foreign presence, and this in no small measure reflects the international financial position of the government, which is based on its trading position.

A final set of factors also carries neomercantilist implications and relates to what Ernest Preeg calls the "conflict between the economic gains from trade and competing national objectives":

> It reflects the growing economic role of government in all industrialized countries. The policy objectives could include regional, . . . development, a higher degree of self-sufficiency for particular sectors of the economy—from agriculture to computers to fuels—or environmental standards. To some extent, these objectives are pursued through the use of protective tariffs but they are also affected by a variety of non-tariff barriers from quotas to public financial support to preferential procurement policies.[24]

These issues of domestic legislation, which affect willy-nilly international trade, have become so integrally a part of governance that many observers have called for a continuing process of international negotiation to avoid their detrimental consequences.

As Schmitt has argued, "for reasons such as these, and perhaps others, a market equilibrium in the overall balance of payments will not be a political equilibrium once the current account balances associated with it are found unacceptable."[25] The pursuit of current account surpluses by all governments presents two bases of economic conflict. On the one hand, it reflects the notion that the domestic and foreign political gains associated with current account surpluses might carry real losses for others. Thus even in the pursuit of general economic cooperation there is recognition that the game is partially conflictual and that one nation's gain might be another's relative loss. On the other hand, as argued earlier, the pursuit of surpluses inevitably results in conflict in that it is empirically impossible for all economies to run surpluses simultaneously. At least one must be in deficit in order to allow others to be in surplus, and this basic characteristic of trade relationships interjects competition into the pursuit of low policies. And if the advanced industrialized societies manage to minimize economic conflict by successfully and simultaneously maintaining current account surpluses, it will be the less developed countries which will have to accept deficits.

[24] Preeg, *Economic Blocs and U.S. Foreign Policy*, p. 152.
[25] Schmitt, "The International Monetary System," p. 203.

The fostering of economic and other low policies results, then, in both cooperative and conflictual behavior. The common interest of all industrialized societies in domestic gains forces them to cooperate with one another. The very act of cooperation and of fostering international interdependence also sets severe restrictions upon the traditional policy of independence and autonomy. With the emergence of high levels of interdependence reflecting both technological change and policies intentionally fostered by governments, the ideal view of state autonomy has been challenged, and this has greatly affected foreign policy behavior. No amount of political will can recreate a world where independence and autonomy can be obtained, except perhaps at costs that no governments are willing to incur because losses in wealth that would accompany increased autonomy would handicap the legitimacy of those governments in the eyes of their citizens.

Increased Domestic Demands and the Allocation of Resources

We have seen that one of the major influences in the transformation of foreign policy goals under modernization has been the replacement of the quest for power by the quest for social and economic wealth. This quest for wealth itself reflects one of the primary domestic consequences of modernization: the politicization of increasingly larger sectors in society, which place increasing demands upon governments to provide an enormous variety of social services. It is also a paradox at the heart of foreign policies in all modernized societies that these increased demands on governments create problems of resource allocation, at least in the short run. One result is that predominantly external goals decrease in priority relative to predominantly domestic goals. This has occurred at the same time that domestic conditions have become increasingly sensitive to international events as a result of the growth in international interdependence as well as of absolute increases in international activities by the citizens of most modernized societies.[26]

----

[26]Where governments try to repress dissent, as in the case of the Soviet Union, significant additional costs result, including costs to governmental legitimacy.

It is a distinctive feature of all governments in modernized societies, be they democratic or authoritarian, capitalist or socialist, that they have assumed great multifunctionality. Governments are looked to as creators of—as well as redistributors of—the common wealth. While the modern social-service state has been created by increasing demands put upon governments, these demands themselves have resulted from the increased politicization of individuals and groups. A government is impaled upon "the dilemma of rising demands and insufficient resources"[27] when domestic demands are greater than available resources and, especially, when it wishes to maintain simultaneously existing levels of commitment abroad. Demands can arise from a variety of sources, including poverty groups desirous of obtaining a greater share of social wealth, military groups wanting new weapons systems, or citizens sensitive to the need for maintaining public order in societies increasingly sensitive to labor or minority group disruption. It is no accident that governmental allocations to education, health services, and other collective social enterprises have increased dramatically in all modernized societies. They reflect demands for a better life by all and increased costs of labor in the social sector, where gains from increased productivity are not great. These costs may be added to the "rising cost and widening scope of activities required to keep mature urban societies viable."[28]

One of the inexorable results for governments of increased demands and rising costs is the curtailment of external commitments, or the decreased relative priority of foreign goals in comparison to domestic objectives. These curtailments add to the costs to any government of defense autonomy and independence. It is debatable whether the multiplier effect generated by the allocation of resources to external commitments produces greater or lesser levels of goods domestically than would allocations that directly met increased demands. Some argue that they are lower, since the production of such goods as armaments is not consumable.[29] Others have argued that government investments in defense-related activities have direct spinoffs to the private sector, as in the development of jet transport, atomic energy,

[27]Harold and Margaret Sprout, "The Dilemma of Rising Demands and Insufficient Resources," *World Politics,* XX:4 (July 1963), pp. 660–693.

[28]Ibid., p. 685.

[29]See Kenneth Boulding, ed., *Peace and the War Industry* (Chicago: Aldine, 1970).

transistors, etc., and that while such investments could take place directly in consumer goods, they are unlikely to without the mobilization of political support that investments receive when oriented toward defense. However, as society becomes highly politicized, it also becomes increasingly likely that externally oriented allocations are highly visible, as in the case of British expenditures on maintaining forces east of Suez, or American expenditures on Vietnam. Such expenditures are therefore likely to be viewed as squandering of domestic wealth or as perverted governmental priorities. This is especially the case in democracies where allocations to external expenditures become weapons in the critical hands of political opposition groups.

The dilemma posed for governmental resource allocation by these demands can be met in several ways, but each has its costs to a government's domestic and foreign policies. The Sprouts summarize them as follows:

> First, efforts may be made to *expand the economy.* . . .
> Second, the rulers may prudentially *revise their order of priorities.* . . .
> Third, the rulers may . . . *divert public attention* to other values. . . .
> Fourth, the men in power may try to *change the opinions of dissenters.* . . .
> Fifth, . . . the rulers may try to *silence dissent and opposition.* . . .[30]

A sixth means of dealing with the dilemma is the fostering of cooperative and compatible efforts with other governments designed to share costs and increase the economic wealth available to all.

Each of the six ways out of the dilemma has been tried by most governments in modernized societies. Economic growth has been the most central and successful means, since it avoids some of the difficulties of redistributing social income. But it can have disruptive effects on some members of society who prefer the stability of the status quo, especially when some gains might be lost as a consequence of technological advance. One obvious example is the fear of shop owners that construction of large stores, including discount stores, will jeopardize their businesses. It also serves to increase international interdependence, which sacrifices national autonomy. Moreover, growth becomes more

---

[30] Harold and Margaret Sprout, "The Dilemma of Rising Demands," pp. 690–691. Emphasis is theirs.

difficult to obtain as natural resources become scarce or rise in cost, as the oil crisis of 1973–74 vividly demonstrated.

Revising governmental priorities also helps meet domestic demands, but usually at the cost of international commitments and potentially at the cost of international stability if security is affected detrimentally. Diverting public attention and changing or silencing the views of dissenters also can be relied upon, but only for short-run gains, given the political repercussions of pursuing such policies over long periods of time. Finally, international cooperation, while it serves to create international goods, also increases international interdependence, which further limits the freedom of a modern state to pursue a traditional policy of national autonomy.

In the final analysis, there is no easy way out of this dilemma for a government. A decreased relative priority for external commitments, especially for military purposes, does seem inevitable, although other external commitments of a predominantly economic nature may be created. This relative decline in external priorities is, of course, reinforced by the international stability created by nuclear deterrence. In a world where international tensions rose dramatically from present levels, governments might well be more able to make domestic sacrifices for security purposes than they are today. The decline in national extroversion, it should be emphasized, has taken place paradoxically at a time when international interdependences have sensitized national economies to external events in an unprecedented fashion. The latter trend ought to require a greater external orientation in governmental policy. Yet the fact that the world remains divided into nation-states and that governments depend for their authority upon national populations restricts the degree to which adequate levels of international cooperation can develop by orienting governmental action to predominantly domestic arenas.

Changes in the Processes of Foreign
Policy Making

It would be surprising if the great changes that societies undergo as they become highly modernized did not have a profound effect upon the processes of policy making in domestic as well as foreign affairs.

At the turn of the century a number of predictions were made that industrialization would breed democratization and that cabinet-style decision making in closed forums would yield to open diplomacy, more likely to lead to international stability and peace. Cabinet-style decision making is apparently something of the past, but despite the predictions concerning the democratization of foreign policy, policy processes have succumbed to administrative politics and have been bureaucratized. This has resulted from several factors, including the amount of information that must be gathered for effective policy making, especially as the number of states and functional areas that a government must deal with increases. Ironically, one rationale for the growth of administration in the policy process has been the need to increase national control; yet with the administrative revolution in government, great losses of control from the top have occurred. Policy, therefore, has become no more—and perhaps a good deal less—rational than it once was, at the very time when growth in complexity of international life has required rational policy making more than ever for state survival.

It is a paradox, then, that just as modernization has bred administrative professionalism and promises the growth of a rational administrative science, rationality models capable of understanding policy have decreased in importance and models of bureaucratic behavior purporting to explain policy making have become more important.[31] In modern bureaucracies, policy making tends to undermine rather than to enhance the ability of political leadership to pursue rationally a set of explicit external goals. Interest group politics have become more important, and foreign policy has tended to reflect what occurs within the bureaucracies upon which leadership depends for information and position papers, more than it does national policy requirements. One result is a form of policy rigidification that contradicts the needs of foreign policy for flexibility and freedom to maneuver.[32]

In modern bureaucracies, policy making involves two sorts of bargaining "games." One is lateral, between members of various adminis-

---

[31] See, in particular, Graham T. Allison, "Conceptual Models and the Cuban Missile Crisis," *American Political Science Review*, LXIII (September 1969), pp. 689–718.

[32] This problem of bureaucracies has been an obsession of Henry Kissinger, both while an academic and in government. See his essay, "Domestic Structure and Foreign Policy," in *American Foreign Policy*, revised ed. (New York: Norton, 1974), pp. 9–50.

trative units, with overlapping jurisdictions in a particular set of issues (as for example, the overlapping jurisdictions of the Departments of Defense and State, the CIA, and the Arms Control and Disarmament Agency in arms control issues). The other is hierarchical, among members of different strata in a single agency (where one encounters crosscutting efforts of different people to advance their own positions and power).[33] The emergence of a single spokesman in foreign affairs, frequently prescribed as necessary for security and policy flexibility, is made impossible by the characteristics of modern bureaucracies.[34] Plurality in the number of foreign policy voices inevitably accompanies the increased significance of routine, daily decision making, especially in areas of low policy. This contrasts with the more unified and consistent nature of decision making which ideally exists in crises and in high politics, although the evidence of Graham Allison's study of the Cuban missile crisis would indicate its absence even there.[35] With increases in routine policy making, control at the top is restricted and the autonomy of lower-level officials enhanced.

Several aspects of controlling routine decision making can be summarized in an examination of two problems, which I shall label the organizational problem and the problem of size.

The organizational problem is one that has perplexed specialists in administrative science and eluded most efforts to reform the processes of decision making for foreign affairs. The problem stems from the need to divide the functions of government according to predominantly domestic areas. Thus all modern governments have ministries or departments such as agriculture, labor, education, transportation, and finance. Unlike such departments under nonmodernized conditions, now each domestic area has a significant international bureau, which represents a response to the breakdown in the distinction between foreign and domestic affairs that fit the nineteenth-century model of administration. With the multiplication of international bureaus, the ability of a foreign ministry to control foreign policy or even to

[33]See Paul Y. Hammond, "Foreign Policy-Making and Administrative Politics," *World Politics*, XVII (July 1965), pp. 656–671.

[34]For an evaluation of the ability of Henry Kissinger successfully to wear his many hats in government, see I. M. Destler, "Can One Man Do?" *Foreign Policy*, No. 5 (Winter 1971–72), pp. 28–40.

[35]Graham T. Allison, *Essence of Decision* (Boston: Little Brown, 1971).

coordinate it on a rational basis is severely restricted. In fact, as low policies gain in importance, this problem is further exacerbated. It is made all the more difficult insofar as the representatives of these departments tend to seek total foreign as well as domestic control over issues that appear to be in their own domain. Thus, for example, the Treasury Department in the United States has sought to maintain control over foreign monetary policy, even though in some cases the interests of the Departments of State and Defense are at stake. This has been frequently detrimental to the pursuit of a policy that ought to take into account the manifold foreign policy stakes of the U.S. government, as, for example, during the monetary crisis of 1971, when the decision to change the exchange rate of the dollar was made without consultation of the Secretaries of State and Defense or the President's Adviser for National Security Affairs.

This problem can sometimes be handled by interministerial committees that cross-cut different departments, thus enhancing the coordination of information and decision making. But the manifold attempts within the U.S. and other governments to reorganize foreign policy decision making to counter the debilitating effects of the organizational problem have largely failed. The problem, moreover, is more difficult to handle the larger the size of the governmental organization involved. Thus the problem is more intractable in the United States than in a smaller government like France, and more difficult there than in Denmark. This leads us to the second difficulty in providing rational decision-making structures, that of size. The larger the organizations involved in foreign policy decision making, the greater is the information provided for decision making and the larger the number of individual stakes in decision making. One result is increased "noise" within the government and a greater propensity for policy rigidification.

In summary, modernization has been associated with the notion that political structures can become increasingly rationalized and thus better able to maintain control over the events within society as well as in the environment of international affairs. Yet modernization also worsens the problem of control by creating roadblocks to efficient and rational policy-making. Modernization has also worsened another problem of control, one that has always been of central concern to foreign policy: the control over events external to the state. Although I shall investigate this problem in greater detail in the next chapter when I analyze the political organization of international society, it would be appropriate to summarize some of its effects on foreign policy at this juncture.

Problems of Control

There is a special problem of control in foreign policy which is not found in domestic affairs and which stems from the inherent nature of international society. The international system is, by definition, composed of a collection of relatively autonomous and legally sovereign political units, with no highly institutionalized and overarching structure of political authority. This creates a perennial problem for foreign policy: how to control and coordinate events which take place outside one's society and which have an immediate impact on one's security and well-being. This problem is compounded when interdependences develop among societies, as they do after modernization begins. This is the case because interdependence erodes the autonomy of governmental action in both domestic and foreign affairs, but it does not necessarily affect the juridical status of the sovereignty of different decision-making units. With the development of interdependence, not only can benefits be gained for all societies, but international catastrophes and costs can also become worldwide, including nuclear war, uncontrolled inflation, or depression.

There are complex reasons why this is the case, and we will examine these in detail in the next chapter. For now, we will accept the assumption that interdependence creates losses of control both within and among societies, so long as mechanisms of international coordination and cooperation remain rudimentary, and we will look at some of the consequences of this problem for the conduct of foreign policy in highly modernized societies.

The major problem for foreign policy that stems from interdependence is that of the autonomy of rational decision making. Interdependence, by definition, makes governments increasingly dependent upon actions taken by other governments for the achievement of both domestic and foreign policy goals. Autonomy can usually be reasserted, but only by reducing international interdependence or by accepting some mechanisms of accommodation with foreign governments, including some forms of political integration. But this option is also highly costly, because of the increased domestic demands on governments to increase social wealth and the national need to maintain interdependences to get that wealth. Autonomy could also be reasserted if governments reduced the number of tasks that they have assumed, but that action would seriously jeopardize governmental legitimacy because it would result in a refusal to accept responsibilities expected by a highly politicized populace.

Governments have been aware of the dilemma that is posed for them by interdependence and have by and large been capable of adjusting to the cross-cutting costs and gains from interdependence. As Rosenau has argued, "the adaptive capacities of the modern nation-state are considerable."[36] What he calls "preservative adaption" is the policy response to an environment that has changed rapidly and that is oriented to the conservative preservation of domestic social and political structures. Samuel Huntington goes further, arguing that interdependence and autonomy grow symbiotically. His claim, however, that "the conflict between national governments and transnational organizations is clearly complimentary rather than duplicative"[37] is contradictated by some of the problems that governments try to confront in wielding effective power in domestic affairs.

Related to the problem of national autonomy is a second problem associated with the increased vulnerability of modernized societies to the actions of others under interdependent conditions. Governmental actions, as a consequence, are oriented less to the achievement of positive goals than they are to the more negative attempt to reduce their vulnerability to the actions of others and to increase others' vulnerabilities to their own actions. The result is a more subtle form of foreign policy than hitherto existed, based on the intended as well as unintended consequences of transnational activities. As Pierre Hassner has argued,

> The essential characteristic of this state [of affairs] is neither force nor cooperation but the constant influence of societies on one another within the framework of a competition whose goals are

[36]James N. Rosenau, "Adaptive Politics in an Interdependent World," *Orbis,* XVI (Spring 1972), p. 163.

[37]"Transnational Organizations In World Politics," *World Politics,* XXV (April 1973), p. 366.

less and less tangible, whose means are less and less direct, whose consequences are less and less calculable, precisely because they involve activities rather than strategies and because these activities are important as much because of their effects on what societies are as on what they *do*. . . .

The real race may be less to increase one's comparative power than to decrease one's comparative vulnerability, to manipulate not only an opponent's weaknesses but one's own, to encourage exported erosion or to control contagious explosions, to modify or maintain not so much territorial borders or even diplomatic alignments as what might be called the balance of will and the balance of expectations.[38]

As a result of this exacerbation of the problem of control, a third issue has become significant in foreign policy in highly modernized societies. With increased interdependences and vulnerabilities, governments tend to pursue short-range and conservative foreign policies. Since interdependence brings about possibilities for uncontrolled change, governments fear the adverse consequences of any change that carries with it a large number of unknown factors. They would prefer generally to maintain the status quo, whose costs and benefits are familiar. The fear of uncertainties created by the international situation are, moreover, compounded by domestic uncertainties. The stability of highly modernized societies rests on political traditions and institutions that developed over a centuries-long process of nation building. Yet these structures submit to a fragility engendered by rapid social change. One result is that governance tends to be based on short-term and daily decision making oriented more to the maintenance of the status quo and operating the machinery of public affairs than to steering a course for the future based on grand political designs.

Conclusions

The argument of this chapter has rested on the hypothesis that under modernization, societies and governments confront a set of common problems and options that result in a convergence of their foreign

---

[38] Pierre Hassner, "The New Europe: From Cold War to Hot Peace," *International Journal,* XXVII (Winter 1971–72), pp. 12–13.

policies along certain specified dimensions. I argued that governments of highly modernized societies may be characterized by the large scope of the objectives they pursue, the depth of demands placed upon them by constituents, the intermeshing of foreign and domestic concerns, the fragility of the societies that they govern, and the withering of governmental legitimacy that results from their inability to perform effectively. As a result of these changes, along with the growth in international interdependence, transformations have taken place in all three aspects of foreign policies. Their contents have become increasingly centered on low policies associated with the achievement of economic growth, but frequently intermeshed with a new form of transcendentalism that reflects the incapacity of governments to perform effectively. Policies have also undergone a radical change in administrative process, which has been designed to enhance the rationality and consistency of policy but which also results in a growth of irrationality and losses of control at the top because of the growth of politics within administrations. The control of policy effects has also been severely withered at a time when the stability imposed by nuclear deterrence has fostered a new type of international stability but when interdependence creates a new exigency for increased control.

These changes in foreign policies offer the citizens of all modernized societies opportunities for increased wealth and welfare that were unthinkable before modernization took place. They also, however, increase international instability insofar as interdependence has grown far in advance of either the instruments capable of controlling it or the knowledge social scientists have of its effects. The transformation of foreign policy, moreover, takes place wherever modernized societies exist, regardless of the ideologies and political myths accepted within them or the political institutions they possess. It will, of course, make some difference whether these institutions are democratic or nondemocratic, whether the society is large or small, and whether its economy is relatively open or closed to international events, in terms of the ability of a government to come to grips with foreign policy problems. In general terms, however, the influences that have transformed foreign policies are apparently necessary concomitants of the modernization process itself.

The generalizations that I have put forward in this chapter are meant to apply principally to modernized societies. But the changes that are reflected in foreign policies conducted under modernized conditions are also likely to be dispersed throughout the international system differentially, with some aspects of modernization appearing far ahead of others. They are therefore likely to characterize the foreign policies of less modernized societies to greater or less degrees before these societies become relatively modernized, or even regardless of whether they do. Before turning our attention to changes brought about by modernization in the international system, it will be worth while to address ourselves to some of the problems of foreign policies in the relatively nonmodernized world in these regards.

FOREIGN POLICIES IN RELATIVELY NONMODERNIZED SOCIETIES

There are major difficulties in any effort to generalize about the foreign policies of relatively nonmodernized societies that are absent in a discussion of modernized societies. Less modernized societies, first of all, do not share a common social base. At a minimum they can be divided into several universes of cases rather than a single universe. Since they have not wholly undergone what Marion J. Levy, Jr., calls "the universal solvent"[39] of modernization, they tend to reflect a plurality of types of social structures that impede any effort at generalization. A secondary issue of importance is their rather different histories. Some, like China, Ethiopia, Egypt, and India, have long traditions of national or cultural autonomy, while others are the artificial creations of European colonialism. Thus the major problems they confront in domestic and foreign policy may be strikingly different. Nation building and the creation of a national identity, for example, are more likely to infuse politics in those states which are artificial creations than where national and cultural identity have grown through a long-term and organic process. Third, these less developed societies tend to have rather different sorts of ties to the outside world. Some are highly dependent upon one relatively modernized society for aid, investment, and trade, while others have greater autonomy, either because they have broken colonial and neocolonial ties or because they

[39]*Modernization and the Structure of Societies* (Princeton, N.J.: Princeton University Press, 1966), p. 14.

were not fully brought into a European colonial system. Finally, these societies have rather different resource bases, with some poorly endowed, others richly endowed, some endowed with a single resource, others with a variety of resources. Their ability to control their own destinies will thus depend to a large degree on a combination of their resource base and size and the nature of the international market for which they can produce. A state like Iran, for example, with a moderately large population, well endowed in oil and other natural resources, is likely to have greater leverage over its own economic growth and autonomy than overpopulated and resource-poor Haiti.

Notwithstanding the great impediments to generalizing about the foreign policies of nonmodernized societies, there has been a striking and apparent singlemindedness about the way foreign policies have been conducted by less modernized societies since the onset of the cold war. Originally this distinctiveness revolved around the efforts of the majority of governments in less developed societies to pursue a policy of neutralism and a refusal to take sides with either of the superpowers.[40] In recent years it has focused upon the seemingly common claims of less developed countries to institute a "new international economic order" based on a radical and more equitable distribution of global wealth and national control over all natural resources.[41] With growing assertiveness since the success of the OPEC cartel in quadrupling the price of crude oil and of some of its members in carrying out an embargo in the aftermath of the October 1973 Middle East war, the less developed countries have tried to force the industrialized countries to meet their radical claims through the creation of other cartels of raw materials producers.

In the next chapter I shall outline efforts to evaluate the potential of the less developed countries collectively to implement their claims. Here we are concerned more with the reasons they are making these

[40]See the analysis in Peter Lyon, *Neutralism* (Leicester: Leicester University Press, 1963); or Laurence W. Martin, ed., *Neutralism and Nonalignment* (New York: Praeger, 1962).

[41]The elements of this order are spelled out in a series of United Nations declarations and resolutions passed by the overwhelming majority which less developed countries have in that institution. See "Declaration on the Establishment of a New International Economic Order" adopted by the Sixth Special Session of the General Assembly of the United Nations on May 1, 1974, and "Charter of Economic Rights and Duties of States" adopted by the Twenty-ninth Session of the United Nations General Assembly on Dec. 9, 1974.

claims than with their ability to succeed. While the apparent unity in foreign policy undertaken by less developed societies is striking, it is less clear why this came about or how it is related to modernization. The policy of neutralism which was evoked stridently during the cold war is a case in point and can probably be explained better by "structural characteristics" of the international system of the 1950s and 1960s than by a theory of modernization. A policy of neutralism with respect to alliance was undoubtedly related to the recency of independence of most Third World countries rather than to the process of modernization. Most newly independent governments, after all, have attempted to rebel against prevailing international alignments in order to concentrate on building domestic political power or to revise what has been considered the perverted diplomacy of a former regime. This was as true of the United States in the eighteenth century as it was of Russia after the Bolshevik Revolution and of India or Indonesia after independence.

Some scholars have argued that the policy of neutralism is in fact a necessary characteristic of most less modernized societies which results from the structure of international society in the contemporary world.[42] The growth in nuclear deterrence, for example, has made it possible for most governments to pursue policies that are far less oriented to the defense of national borders than was the case in the past. The security of territorial borders in nonmodernized societies is, moreover, enhanced by the fears in most newly independent societies of changes in the territorial status quo. Since many of them are artificial creations trying to develop their own national identities, they have recognized that any claims they may put forward against other newly independent states may well be reciprocated, and, by and large, they have refrained from doing so. Yet wars concerning territorial borders remain frequent among less modernized societies, and are at least far more prevalent there than among modernized societies. This is especially true when different nationalist groupings have laid irredentist claims to the same territory, as in the case of Palestine or the borders between India and Pakistan.

In spite of the more ambiguous nature of territoriality in the foreign policies of relatively less modernized societies, it is apparently the case that a policy of neutralism fulfills at least two purposes. First, most

---

[42] See, for example, John Burton, *International Relations: A General Theory* (London: Cambridge University Press, 1967).

governments in less developed societies are likely to concentrate their efforts on increasing the power of a centralized state both as an end in itself and as a means of achieving other policy goals. They are therefore likely to pursue policies of autonomy in international affairs, which will at times be infused with some pan-national and cross-cutting claims, as in pan-Africanism or pan-Arab unity. Such a policy would also be designed to decrease dependence on any one individual or group of modernized societies. Thus, simply in terms of autonomy, a less modernized society is likely to try to maximize the number of sources of foreign aid, the number of markets providing it, and that it provides.

Second, a policy of autonomy, smacking of neutralism, is also likely to be pursued as instrumental to an additional set of goals associated with economic growth and modernization. The content of foreign policy in less modernized societies is thus as likely to concentrate on areas of low policies as is the content in highly modernized societies. Economic growth will be seen, together with autonomy and the enhancement of national culture, as the primary stake of politics, for reasons similar to those we reviewed earlier. There will, however, be a major difference in certain aspects of the way these low policies will be pursued. First, the inherent incompatibility between national autonomy and modernization will not be as apparent in the case of nonmodernized societies as it is in modernized societies. This is due partially to the fact that for the modernized societies that now exist, national autonomy was achieved before high levels of modernization. For the less modernized societies, governments are more likely to see in industrialization and growth the means of creating national autonomy. Second, low policies pursued in less modernized societies are far more likely to focus on distributional aspects at the international level than are low policies pursued in modernized societies. The latter are likely to see economic growth and the growth in trade as "trickling down" to poorer regions of the world and will be unwilling to pay more than lip service to the need to redistribute world wealth. They will be, in short, far more oriented toward the status quo than governments of less developed societies, which are likely to make increasingly vocal revisionist claims for a redistribution of global wealth.

It would thus appear that the shift from a policy of neutralism to one based on the elements of a "new economic order" is related to a shift in importance from structural aspects of the cold war to the modernization process itself. If neutralism is related to the movement toward independence and decolonization and to the cold war bipolarity between the United States and the Soviet Union, claims for egalitarian distribution of wealth and justice seem an inevitable part of the modernization process. Yet some observers claim that this is not the case and that the modernization process is less important than it may seem to be. One observer, for example, argues that just as the cold war gave rise to claims of Third World neutralism, so too the decline in the cold war and the onset of détente between the Soviet Union and the United States served to shift Third World policies toward distributive claims:

> It is not without irony that the decrease in the significance to the two great powers of the Third World states coincided with the rise in the demands of the latter for a greater measure of equality. Although by the middle to late 1960's the restraints imposed upon the states of the Third World by the cold war had clearly begun to recede, the burdens an increased measure of independence imposed upon political leaders of these states had just as clearly not receded. However persistent many Third World governments had been in their criticism of the cold war, the attention they had received as a result of that conflict had assuaged deep anxieties over their very viability as states. If the cold war restricted their freedom of action, it also gave them a much needed sense of importance and worth.[43]

The evolution of the cold war system alone is, however, an insufficient explanation for the unity of Third World societies since the formation of the Group of Seventy-seven in UNCTAD (United Nations Conference on Trade and Development) in 1967. At a minimum the claims for redistribution emanate from multiple factors which characterize much of the less developed world and which also are related to modernization. In part they relate to the desire for autonomy and prestige which Third World leaders feel is due them in a world in which rich societies and their "alien" values prevail.[44] They also revolve around efforts by Third World leaders to maintain their own authority in domestic societies which are undergoing rapid change and social dissolution and even have a history of mismanagement. Such problems

[43]Robert W. Tucker, "A New International Order?" *Commentary*, February 1975, p. 40.

[44]See Rajni Kothari, "Dyason Memorial Lectures: I. Changing Nature of Human Conflict in Our Times; II. Choices Facing a Divided World," *Australian Outlook*, 28:3 (December 1974), pp. 221–244.

of stability and control will also likely be greater for governments in less developed economies than for those in modernized societies. This is true because of the inherent instability of societies undergoing modernization, as traditional ties are broken without being replaced by stronger and more legitimate new governmental ties. But it is also true that less modernized societies are found to have extremely difficult problems in achieving their goals of autonomy and growth. Population growth, the mercurial nature of international markets, rival claims for domestic power, and a host of other problems make it relatively unlikely that more than a few less modernized societies will transcend the divide between them and the increasingly richer more modernized world. Not only is social chaos engendered by famine or frustration more likely there than in the more modernized world, but bold foreign policy initiatives may also be more forthcoming. This would result from the lower stakes that most nonmodernized societies have in the status quo and their consequent greater willingness to accept risks for potentially great gains. It also might stem from the desire to take bold actions, including those involving the use of force, simply as a means of maintaining domestic social cohesion or power for the ruling groups.

Nonmodernized societies, in short, are significantly affected by the same trends analyzed in our examination of foreign policies in highly modernized societies. For them, too, one can say that the ideal and actual patterns of classical statecraft are largely irrelevant. But it is far more difficult for us to make generalizations concerning the content, processes, and problems of control or future evolution in their foreign policies.

5

The Transformation of the International System

The contemporary international system represents as dramatic a contrast with that of classical statecraft as do the major elements of foreign policy. Instead of five or six major powers encountering each other in the eternal ballet of balance-of-power diplomacy, two superpowers predominate in a system whose stability and rigidity rest upon the ambiguous presence of weapons of massive destruction and, in spite of efforts at détente, represent an apparently permanent divide between East and West, as well as between the superpowers and the others. Rather than some two dozen or so smaller states in the international hierarchy, some 150 sovereign political units now exist and represent a diversity in type of state systems, range of power, and importance that is unparalleled in history; yet each seems able to voice its concerns as a result of a polycentrism[1] fostered by the paradoxical paral-

[1] For a discussion of bipolarity, multipolarity, and polycentrism in the contemporary international system, see Stanley Hoffmann, *Gulliver's Troubles, or the Setting of American Foreign Policy* (New York: McGraw-Hill, 1968), Chap. 2. Hoffmann defines these terms as follows: "Bipolarity, i.e., the existence of the United States and the Soviet Union, whose power far exceeds that of other units and which are sufficiently matched to be placed in the same top league, if one applies to the present system the customary yardstick of power, namely, the capacity to wage war and to inflict damage on an enemy" (p. 17). Polycentrism "results from the devaluation of coercive power. The 'centers' are states many of which lack the traditional ingredients of military might, but which are well supplied in the new factors of power and eager to play the game" (p. 34). Multipolarity emerges from the trend toward nuclear proliferation (pp. 43–46).

ysis in the use of force by the superpowers in a world of nuclear weapons. Moreover, tremendous diversity and unevenness exist in the development of societies that tend to counterpose rich against poor over issues across the great divide between modernized and less modernized societies, a divide which itself cross-cuts the ideological and security divisions between East and West. Additionally, a variety of new types of nonstate units with impressive economic wherewithal have arisen, with which governments must interact at least indirectly and often directly and actively. These new units range from international organizations of states or of nongovernmental interest groups (labor unions, parties, etc.), to transnational or multinational corporations and other transnational groupings. Their existence challenges the state-centric theory of international politics, although their importance varies with the state and unit in question.

The growth of these new structures of international society is perhaps as difficult to trace as are their effects on contemporary statecraft. Some are the result of long-term secular trends, including those depicted in Chapter 1. Others stem from the more accidental qualities of warfare, including the Soviet and American victories in World War II, which both accelerate and change these long-term trends. In this chapter our concern will not be with a descriptive history of the balance of power, or of how it was disrupted by the French Revolution and restored as a workable structure of European stability for a century. Nor will we trace out the means by which extra-European powers, including Japan, China, Russia, and the United States, entered that system and eventually came to play central roles in it. Nor, again, will we look at the evolution of force in the international system from the days of Westphalian field armies to those of ballistic missiles and nuclear weapons. Rather, our central concerns will be centered around issues raised in our discussion of the transformation of foreign policies. We will review, in particular, the emergence of new structural relationships in international society that are related directly to the processes of modernization—those, especially, that relate to the growth of transnational economically based activities that have served to circumscribe national autonomy. We will review and I will offer an explanation of how various structures of interdependence have developed during the modernization process and what their major effects have been on statecraft.

Arguments concerning the growth in international interdependence were reviewed in Chapter 2 in the discussion of ideological explanations of the modernization process. There I argued that two ideological schools of thought, liberalism and Marxism, presented normative views concerning the growth in international interdependence. In liberal thought, interdependence became a goal of foreign policy that should be implemented with global industrialization and that should result in a framework in which natural harmony of interests among nations could unfold. Marxism argued that industrialization brought about a global division of labor, especially between financial and proletarian classes, which would succumb to the proletarian revolution and permit the growth of a natural harmony of interests among working classes, and eventually among all nations in a classless world. The arguments of liberals and Marxists were essentially normative, even though they were based on empirical observations. As the protectionists of the nineteenth century argued, interdependence cannot dissolve political divisions or asymmetries in the world of power politics. As a result, the emergence of universal structures of international society can represent a form of disguised nationalism, or imperialism, with the larger and more industrialized nations reaping disproportionate gains. Moreover, the failure of either liberalism or Marxism to create a world of international harmony that could justify its claims has also served to give the term "interdependence" a pejorative connotation.

In using the term "interdependence" in this chapter, I shall avoid normative biases as much as possible. In fact, it is the argument of this chapter that the growth in international interdependence does not warrant any optimistic conclusions concerning the development of regional or universal supranational governments or of the institutionalization of world peace. Rather, interdependence in a world of nation-states is far more destabilizing than its earlier proponents or current detractors would admit.[2] It leads to breakdowns in both domestic and international mechanisms of control and does not guarantee the development of new instruments to maintain political order. Moreover, no

---

[2] The major criticism of views like those put forward in this chapter can be found in Kenneth N. Waltz, "The Myth of National Interdependence," in Charles P. Kindleberger, ed., *The International Corporation* (Cambridge, Mass.: M.I.T. Press, 1970), pp. 205–223. Also see David P. Calleo, "The Political Economy of Allied Relations: The Limits of Interdependence," in Robert E. Osgood and others, *Retreat from Empire: The First Nixon Administration* (Baltimore: Johns Hopkins Press, 1973), pp. 207–240.

scholar of international politics has yet developed a convincing analysis depicting the political and organizational requisites of different forms of interdependence in international society.[3]

I shall now turn to a general analysis of the phenomenon of interdependence, offer definitions for several of its forms, trace their historical development, and conclude with some observations concerning the political ramifications of its growth.

TYPES OF INTERDEPENDENCE

The analysis of interstate interdependence begins with a central political problem that arose in international economic interchanges after World War II among the advanced industrialized societies of the non-Communist world. This was no accident. As we have already seen, with the growth of the nuclear stalemate and the increased importance that economic relations grew to have both for plays for international power and for increasing domestic wealth, economic phenomena came inevitably to be viewed as political. Yet the growth in economic relations posed a fundamental dilemma for the autonomy of national governments. As Richard N. Cooper argued in his classic study of interdependence,

> The central problem of international economic cooperation . . . is *how to keep the manifold benefits of extensive international economic intercourse free of crippling restrictions while at the same time preserving a maximum degree of freedom for each nation to pursue its legitimate economic objectives.*[4]

As societies are drawn closer together in the pursuit of predominantly national goals, the autonomy of national decision making remains critical to the ability of governments. The achievement of policy

---

[3]Neofunctionalist theorists of international integration still maintain the view that the erosion of economic barriers between nations contains the seeds of spillover for political union. For a survey of the current state of this field, see Leon Lindberg and Stuart Scheingold, eds., *Regional Integration: Theory and Research* (Cambridge, Mass.: Harvard University Press, 1971). It was originally published as *International Organization*, XXIV (Autumn 1970).

[4]Richard N. Cooper, *The Economics of Interdependence: Economic Policy in the Atlantic Community* (New York: McGraw-Hill, 1968), p. 5. Emphasis is his.

goals, including those that derive from the demands placed on governments by their politicized populations, is never likely to be made willingly on the good faith of other governments' cooperative actions. Yet this is exactly what must emerge from a world of interdependence. If interdependence is the opposite of state autonomy and if autonomy is defined as the ability of a government to achieve its goals by itself, then interdependence may be generally defined as follows: it is the outcome of specified actions of two or more parties (in our case, of governments) when the outcomes of these actions are mutually contingent.

It is important to note that interdependence as thus defined relates to specific kinds of actions in specific issue areas. It refers to such actions as those taken in implementing monetary policies, or defense and security arrangements. It need not refer and in fact almost never refers to the whole range of actions that two or more governments take with respect to one another. The Soviet and American governments, for example, are highly interdependent in terms of their security arrangements, and this has led them to take a wide range of arms control measures in common. The security of each is contingent upon actions taken by the other. At the same time these two governments are hardly interdependent at all in commercial affairs, in spite of the recent growth in their trade. Nor are they interdependent in implementing domestic social welfare programs or in most other issues.

Interdependence need not be perceived in the actions and activities of governments. Indeed, as interdependence grew during the twentieth century, its perception by government officials took a long time to develop. The monetary and trade policies of governments in the 1930s, for example, reflected the belief of many officials in America and Europe that they could deal with domestic problems of unemployment and deflation through national encapsulation and the limitation of imports. But competitive devaluations and restrictive trade practices had deleterious consequences for all, and the lesson was learned and incorporated into such postwar institutions as the General Agreement on Tariffs and Trade and the International Monetary Fund that actions taken by governments in these fields are of concern to others. The perception that intergovernmental actions are contingent upon one another has thus benefited the economic management of all governments. It has also, however, created some new dangers in that the contingency of action can be manipulated by some of the governments involved.

We will now review several forms of interdependence that have become characteristic of international society today. One form, strategic interation, which involves the interdependence of purposeful unitary actors, is as old as international politics itself; but it has some unique characteristics in contemporary statecraft. The other two, systemic interdependence and the interdependence associated with the outputs of collective decision making, are relatively new and depend upon the development of high levels of modernization. The former refers to the conditions that enhance the reverberation of events occurring in one part of the world in other parts; the latter is associated with actions taken by global and regional international organizations.

Strategic Interaction

The bargaining process between states, upon which rests the basic structure of international society, is essentially a form of interdependent behavior. In fact, it is the most traditional form of behavior in the international system. Strategic interaction involves the purposeful action of two or more governments when the choice of actions of each depends upon the choices of others.[5] In a world of states where there is no overarching structure of political authority, rational strategic behavior has been generally thought to be imposed on governments, each wishing to maintain its autonomy and security and fearful of the motivations of others.[6] In such a world, which is thought to be dangerous in that its structure is fundamentally anarchic, strategic interaction is perhaps the most common way to structure and stabilize relationships. It has been, for example, one of the primary foreign policy strategies that governments have pursued and one that has made the metaphor of the chessboard suitable for international affairs. Alliances were typical outcomes of strategic behavior. In forming them, governments intentionally created an interdependence in order to assure themselves the support of others in case of war with a third party, or in

---

[5]See, for example, Erving Goffman, *Strategic Interaction* (Philadelphia: University of Pennsylvania Press, 1969), especially pp. 127-218.

[6]See Hans J. Morgenthau, *Politics among Nations,* 5th ed. (New York: Knopf, 1973), Chap. 3; and Stanley Hoffmann, *Contemporary Theory of International Relations* (Englewood Cliffs, N.J.: Prentice-Hall, 1960), pp. 1-26.

order to constrain the actions of allies so as to prevent them from engaging in some activity that might lead to war.[7]

Strategic interdependence, then, has always been central to international politics, and it has been reaffirmed by the development of nuclear deterrence, which is essentially a process of strategic interaction. Yet its applicability and use for most governments, including the superpowers, have changed radically along with the general transformation in foreign policy that takes place under modernization. This can be seen in a brief review of some of its traditional assumptions, which we examined from a somewhat different angle in Chapter 2.

Strategic interdependence was based traditionally upon a system of relationships in which national borders were relatively impermeable to external activities. Each state could be viewed as a separate national unit, and clashes among states would in some measure be conceptualized in terms of a set of billiard balls which occasionally smacked against one another. In short, there was virtually no interpenetration of societies, so that governmental control over domestic affairs was secure and the state could be conceived as a unitary and rational actor. Accordingly, domestic policy and foreign policy were insulated from each other, as under classical statecraft, and governments were free to behave strategically in international affairs, limited by the resources they controlled rather than by domestic interests and concerns.

The use of force by governments was deemed to be both necessary and legitimate, and this constituted a second assumption of strategic interaction. Threats to use force were ubiquitous in a world in which each government believed that the enhancement of state power and encroachments upon others were inherent in international affairs. Such threats existed overtly or covertly at all times, even against allies, whose loyalties might shift radically in the implementation of a grand design or as a response to other changes.

Critical to a system of strategic interaction, however, was its third assumption: that governments always behaved rationally in foreign policy in their efforts to maximize their capacity to survive or to enhance their power.[8] It is the undermining of this assumption under

[7]The motivations for alliances in traditional statecraft are discussed in George Liska, *Nations in Alliance: The Limits of Interdependence* (Baltimore: Johns Hopkins Press, 1962), pp. 26–41.

[8]Rationality has three distinct meanings in studies of foreign policy. In theoretical writings, rationality assumes that behavior conforms to the following

the transformation of foreign policy in the modernization process that makes strategic interaction so much less central to international politics today. Borders have become highly permeable to activities arising outside of them, foreign and domestic affairs have become intermeshed, and the rise of interest group politics in domestic and foreign affairs has severely restricted the utility of assumptions of rationality. Moreover, the use of force as an instrument of diplomacy has become too costly and ineffective for many of its traditional purposes.

The assumptions of strategic interaction have been perhaps most severely undermined in Western and highly industrialized countries, which have for all practical purposes given up the use of force as an instrument of diplomacy vis-à-vis one another since World War II. They have also been undermined in many parts of the less developed world. But if the factors that once made strategic interaction a fundamental condition of international life are decreasingly relevent, we might well ask what their future role may be. It would be foolhardy to predict that strategic interdependence will be completely outmoded. It remains of central significance in the study of military strategy and, especially, in gaining an understanding of how and why deterrence

---

criteria: (1) when faced with a set of choices, a rational individual will choose one alternative; (2) his choice will be based on a transitive ordering of preferences, so that if he prefers A to B and B to C, he will prefer A to C; and (3) the individual always and consistently chooses the most preferred alternative. See, for exposition, Kenneth J. Arrow, *Social Choice and Individual Values,* 2d ed. (New York: Wiley, 1963), Chap. 1.

A second definition of rationality in foreign policy has to do more with a just balance than does this first, more technical definition. Here, a rational foreign policy is one in which the goals of policy and the means selected to implement the goals are in balance, or just proportion, as are the stakes involved and the risks that the government will take to support those stakes. Thus for a number of writers the U.S. engagement in warfare in Vietnam was irrational, although it might well have been rational from the point of view of the first definition offered above. Here the means used were disproportionate to the ends, and the risks assumed were far greater than the American stakes involved. See, for example, Hans J. Morgenthau, *A New Foreign Policy for the United States* (New York: Praeger, 1969).

Finally, rationality in foreign policy has also been associated with the emergence of modern regimes based more on application of laws passed in parliamentary bodies than on more traditional and presumably less rational forms of authority. The more that foreign policy related to the application of law and the less to other forms of authority, the more rational it would be said to be. See Max Weber's formulation in *Wirtschaft und Gesellschaft* (Turbingen: Mohr, 1925), Vol. 2, Part 3, Chap. 6. The English version is found in *From Max Weber: Essays in Sociology,* translated and edited by H. H. Gerth and C. Wright Mills (New York: Oxford University Press, 1947), pp. 650-678.

works or under what conditions it might fail to work. In this sense, it is clear that strategic interdependence has shifted from the former European great powers to the interactions of the two (if not three) major global powers, the U.S. and the Soviet Union (and perhaps China).

Nor has the utility of this most traditional of all structures of international society been eroded in relations between non-superpowers. It has been transformed in relations among the highly modernized societies and also seems to have been given new life on the periphery of the modern world. In the latter area, where superpowers have increasingly resisted temptations to intervene because of the decline in the efficacy of the use of force, governments may well be freer to criticize others without fear of recrimination and thus "act out" strategic interactions in political rhetoric more than in political actions. Among the more modernized societies strategic interactions may well prove to be one of the central means for handling problems of instability that have arisen from the development of other forms of interdependence, which will be discussed presently. As levels of systemic interdependence (defined below) have increased among these societies, policy instruments capable of controlling their effects have not been developed. This is especially true in areas of low policies and is associated with such contemporary phenomena as the rapid flow of capital across borders during monetary crises. Thus, both within the European Communities and among the most important monetary reserve countries, bargaining relationships have evolved primarily over issues of low politics and for the principal purpose of crisis management.

At times, but less frequently than has often been asserted, one or more governments may attempt to manipulate a crisis for egotistic ends which smack more directly of the conditions of classical strategic interactions, yet which are also quite different from them. For example, bargaining is based less on the decisions of a head of state, or of a unitary actor, than those of specialized ministers and nonministerial officials (e.g., central bankers), whose policy positions frequently reflect both bargains struck within governments and long-term relationships developed with colleagues of similar rank abroad. Also, here, in contrast to the situation in classical strategic interdependence, the interests of the various governments tend to be highly convergent and complementary most of the time, especially insofar as the interests of all are to preserve the stability of their relationships and this concern overrides particular and divergent national policy goals.

Systemic Interdependence

Perhaps the most prominent form of structural relationship in international society today is one that can be labeled systemic interdependence. This condition is in many ways the opposite of strategic interaction, and it has arisen from two very general sets of conditions: technological change and governmental policy. Technological change, by creating a rapid decline in transportation costs around the globe and developing a vast network of communications among societies, certainly made an enormous difference in overcoming "natural" barriers to the flow of factors of production (labor, technology, capital) and of goods, services, and ideas across political boundaries. Governmental policies, especially in reaction to more overt neomercantilist and restrictive policies in the 1930s, also resulted in conspicuous efforts to lower political barriers to the flow of goods, manpower, investments, resources, and technology on an international level.

As a result, systemic interdependence has become highly significant in international affairs. It can be defined along a continuum, and measured by

> the extent to which events occurring in any given part or within any given component unit of a world system affect (either physically or perceptually) events taking place in each of the other parts or component units of the system.[9]

Here, as is not the case with strategic interactions, borders are highly permeable to certain kinds of flows between both official and nonofficial groups. The utility of force in relations between the interdependent units tends to be more marginal than in the first instance, either because of treaty (NATO), tradition, and habit (U.S.-Canadian boarder or because of nuclear deterrence. And rational calculus is far less marked, because of the breakdown in the foreign-domestic distinction and the permeation of national affairs by pressure group politics.

As we saw in the last chapter, the transformation of foreign policies

---

[9]Oran R. Young, "Interdependencies in World Politics," *International Journal,* XXIV (Autumn 1969), p. 726.

goes hand in hand with the growth in systemic interdependence. Non-security activities in particular assume a major and central importance in the content of foreign policy, and governmental concern for these activities increases as a function of the expanded range of governmental goals. Consequently, activities that were once thought to be predominantly economic now also seem to have significant political overtones. Recently, for example, Cooper argued that the two-track system separating commercial policy from security policy after World War II began to erode as a result of governmental refusal, under domestic group pressure, to adhere to GATT's trading rules. "When trade relations sour, they infect other areas of policy, even 'high policy,' via domestic political attitudes and pressures."[10] In short, foreign economic policy has become politicized for all parties. The traditional security focus on foreign policy seems to have lost its predominant significance for all but the superpowers, and all powers have assumed a new emphasis on what might be termed economic security: maintaining an acceptable level of economic growth to insure increases in income for all members of society and, not inconsequentially, also to insure governmental stability. The transformation also takes place, as argued earlier, as the international stalemate created by nuclear deterrence makes it easier for governments to seek their national ambitions in international economic affairs. And in turn this kind of behavior is more salient as the societies of the world become increasingly interdependent in their economic relationships. Thus the manipulation of systemic interdependence by governments becomes of vital interest for domestic as well as foreign policies.

One of the central characteristics of systemic interdependence has to do with the relationship between policy instruments and policy goals, and with the number of instruments that are available to control the outcomes of governmental policies. Unless some sort of supernational government is instituted along with systemic interdependence, the number of policy instruments capable of controlling the outcomes of governmental policies decreases.[11] Interdependence does this, in the first instance, by removing from governments a whole set of border

[10] Richard N. Cooper, "Trade Policy Is Foreign Policy," *Foreign Policy,* No. 9 (Winter 1972–73), p. 32.

[11] This crucial relationship among policy instruments, policy targets, and policy objectives is formalized in Jan Tinbergen, *On the Theory of Economic Policy,* 2d ed. (Amsterdam: North-Holland, 1963). Tinbergen argues that an optimum policy situation exists when the number of instruments available for use exceeds

controls (which once limited transactions in goods and services, ideas, or production factors) and thus decreasing the level of control over activities both within and beyond the state. The loss of control that accompanies this form of interdependence means that any government's range of political options is highly restricted. A government may wish to foster political integration in those areas where interdependence is high; or it may wish to restrain the further growth in interdependence, perhaps even at the cost of hindering the achievement of fundamental domestic goals. The first option is made difficult to accept, since it requires that the government give up aspects of sovereignty, never an easy thing to do. The latter option is, however, equally difficult, in that it would weaken the government's legitimacy by causing a growth in public dissatisfaction with governmental performance.

Systemic interdependence requires multilateral rather than bilateral diplomacy, and it is generally accompanied by a relative increase in the former and decline in the latter. Frequently, too, systemic interdependence leads to the formation of multilateral institutions, which are designed to control the destabilizing effects that accompany interdependence. Indeed, most of the major international economic institutions created after World War II were formed as a result of the perception gained during the depression of the 1930s that the societies and economies of the world had become more highly interdependent. One of the primary fears of some governments in the immediate aftermath of World War II was the recurrence of depression and fear that new outbreaks of domestic turmoil might lead to right-wing or Marxist revolutions.[12] Partially in order to prevent the realization of

---

the number of goals. In principle, an infinite number of policy mixes then exists, in that one instrument can substitute for another and "it will always be possible to find one among the infinity of solutions . . . for which welfare, however defined, is at a maximum" (pp. 37–38). This is not only the most efficient but also the fairest situation, because it allows any pressure to be "distributed more evenly over the various social groups" (p. 41). With the opening up of borders to new activities, governments give up certain instruments, like trade or exchange rate policies needed for control since the number of instruments becomes too limited to assure policy consistency and control. When the number of instruments is fewer than the number of goals, no clear solution exists on grounds of efficiency or fairness. Also see on this central point Cooper, *The Economics of Interdependence,* pp. 153–157; and Warren L. Smith, "Are There Enough Policy Tools?" *American Economic Review,* LV (May 1965), pp. 208–220.

[12] See, for example, Stephen E. Ambrose, *Rise to Globalism: American Foreign Policy 1938–1970* (Baltimore: Penguin, 1971), pp. 11–22.

these fears, a network of new international economic organizations was created to assure the prosperity of all members under the belief that the prosperity of the world was indivisible and that the domestic and foreign policies pursued by any one government were of legitimate concern to all other governments. Thus the International Monetary Fund (1944) was to provide an orderly means for governments to change their exchange rates and to replace competitive devaluations or a world of currency blocs; and the General Agreement on Tariffs and Trade (1948) was designed to facilitate a world of multilateral bargaining through which barriers to trade could be progressively dismantled on an international and universal basis.

The organizational structure of the postwar international economic order thus reflected a number of concerns about growing international interdependence, which were crystallized in the ideas of American Secretary of State Cordell Hull (1933-44). Hull was firmly committed to a world in which the principles of liberalism could be permitted to develop. In particular, he felt that international peace and stability required that governments remove their international economic activities from the sphere of high policy and permit economic interdependences to grow. A network of interdependent relationships would then result and would be based on universal and general rules in which national governments would have such great stakes that they would also have an inducement to transcend a world of power politics. Thus, as Cooper has argued, the creation of the IMF, IBRD, (International Bank for Reconstruction and Development) and GATT resulted in the creation of a "two track system," which

> kept trade issues off the agenda of high diplomacy, except when governments deliberately put them there for reasons of high policy. In other words, trade issues per se did not intrude into high policy, although high policy did occasionally, and in important ways, intrude into trade relationships, for example in formation of the European Economic Community and in proscriptions on trade with Communist countries.[13]

[13]Cooper, "Trade Policy Is Foreign Policy," p. 19. Robert Gilpin provides a strikingly different interpretation of the establishment of a system of interdependent relationships in "The Politics of Transnational Economic Relations," in Robert O. Keohane and Joseph S. Nye, Jr., eds., *Transnational Relations and World Politics* (Cambridge, Mass.: Harvard University Press, 1972), pp. 48-69. He argues that "economic and technological factors have been able to exercise

These organizations were able to provide both a framework in which interdependence could develop and a set of mechanisms for intergovernmental consultation that could control some of the destabilizing (and unintended) effects of interdependence.

Systemic interdependence as defined here bears great similarity to some concepts of economic integration, and it would be useful to make some distinguishing definitions. When integration is viewed as a state of affairs rather than as a process, it relates to a set of conditions brought about usually by the removal of discriminations along borders, or what has been called "negative integration." "Positive integration" is far more process-related. It involves, in Tinbergen's terms, the

creation both of new institutions with their instruments and the modification of existing instruments and applies, in principle, to the institutions and instruments requiring centralized handling. As a minimum, this refers to measures needed to *avoid a distortion* of the processes of free competition.[14]

Positive integration connotes *dirigiste* policies that are uniform in a given area, and also the emergence of centralized political authority.

For many theorists of integration, negative integration, or the development of system-wide interdependences, is a strategy of political unification; interdependence breeds instability, or spillover effects that are likely to require political actions and the creation of centralized institutions to control them. To date, increases in flows of trade or of capital have reflected growth in interdependence, especially among the highly industrialized societies. This region of world politics has also certainly not been characterized by any significant amount of positive

their profound effects because the United States ... has created the necessary political framework" (p. 54). He finds that the U.S. enabled and encouraged the Europeans to develop and create discriminatory trade policies in exchange for enhancing American security via support in NATO; that it granted preferential access by the Japanese to the U.S. market in exchange for bases in Japan; and, finally, that "just as a particular array of political interests and relations permitted this system of transnational economic relations to come into being, so changes in these political factors can profoundly alter the system and even bring it to an end" (p. 63). Also see the essay of Benjamin J. Cohen, "The Revolution in Atlantic Economic Relations: A Bargain Comes Unstuck," in Wolfram F. Hanrieder, ed., *The United States and Western Europe: Political, Economic and Strategic Perspectives* (Cambridge, Mass.: Winthrop, 1974), pp. 106–133.

[14] Jan Tinbergen, *International Economic Integration,* 2d ed. (Amsterdam: Elsevier, 1964), p. 78.

integration. Some exceptions exist, as when governments come together in an ad hoc way to arrange special controls for emergencies (as in the creation of the Group of Ten major monetary countries in the early 1960s to pool resources in dealing with speculative crises). Positive integration has proceeded to a more significant level in the European Communities, but even there its growth has been limited, since the removal of barriers to factor movements has been much easier than has the adoption of common policies, which require the relinquishing of sovereign rights by member states.

Since systemic interdependence involves loss of governmental autonomy as activities across international borders increasingly evade governmental control, it is also related to transnational politics. Both arise from the increasing number of transactions among societies in nongovernmental contexts. Karl Kaiser draws a distinction between transnational and intergovernmental systems that is clear. For him, a "transnational society subsystem" exists when "relations" between national systems are handled and decided upon by nongovernmental elites and pursued directly between social, economic, and political forces in the participating societies."[15] "Intergovernmental transactions", on the contrary, are those where "relations between national systems are handled and decided upon by elites located in governmental institutions."[16] Thus, exchanges of goods, services, materials, and so forth among people in different societies are examples of the former type of relationship, and traditional alliances exemplify the latter.

Transnational interactions, then, reduce control over the foreign activities of citizens by their governments *if* no positive integration takes place. Transnational activities may bring about situations in which governments are forced to take action, frequently with their freedom of choice highly restricted. This has been most noteworthy in matters affecting the international monetary system, where as transnational flows have increased (via the banking and multinational corporation structures), the capacity of a single government to affect their scope or the direction of their change has decreased.

In the last chapter I argued that the diminished loss of control over

[15] Karl Kaiser, "The Interactions of Regional Subsystems: Some Preliminary Notes on Recurrent Patterns and the Role of Superpowers," *World Politics,* XXI (July 1968), p. 91.

[16] Ibid., p. 92.

foreign and domestic policies as a result of increased international interdependence has had two general effects. On the one hand, it creates incentives for governments to reduce their own vulnerability to outside pressures and to increase the vulnerability of others. On the other hand, it pushes governments toward the adoption of short-term, conservative types of foreign policy. Here I will extend my analysis of the effects of interdependence on policy and policy control.

It appears that the higher the level of interdependence among a set of political systems, the greater will be the likelihood that the system of interactions will undergo crises. Loss of control that accompanied the growth of transnational politics thus inevitably contributes to the likelihood of international economic crises.[17] In international finance, the enormous growth in short-term flows of liquid capital across borders eludes the closest government controls and can threaten domestic anti-inflationary measures, exchange rates, and other policies. These flows seem to be the inevitable consequences of interdependent relations in the economic field, just as the spread of ideas, habits, fashions, and even rebelliousness are destabilizing cultural and political consequences.

The crises that arise out of interdependent relationships also reflect a growing set of ties that bind societies together. As a result of these ties, with increased interdependence there also results an increased ability of any one government to manipulate the internal affairs of others. For example, when the effectiveness of credit restrictions in one society is dependent upon policies pursued elsewhere, other governments can manipulate the results. A high interest rate designed to curtail the growth in the money supply of an economy can attract funds from abroad unless other governments also raise their interest rates. The Federal Republic of Germany has periodically confronted this problem in its attempts to curtail inflation, only to find its high interest policy undermined by loose credit policies in the United States causing dollar outflows to Germany.

A new form of interventionism thus accompanies the growth in international interdependence. Now a government is able effectively and frequently to intervene in another society by changing its own domestic policy. This has been illustrated in trade diplomacy in recent years between the United States and the Soviet Union, with Moscow trying

[17]I argued this in greater detail in "Crisis Diplomacy, Interdependence, and the Politics of International Economic Relations," *World Politics,* XXIV, Supplement (Spring 1972) pp. 123–150.

to liberalize its policy toward the emigration of Jews to Israel without at the same time overtly admitting to a change in domestic policy that certain American proponents of trade and credit restrictions have fostered. Similarly, when the Mansfield Resolution, designed to reduce the number of American troops stationed in Europe, was being debated in the U.S. Senate in spring 1971, Chairman Brezhnev agreed to pursue discussions with the U.S. on mutual and balanced force reductions in Europe. This served to bolster the position of the U.S. administration in combating Mansfield in the Senate.

The same factors that enable governments to manipulate the domestic affairs of others can also result in the playing out of domestic policies in an international context. West German legislative elections have traditionally involved speeches by leading spokesman for all parties in the United States, just as the domestic debates over ratification of Eastern treaties negotiated by the Brandt government led other parties to send their leaders to the U.S. to make speeches reflecting their views of German security and German-American relations in the hopes that they could sell their own views as American-supported to their constituents in Germany.

Interdependence does not only breed crises and various forms of linkage; it also increases the potential for any single party to manipulate a crisis for its own domestic or foreign political ends. With the increased number of crises in areas of systemic interdependence and the growing interrelatedness of issue areas (including trade systems, monetary systems, and security systems), negotiations normally will involve a wide range of issues for the development of possible trade-offs among governments in their attempts to reach decisions or consensus. At the same time, possibilities for political "blackmail" are also enhanced with the growth in the links between different issues and stakes.

The linkage of issues and stakes has been of special significance in the European Communities, where interdependence has reached its highest levels. There is some general debate concerning whether the emergence of multiply linked issue areas tends to create greater stability or instability in international politics.[18] In Europe, the results are somewhat mixed. The decisions to implement the original provisions of the Rome

---

[18] See, for example, Seyom Brown, "The Changing Essence of Power," *Foreign Affairs* Vol. 1 (January 1973), pp. 286–299.

Treaty concerning a customs union were, by French demand, made dependent upon the development of a common agricultural policy (CAP). That policy itself depended upon relatively fixed parity relations among the member countries, so when the fixed-rate monetary system began to unravel after 1969, the French added the quest for a common monetary policy to that for the operation of the CAP. All of these eventually became linked to British efforts to create a larger regional aid fund and to German efforts to harmonize fiscal policies. They had, in sum, the making of a package deal upon which all could agree, but also on which each government exercised a unit veto, since withdrawal of any one government's support could bring apart the whole agreement. The French did this in the mid-1960s, but the policy of blackmail had only mixed results.

It is a paradox of this situation, however, that with the increased incidence of crises in an interdependent world, governments have tended to grow to rely upon crises for effective decision making. Administrations have become aware of their inability to cope with the increased demands placed upon them, the undermining of their own domestic authority, and the costs of making effective decisions, for reasons reviewed in Chapter 4. But they have become somewhat more willing to see crises erupt as a means of short-cutting decision-making processes. Most governments, as argued earlier, have become fearful of changes from the status quo, especially the more modernized governments. Yet none can escape decision, through disruptions either from interdependence or from domestic unrest. In periods of crisis governments are frequently able to take decisions that the loss of domestic support in normal times would rule out. Indeed, under such circumstances, forceful action has its own reward, in that it is likely to be highly appreciated by most citizens and, even if it involves domestic sacrifices, may well bolster sagging governmental authority. It is interesting to note that many of the new institutional arrangements that have been created to deal with interdependences have emerged from ad hoc decision making during crises.

Crises, then, have accompanied interdependence and have a mixed effect upon international society. Although one might well predict that the number and incidence of crises of interdependence will spread in future years, one can also anticipate that mixed solutions, toward retrenchment from interpendence or toward increased policy coordination, will be in order. Cooper summarizes the economic policy choices for the societies of the highly interdependent Atlantic states, positing options that are applicable to noneconomic problems as well:

> (a) to accept the integration and the consequential loss of national freedom, and to engage in the *joint* determination of economic objectives and policies;
> (b) to accept the integration but attempt to preserve as much national autonomy as possible by providing . . . accommodation[s] . . .
> (c) to reject the integration by deliberate imposition of barriers to the integrating forces, freedom of foreign trade and international capital movements.[19]

Systemic interdependence, in summary, has created transnational structures that have diminished governmental controls over domestic activities; but it has also induced governments to cooperate with one another. The stakes involved in the preservation of interdependences have thus far proved greater than the costs of untangling the relationships. And some losses in governmental control either are not very serious or have been complemented by collective measures taken for policy harmonizing and achievement. Yet as a result of some of these new international commitments and agreements, some sorts of control over domestic phenomena become less rather than more effective. The crisis of control on the international level is thus mirrored within states when increased demands on governments are greater than ever and the inability of governments to achieve all demands serves to question governmental authority.

Interdependences, Public Goods, and Asymmetries

There is a third form of interdependence that is associated with the production and consumption of collective goods, usually in the context of international organizations, where member states are presumptively equal to one another. Paradoxically, however, such public goods are most helpful in the analysis of highly asymmetrical interdependent relations, where inequalities among nations are pronounced.

While public goods may involve both strategic interaction and systemic interdependence, their distinguishing characteristic is their property of nonexclusion in the use derived from a good by the members of

---

[19]Cooper, *The Economics of Interdependence,* p. 262. Emphasis is his.

a group.[20] The concept denotes a large number of goods consumed jointly by nations, including security, a stable network of trade relationships, accepted rules of international finances, and so forth. What is significant is that once such a good is supplied for any one unit, it also can be provided at no or little cost to others. In other words, the costs of excluding members of a set from consuming a good produced by or for the set are very high, and "it is of the essence of an organization that it provides an inseparable, generalized benefit."[21] Rational action (as defined technically above) by the leaders of small units in the group would lead them to provide suboptimal contributions for the supply of the good. This has been the case in many organizations, such as the UN or NATO, where smaller countries pay disproportionately less than larger ones.

The reasons for disproportionate payment according to size are debatable, and in many instances reasons other than size seem more compelling. For example, with regard to contributions to NATO, it may well be that the value placed on NATO by the U.S. or Germany is higher than that placed by France or Iceland. Regardless of the reasons, however, disproportionality of payments for a collective good leads to an examination of one of the most significant aspects of interdependent relations: asymmetries exist among nations, and will always affect interrelationships. As just noted, this phenomenon has most frequently been discussed in the context of public goods with reference to size, where, as Olson and Zeckhauser put it, there is "a tendency for the 'larger' members—those that place a higher absolute value on the public good—to bear a disproportionate share of the burden."[22] The interests of the group and of an individual member are likely to differ, and as a result, individuals

will not act to advance their common or group objective unless there is coercion to force them to do so, or unless some separate

[20] Frohlich and Oppenheimer formally define a public good as follows: "Whenever each of the consumers in a given group receives a consumption unit derived from the same production unit, that production unit will be defined as a *public good* for that group." See Norman Frohlich and Joe A. Oppenheimer, "Entrepreneurial Politics and Foreign Policy," *World Politics,* XXIV, Supplement (Spring 1972), pp. 157. Emphasis is theirs.

[21] Mancur Olson, Jr., *The Logic of Collective Action: Public Goods and the Theory of Groups* (Cambridge, Mass.: Harvard University Press, 1964), p. 15.

[22] Mancur Olson, Jr., and Richard Zeckhauser, *An Economic Theory of Alliances* (Santa Monica, Calif.: Rand Corp., 1966), p. 4.

incentive, distinct from the achievement of the common or group interest is offered to the members of the group individually on the condition that they help to bear the costs or burdens involved in the achievement of the group objectives.[23]

Frohlich, Oppenheimer, and Young have argued that it is a different asymmetry which is determining. In particular, they place a special emphasis on the value to the individual of consuming the good, or the value earned in exchange for supplying the good.[24] An individual who seeks to supply public goods in exchange for other values is an entrepreneur whose role is "conceptualized as the set of rewards and costs which an individual can expect to incur by supplying consumption units in exchange."[25] It is the political entrepreneur who supplies goods collectively. Under this notion what makes NATO and the Warsaw Pact different from more traditional alliances is that they involve a public good supplied by a leadership whose profits are "revenues" from the recipients of the goods (plus the value attached to the act of political entrepreneurship).

One virtue of this public goods concept of interdependence is its embodiment of notions of interest-maximizing behavior on the part of different members in a group. This facilitates the analysis of collective processes, especially when combined with other forms of interdependence. In our own discussion we will now look more closely at politics within the Atlantic community, both as involving a public good individualistically supplied by the U.S. (NATO's nuclear deterrent) and as a network of interdependent economic relationships. We do this in order to see how the two sets of relationships affect one another, and in order to examine symmetries and asymmetries within the system and their interaction in what are seemingly different and separate aspects of a single set of relationships.[26]

[23] Olson, *The Logic of Collective Action,* p. 2.

[24] Norman Frohlich, Joe A. Oppenheimer, and Oran Young, *Political Leadership and Collective Goods* (Princeton, N.J.: Princeton University Press, 1971), pp. 145-150.

[25] Frohlich and Oppenheimer, "Entrepreneurial Politics," p. 159.

[26] A somewhat different set of notions concerning asymmetries and interdependent relations has been formulated by Robert O. Keohane and Joseph S. Nye, who distinguish "sensitivity interdependence" and "vulnerability interdependence." The former concept "is appropriate for the analysis of state behavior when the structure of relations is well established and generally accepted

Certainly, in the real world, questions of "burden sharing" in NATO are intermixed with monetary and commercial matters, since the U.S. and other advanced industrialized societies in the non-Communist world have become economically interdependent. Fundamental symmetries and asymmetries exist in these relationships and cross-cut one another. In security matters, the U.S. has a role that remains unique. Since the onset of the cold war its nuclear wherewithal has provided the basis of NATO's defense, and no other state in the organization can rival the U.S. in nuclear capacity. In international monetary relations, the U.S. has been responsible for provision of dollar assets to meet others' demands for reserves, liquidity, private transactions, intervention in private markets, etc. Although the American government has grown reluctant to provide such sources, since this involves continuing overall balance-of-payments deficits, and although the Europeans also apparently would like to develop a system that would assure for the collective supply of reserve assets, Richard N. Cooper has argued that a fundamental asymmetry will continue here, too, so long as the Europeans fail to create a unified currency, the start-up costs for which are prohibitive. He argues,

> The basic asymmetry is the dominant economic size of the United States reinforced by the closely related asymmetries in scale and sophistication of financial markets. . . . These asymmetries in turn lead through a complicated process . . . to two separate but related asymmetries in the operation of international payments: the extensive private use of the U.S. dollar as a medium of exchange, a unit of account, and a temporary store of value; and the use of the dollar as an official intervention currency in a payments system that relies on private markets for multilateral clearing. . . . The reasons for these asymmetries are deep-seated, residing in the enormous efficiency of money as an intermediary in the process of exchange.[27]

but where marginal effects of changes in flows within that structure can have significant effects." Their second form of interdependence stresses asymmetries that result from differential opportunity costs: "the less dependent state incurs relatively lower costs from the termination or drastic alteration of the relationship." "World Politics and the International Economic System," in C. Fred Bergsten, ed., *The Future of the International Economic Order: An Agenda for Research* (Lexington, Mass.: Lexington Books, 1973) p. 124.

[27] Richard N. Cooper, "Eurodollars, Reserve Dollars, Asymmetries in the International Monetary System," *Journal of International Economics,* 2 (November 1972), pp. 327–328.

In commercial affairs, however, the United States and Western Europe are on more or less equal footing, if one accepts the European Communities as an individual unit. By 1970 the Europe of the Nine (it actually expanded from six to nine on January 1, 1973), had a slightly larger population than the U.S., a GNP about two-thirds as large, and a larger share of world exports (25% versus 20%) and imports (25% versus 17%). This relative equality in weight as trading units, however, is obviously affected by the fundamental and long-term asymmetries in the other situations, and this disparity strongly influences the selection of bargaining choices on both sides of the Atlantic.

It might generally (and controversially) be argued that one of the most significant political effects of interdependence is that as it increases, it tends to equalize the relative power that any government can use vis-à-vis others. This should normally be the case whether one looks at the systemic interdependences in the international economic order or the more public goods–related interdependences in the security field. Among these factors is the increased cost of exercising power in the contemporary world, as I argued in the last chapter at some length. Interdependence increases the linkages between states, and even great powers must give up political instruments as they become more interdependent with others. This increases the blackmail power of smaller states when their stake in the stability of an interdependent system is lower than the stake of larger units.

An additional feature of this lowering of relative asymmetries—one which indeed follows from it—is that the more interdependent a set of political systems becomes the lower becomes the capacity of any one of them to achieve positive goals and the greater its ability to threaten others with harm through the use of negative sanctions. Stanley Hoffmann observes this in his portrayal of the United States as Gulliver among the Lilliputians:

> Today the most fascinating aspect of the utility of military power is that this once fairly persistent link between military strength and positive achievements has been loosened. The power to coerce has never been so great or so unevenly distributed . . . , but its nature is now such that its possessor must restrict its uses. The fullest use of nuclear power is in *denial,* but this must consist in threats—in deterrence—and by definition shuns execution.[28]

[28] Hoffmann, *Gulliver's Troubles,* p. 29.

This decline in the role of positive inducements and increase in the power of denial is evident not only in the nuclear diplomacy of the superpowers but also in the recent international monetary crises. The United States government was unable to rectify its balance of payments before the monetary crisis erupted in August 1971. It had failed to convince surplus countries (Europe and Japan) to revalue their currencies or to lower their barriers to imports from the United States. The European Community members continued to maintain their discriminatory arrangements, which the U.S. government felt were in violation of the most-favored-nation principle embodied in the GATT. The U.S. in short, was in a crisis, but was also unable to achieve the goals required to get out of it. Therefore, the U.S. government resorted to a series of negative maneuvers after August 15 that threatened others with harm, by imposing import restrictions and by attempting to force them to float their exchange rates. The use of these tactics was in part responsible for the U.S. government's ability to achieve its short-term objectives in the Smithsonian agreements of December 1971.

In the real world, of course, the degree to which asymmetries are reduced by interdependence or the degree to which the capacity to deny others the achievement of their goals as opposed to one's ability to achieve one's own depends on a number of factors. Among these is the entrepreneurial capacity of the members of a group. I will now argue, that the entrepreneurial capacity of the U.S. in providing collective monetary mechanisms also limits to some degree the adverse affects of interdependence that we have just examined. This role can perhaps best be understood if we adopt some of the language in current usage in "dependence" theory and treat the U.S. as a "core" area, and Europe and Japan (among others) as its "periphery."[29] While a core

[29]The distinction between core, or center, and periphery is now commonplace in the literature on economic and political development, but especially in neo-Marxist and in ultra-Keynesian analysis, and seems to have had its first major usage in Raul Prebisch, *The Economic Development of Latin America and Its Principal Problems* (New York: United Nations, 1950). The neo-Marxist position is frequently based upon some application of the Leninist notion of the law of uneven development, as in Stephen Hymer, "The Multinational Corporation and the Law of Uneven Development," in Jagdish N. Bhagwati, ed., *Economics and World Order: From the 1970's to the 1990's* (New York: Macmillan, 1972), pp. 113–140. The ultra-Keynesian view is based on notions of the economies of agglomeration and the economic bases of market expansion, as in Hans O. Schmitt, "Integration and Conflict in the World Economy," *Journal of Common Market Studies,* VII (September 1969), pp. 1–18, or John Knapp, "Economics or Political Economy?" *Lloyds Bank Review,* No. 107 (January 1973), pp. 19–43.

area may be understood in terms of the leadership it provides in establishing a shared mechanism or good, entrepreneurship is *not* essential for the development of a core area. Economic and political growth is willy-nilly a nuclear process:

> Particular peoples and nations have tended to crystallize around particular concentrations of capital and technology, core areas whose superior rates of economic growth raised expectations of economic reward from political association with them.[30]

One feature of core areas is their ability to attract all factors of production (technology, capital, labor) due to the higher expectations as well as the lower risks that they provide. Indeed, it may well be the process of concentration that affects an acceleration of innovations, which is responsible for a self-maintaining process. Nucleation at a core also results in some real losses at the periphery, where the ability of governments to achieve political and economic goals on their own declines in a relatively open world. Leaders of peripheral states must thus accept high costs to the well-being of their own populations if they attempt to create new core areas of their own, yet such costs may be willingly accepted. As Schmitt argues,

> There are several reasons why a citizenry may willingly bear such costs. Fear of excessive concentrations of power could in many minds justify even permanent losses in material welfare. Residential preferences of a population with cultural and political memories may not in any case be shared to the same extent by managements of foreign origin. Finally, the survival of a distinct culture as a source of collective pride may be thought precarious in the context of a new and amalgamated society.[31]

Even though it is usually applied to relations between rich and poor societies, the core-periphery model sheds a great deal of light on U.S.-Europe relations as well. In many ways frictions between the two reflect the pains that must be inflicted in any conscious effort by Europeans to create a new core area. This has been an explicit goal set by the nine heads of state of Europe since the time of the expansion of the Community in the early 1970s. It was originally also encouraged by the U.S. government, since European political and economic inte-

[30] Schmitt, "Integration and Conflict in the World Economy," p. 2.
[31] Ibid., pp. 6–7.

gration has been a principal and, until recently, an unquestioned goal of American policy. In return the U.S. government received, implicitly at least, a free hand to run the security policies of the Atlantic region and also received benefits of seignorage from use of the dollar in international monetary relations.[32] American dominance in the international monetary system assumed growing costs in recent years, and, as European restrictions against American exports were maintained, the original bargain seemed less worthwhile. Moreover, as the U.S. security role assumed less significance with the development of East-West détente and as European suspicions of the U.S. guarantee increased, the bargain also lost some of its support on the other side of the Atlantic.

The whole structure of U.S.-West European relations has now entered what might be termed a "crisis zone,"[33] and this has greatly affected trans-Atlantic politics. In a crisis zone, potential areas for bargaining between core and periphery increase as the basic issues dividing the two become clearer. Here, the natural interests and foreign policies of the two naturally tend to differ, and these differences are likely to be acute concerning the "rules of the game" between them. The core area state

[32] See especially Cohen, "The Revolution in Atlantic Economic Relations," and Gilpin, "The Politics of Transnational Economic Relations," for analyses concerning the nature of this implicit general trade-off. On the costs and benefits of having one's currency widely used in private and public transactions outside one's jurisdiction, see Benjamin J. Cohen, *The Future of Sterling as an International Currency* (New York: Macmillan, 1971), pp. 34–52.

[33] I have borrowed this term from discussions concerning bargaining within the international context, where "crisis zone" has a well-defined technical meaning. It is that area on a graphic depiction where dollar liabilities are greater than the gold backing in American reserves. This situation was realized by the mid-1960s. Originally it was feared that when the international monetary system entered this zone, it would be prone to a great number of instabilities. See the original analysis of Robert Triffin, *Gold and the Dollar Crisis* (New Haven, Conn.: Yale University Press, 1960). The system, it was felt, would be liable to "runs on the central bank" (i.e., the stock of U.S. gold reserves), since there would be no international leader of last resort or central bank to inspire confidence in the value of the dollar. See also the arguments in *International Monetary Arrangements: The Problems of Choice; Report on the Deliberations of an International Study Group of Thirty-two Economists* (Princeton, N.J., International Finance Section, 1964), p. 35. Also see the criticism of this view in Lawrence Officer and Thomas D. Willett, "Reserve-Asset Preferences and the Confidence Problem in the Crisis Zone," *Quarterly Journal of Economics,* LXXXIII (November 1969), pp. 688–695. This article argues that the effects of mutual interdependence in the monetary system (in terms of benefits derived from the system's operation and of the shared desire to preserve the system) make the crisis zone far more stable than had previously been expected.

will likely try to prevent the coalescence of a new opposing group of peripheral states, which will attempt to create a new core area of its own. The core area state will tend to strike bargains in a variety of issue areas simultaneously so as to maximize its leverage over the periphery, which will resist this strategy.

After the monetary crisis of 1971, then, it was no accident that the American government emphasized bilateral ties it had with governments on its economic and security periphery. This strategy had the effect of impeding the development of a unified coalition against the U.S. The security provided to the German government by the deployment of American troops was stressed as a means of discouraging the Federal Republic from committing itself to new monetary rules for Europe that also would prove to be antithetic to U.S. goals. The U.S. government also made efforts to link together issues of reform in NATO and in international monetary and commercial affairs, since from the point of view of the core, these necessarily form part of a coherent whole. Given the growth in systemic interdependences among NATO members, the U.S. government did not refrain from manipulating economic and political forces in the peripheral states to induce compliance with the American will.

The objectives of the peripheral countries are rather different. This can be seen in the ways they responded (or failed to respond) to an American initiative in April 1973 to come up with a new "Atlantic Charter" outlining the rules of the game by which Americans, Europeans, and Japanese should deal with one another. Rather than regard these as an effort to inject stability into an unstable situation, the European governments almost unanimously felt that this was an American initiative to manipulate the Europeans into compliance. The only way that states on the periphery can compensate for the costs of change in rules of behavior that principally benefit the core area or can minimize the costs of their own nucleation process is by forming a united coalition so that they can deal with the political authorities in the core area on more even terms. They must simultaneously prevent the core area from manipulating the coalition across issue areas. Here we find that the European governments have in fact largely succeeded in preventing the U.S. government from tying together reforms of the monetary, commercial, and security relationships, by insisting that they be separately negotiated.

Table 1. International Market Interpenetration, Selected Countries (Ratio of Imports to Gross National Product)

	1960	*1973*
Netherlands	40.3	41.1
United Kingdom	18.1	22.1
Italy	14.0	20.1
Canada	14.3	19.6
Federal Republic of Germany	14.3	15.8
France	10.5	14.7
Japan	10.6	9.4
United States	3.0	7.2

Source: U.S. Department of Commerce, *International Economic Indicators and and Competitive Trends,* Vol. 1, No. 2 (May 1975), p. 60.

While, in general, asymmetries tend to become reduced as states become more interdependent, the core area has several advantages, especially after the system enters the crisis zone. The U.S. government holds more levers over each of the European governments than any of them holds over the U.S. American strength in economic bargaining relates to the large position of the U.S. in the world market and to its low vulnerability. As can be seen from Table 1, the U.S. economy is relatively unopen to outside activities, since its external sector is comparatively far smaller. While threatening to disrupt world trade, the U.S. government might be expected to be affected least of all industrialized non-Communist societies. Fears of the eventual consequences of manipulative behavior, and the fear in particular of helping to spur on nucleation along the periphery, damp the vigor of manipulative American actions. The system, in short, is stalemated, and manipulative behavior like that adopted by the U.S. in 1971 can be practiced seldom.

Whatever the prognosis may be for the stability of relations among the industrialized societies, they do currently illustrate different aspects of the three types of interdependence outlined in this chapter. Strategic behavior has become important, but it has shifted its focus largely to economic affairs and to a new style of statecraft. These societies have become highly interdependent in the achievement of their basic politico-economic goals. In terms of systemic interdependence, their interrelationships seem to have risen to an unprecedented degree.[34] And the common goods they have produced collectively have multiplied in far greater numbers than most observers could have predicted at the close of World War II.

INTERDEPENDENCE, DEPENDENCE, AND RELATIONS BETWEEN RICH AND POOR SOCIETIES

Two sorts of criticisms have been levied against those who argue the position put forward in this chapter. On the one hand, some argue that the external sector has become less significant for the foreign policies of most societies and that if modernization has any effect on the international system, it is one which heightens national divisions. They maintain that the fundamental nature of international politics stems from the largely anarchic milieu in which they take place and "a comparison of the conditions of internal and external interdependence is always a marginal affair."[35] On the other hand, there are those who maintain that the growing divide between rich and poor societies which has accompanied modernization makes it not simply misleading but perhaps perverse to discuss the growth in international interdependence. If there has been a great change in international affairs during the course of the twentieth century, it is one that reflects the increased gap between rich, industrialized societies and the poverty areas of the world and an increase in global dependence of the poor upon the rich.

Those who argue the first position either tend to ignore some of the

---

[34] I have put to one side an examination of empirical indices of interdependence, both because I regard them as unreliable and because their linkage to general hypotheses has been rudimentary. For some good reviews of empirical indices of interdependence, see Richard N. Rosecrance and Arthur A. Stein, "Interdependence: Myth or Reality?" *World Politics,* XXVI (October 1973), pp. 1-27; and Robert D. Tollison and Thomas D. Willett, "International Integration and the Interdependence of Economic Variables," *International Organization,* XXVII (Spring 1973), pp. 255-273.

[35] Waltz, "The Myth of National Interdependence," p. 206. Samuel Huntington has argued that both Waltz's position and that put forward by proponents of interdependence may be reconciled by looking at the way nationalism and transnationalism grow symbiotically. Hence the "conflict between national governments and transnational organizations is clearly complementary rather than duplicative." *World Politics,* XXV (April 1973), p. 366.

trends we have examined or have insisted that all states are alike in that their leaders must maximize state security and this gives rise to international drama which is similar regardless of conditions involved or the kinds of political units that participate in the system. In short, their argument rests on a faith that international society is by definition anarchic. Regardless of the kind of structural relationships one might posit, international politics remains *sui generis*. I have tried to show how classical assumptions have changed under the processes of modernization, and I have presented both logical analysis and empirical evidence to support the points made.[36]

Arguments supporting the second case are more plausible. They admit that while interdependence has proceeded apace in relations among industrialized societies and that it has also brought unprecedented wealth, it has, far more importantly, created a gap in global society between the haves and have-nots which is distressing and which is likely to create great instabilities in the future. A wide variety of arguments and normative positions support this view.

We may divide these viewpoints, first, according to whether the threats to instability are seen to come from the rich or the poor societies. Second, we may divide them according to strategies to be adopted —by either a less developed country (LDC) or a highly industrialized society—to reduce this gap between rich and poor societies. It should be emphasized that this great divide is in many ways the major problem of global politics in the twentieth century. The gap between rich and poor societies certainly is a central normative issue of global society. As such, it has received an enormous amount of attention in scholarly and political literature. I can do no more here than offer some general observations about the gap and recognize two major points. On the one hand, the creation of the gap is certainly one of the most significant effects of modernization in the world. The processes of modernization have centered in small core areas of the world, and while they have affected politics and societies everywhere, they have done so differentially. On the other hand, the questions of whether and how the gap can be overcome are far from solution. They remain major intellectual and political problems of the twentieth century.

---

[36]For a more detailed criticism of the view that international politics have not changed under modernization, see Edward L. Morse, "Transnational Economic Processes," *International Organization*, XXV (Summer 1971), pp. 373-397.

Those who argue that the existence of this gap poses a major threat to global stability can be divided into two groups, which reflect rather divergent philosophical and normative positions. For some the instabilities have arisen in the less modernized world, while for others they stem from conditions within industrialized societies as they affect the others. An amalgam of liberal and Marxist arguments has been made to support the position that modernization has created instabilities in the less developed world and that these instabilities pose a major threat to global stability that must be dealt with. The liberal position stresses certain salient factors,[37] including the following: The less modernized world, it is argued, has been affected by some of the processes of modernization but by no means all. Thus it has received the benefits of modern medicine, enabling societies in it to reduce mortality rates without having a significant effect on fertility, resulting in uncontrollable growth in population. Population growth geometrically increases the difficulty of achieving real increases in economic well-being, as measured on a per capita basis. It also exacerbates the problem of meeting new demands from rising domestic expectations, thus creating inherent problems of political instability and social dissatisfaction in virtually all relatively less modernized societies. When this problem is coupled with neo-Malthusian arguments concerning inadequate food supplies, it makes the prognosis for political stability even more grave. It is worsened by prospects of limitations on supplies of raw materials that are required if these societies are to become industrialized.

Two sorts of threats to the industrialized societies of the world emerge from these instabilities. On the one hand, some less developed countries may purposely involve specific industrialized societies in international conflict. Three major possibilities exist. First, the development of nuclear wherewithal for purposes of prestige, for economic development, or for some immediate security problem may well continue, as in the cases of India's recent development of a nuclear capability and of the virtual certainty of several Middle East governments following suit. The use of nuclear weapons by some less developed

[37]See, for example, C. Fred Bergsten, "The Threat from the Third World," *Foreign Policy*, No. 11 (Summer 1973), pp. 38-56; Lester Brown, *World without Borders* (New York: Random House, 1972); Miriam C. Camps, *The Management of Interdependence* (New York: Council On Foreign Relations, Council Papers on International Affairs, No. 4, 1974); and Richard C. Falk, *This Endangered Planet* (New York: Random House, 1971).

country is of immediate interest to the sort of global stability desired by all industrialized societies, including the U.S., the Soviet Union, and others, which would almost certainly be involved however indirectly in any situation that threatened the stability of their international environment. Second, the use of economic resources for political ends, as in the case of the oil-exporting countries' organization of an oligopolistic market to pursue political and economic ends, can threaten the necessary chain of production upon which the wealth of industrialized societies depends. Appeasement of economic aggression is an easy route for an industrialized society to take to preserve its economic well-being, even if the long-term consequences of blackmail are great. Third, superpowers may themselves have vital interests at stake in certain areas of the less developed world where local conflict might well become uncontrolled and lead to great power collisions. The situation in Palestine is by no means unique here even if it has been the most persistent danger area for world conflict in the less developed world. Instability in Yugoslavia would inevitably lead to confrontation between the Soviet and American governments, and new outbreaks of warfare in South Asia between Pakistan and India have the potential for engaging China as well.

On the other hand, intervention by industrialized societies in the nonmodernized world may come about simply as a result of attempts to control domestic instabilities and for humanitarian rather than for strategic reasons. The rise of famine in widespread areas of the less developed world, including the Indian subcontinent, and the enhanced likelihood of rioting and the breakdown of social order might well lead to efforts on the part of superpowers to come to the aid of people in those societies for humanitarian purposes. It is not difficult to depict a wide variety of scenarios in which intervention for the purposes of distributing food or providing social order also would lead to the widespread use of force in the less developed world.

Liberals are not alone in arguing the case that it is from the relatively less modernized sectors of international society that threats to instability arise. Some Marxist and Maoist views lead in the same direction. Certainly, in terms of ideology, this is the thrust of Lin Piao's argument concerning the future global revolution,[38] which was based on an

---

[38] Lin Piao, "Long Live the Victory of the People's War!" in Samuel B. Griffith, II, ed., *Peking and People's Wars* (New York: Praeger, 1966), pp. 51–114.

analogy between the rural-based revolution in China and prospects for global revolution. Accordingly, the dependence of industrialized societies upon raw materials from the less developed world creates leverage points for governments on the periphery of the modernized world to induce global change. By withholding raw materials and other supplies from the industrial core areas, including the Soviet Union, and by depriving them of markets for their surplus production, the less developed world can strangle off the wealthy, just as the Chinese Communists isolated and suffocated Chinese cities by taking control of the countryside. From this perspective the liberal fear of the proliferation of oligopolistic markets for raw materials and Lin Piao's prescriptions for global revolution are rather alike.

Both liberal and Marxist arguments concerning the locus of global instability work the other way as well. One theorist of modernization places the instabilities in the modernization process itself and argues that they are created everywhere that modernization takes hold, not only among the less modernized world but in the modernized as well.[39] Here the prognosis for the first modernized societies is not good, since the destruction of family bonds and other social ties within them creates a situation that is historically unique and where social stability and integrity cannot be weighed against precedents.

This sort of argument is far more familiar in theories of dependence between rich and poor societies, and especially in arguments that have been made concerning U.S. relations with most of Latin America.[40] Dependence may have begun with Spanish imperialism, at least in the way the latter served to create a chain of dependent relations in Latin America. Dependences emerged between tenants and landlords and between export sectors and the economy of the metropole. However it developed, it is perpetrated by U.S. governmental policy and the nexus of government and business elites. Direct investment by American multinational corporations and U.S. governmental aid are the primary agencies of this new dependence. Direct investment usually takes place in the export sector, and especially in raw materials, although sometimes it takes place in manufacturing sectors (e.g., automobiles) when

[39] See Marion J. Levy, Jr., *Modernization: Latecomers and Survivors* (New York: Basic Books, 1972), pp. 135–149.

[40] Different theorists, of course, reflect differences of view on the details of the argument. For examples, see the essays in K. T. Fann and Donald C. Hodges, eds., *Readings in U.S. Imperialism* (Boston: Porter Sargent, 1971).

exports are otherwise blocked from the U.S. This investment orients economic growth in the less developed country to the needs of the metropole or rich societies rather than the needs of national economic and political development. It also creates elite groups whose rise to power and wealth depends on external investments: their own interests, in short, are more closely oriented to the needs of the multinational firms for which they work than they are to the needs of national development. Moreover, one of the effects of multinational investment by foreign firms is the sucking of capital along with raw materials out of the less developed society, which deprives it of the capital and material wherewithal for growth. U.S. aid, which has been designed either to foster pluralistic groups in the less developed society or to maintain the power of a ruling elite amenable to American economic and political interests, also serves to prevent the development of a national government willing to put national interests first.[41]

In summary, this theory argues that instabilities associated with rising expectations in the less developed world stem from an institutionalized structure of dependence. The only way to break the chain of dependence is to nationalize industry and sever ties with a global economy that has helped to preserve the dependent relationship between a neo-imperial core and a relatively impoverished periphery.

Whether one argues that one ought to try to do something about the gap depends in part upon whether one believes it can be overcome. There has been a growing sentiment in political circles in industrialized societies that little can be done about the gap through positive actions taken by the wealthier societies. This argument usually, but not always, reflects the viewpoint that the threat from the Third World is not that great. It would argue that nuclear proliferation may have its own logic apart from the development process and that it might just as well create stability (as it has between East and West) as instabilities. It would also argue that the likelihood of the OPEC arrangement on oil being replicated in other raw materials is very low, since most other raw materials, unlike oil, have substitutes at slightly higher prices and, at any rate, the suppliers of these materials are generally far more heterogeneous than is the case in oil.[42] Almost always some highly industrial-

[41] See Robert Packenham, *Liberal America and the Third World* (Princeton, N.J.: Princeton University Press, 1973).

[42] See Philip Connelly and Robert Perlman, *The Politics of Scarcity: Resource Conflicts in International Relations* (London: Oxford University Press, 1975).

ized society is also a major supplier of these raw materials on world markets and would have little interest in raising prices through the creation of a cartel. Moreover, this argument would also probably maintain that any direct action on the part of rich societies, individually or collectively, in relations with less developed countries would be bound to appear interventionary and would not likely have the desired political effects. It would hence be better for the rich societies to "put their own houses in order" and hope that the stability of relationships and prospects for growth in the less developed world that would thus be held out would serve to overcome the gap between rich and poor.

Arguments for action on the part of rich societies stem from one of three major beliefs. First, it can be argued that the threat to the viability of industrialized societies from the less developed world is so great that some action is required.[43] Second, it can be argued that on normative grounds one ought to strive for a just distribution of the world's wealth. Third, arguments have been made that the gap really reflects a growth in interdependence between rich and poor. No less developed society can hope to achieve a stable and continuous level of economic growth in isolation from the rest of the world. Technical aid and capital are certainly required from the rich areas, as are stable market conditions and international financial arrangements. Similarly, the rich societies cannot isolate themselves from the less developed world and hope to live either without their raw materials or without contagion of social unrest.

Arguments from the perspective of poor societies similarly reflect a wide spectrum of viewpoints. For some, the prospects of modernization lie in the ability of less developed societies to create united fronts against the rich societies and to prevent the latter group from dividing them on major issues. This position has largely reflected ideological sentiment more than rational strategy. The societies of the less developed world are so heterogeneous in terms of size, population, resources, and level of cultural homogeneity that any effort at united action is bound to disguise fundamental conflicts of interests. For others, independent national action is more promising. It may permit a degree of autonomy that was impeded by links with one rich society. The diversification of sources of supply and of markets thus can help

[43] See Bergsten, "The Threat from the Third World."

to assure national autonomy even if it does not visibly increase a society's relative level of modernization.

Regardless of how the problem of the divide between modernized and less modernized societies is viewed, there is little doubt that it is a major problem of politics in the contemporary world. It does not, however, in my view, reflect any lower level of interdependence than may have existed in the world before high levels of modernization were achieved in the relatively modernized societies. Interdependence across the planet remains a striking characteristic of contemporary international politics. In relations between rich and poor societies it is made more difficult by fundamental asymmetries that seem to persist. It is, however, clear that modernization has become a goal of virtually all societies. It is no less clear that it is extremely unlikely for any society to be able successfully to achieve high levels of modernization by isolating itself from the rest of the world. Which if any of the less developed societies will succeed in this is an empirical question. Prospects for oil-rich Iran are certainly greater than for population-poor Saudi Arabia or resource-poor Haiti. Wherever prospects seem great, it also seems clear that accommodations can be made between poor and rich societies that are of mutual advantage. Algeria, for example, has been seeking development capital from the United States, even in the absence of diplomatic ties.[44] And many governments in less developed societies have ceased their wholesale nationalization of foreign-based multinational corporations lest foreign sources of needed capital dry up. Instead, they have been increasingly making contracts with those firms that are profitable for all and that undertake "joint ventures" containing specified timetables for domestic takeovers.

A WORD OF CONCLUSION

I have argued in this chapter that the development of a highly interdependent world has been an inevitable concomitant of modernization. While this was recognized by some of the early proponents of modernization, the effects of modernization were not. Instead of laying the

[44]See William B. Quandt, "Can We Do Business with Radical Nationalists? Algeria: Yes," *Foreign Policy*, No. 7 (Summer 1972), pp. 88–95.

basis for a new era of international harmony, interdependence seems to magnify international tensions and to stress national differences. This is most visibly the case in relations between rich and poor societies, but it also is seen in the rather different form that interdependence takes among the more modernized societies themselves. Interdependence inevitably brings with it a reduction in governments' abilities to achieve domestic and foreign policy goals in isolation. But it comes in several different forms, which I have tried to describe. These forms overlap significantly with one another, and this overlapping may itself be responsible for some of the stability that has characterized international society in recent years. While interdependence exacerbates problems, it also creates stakes that are important for all societies and significantly reduces any government's freedom of action.

While interdependence has become a key element of contemporary international society, it is important to note that it brings with it a host of uncertainties. Neither the knowledge of how to deal with it nor the will to do so seems available. For many governments the status quo has become a comfortable retreat in which they know how well off they are rather than think of the risks they confront in an unknown future. Yet interdependence also brings with it its own momentum for change, and almost everywhere political leaders know that in security matters, economic, and social affairs the status quo must inevitably give way. The contemporary situation is so novel historically that reliance on the continuity of a particular status quo or on historical experience is a rather uncertain guide for statecraft.

The emerging international system may, however, reflect far more than the breakdown in old social values. In many ways it reflects a growing international consensus concerning fundamental human and political values. The degree to which consensus exists on value-oriented issues may well be a key to future international stability and to success in handling problems of interdependence. In the next chapter we will turn our attention to shifts in international values and in the final conclusions we will try to compare these shifts to the requisites of political stability in the contemporary world.

6

The Transformation of International Values

In the past two chapters we have reviewed a series of fundamental and contradictory changes that have taken place in international society during the past few decades. Increased interdependence among the societies of the world, especially among the advanced industrialized non-Communist states, has led paradoxically to both loss of national autonomy and, in many respects, its reaffirmation. It also has placed a great emphasis on economic aspects of statecraft, which have become politicized in unique ways. The gap between rich and poor societies, also brought about by modernization, has become a significant political problem for all governments—one whose resolution is as intractable intellectually as it is politically. Rising demands everywhere have confronted short- and long-term problems of insufficient resources to meet them, thus exacerbating tensions in the domestic social order and problems of international control. Partially as a result of these demands, there has been a dramatic shift in the way foreign policies are conducted and the primacy of foreign policy has almost everywhere given way to the primacy of domestic concerns. These changes have been coupled with a decline in the political efficacy of military power to serve as an arbiter between conflicting international claims, with a consequent rise in difficulties in adjusting a wide range of international disputes.

The international system has, in short, undergone great change. This change has not simply represented a transition from one type of international society to another. It has also involved the nature of change itself; for continuous change within and among societies, between various social units and within them, and in the relationships between people on the individual level has become perhaps the key feature of contemporary life. Governments no less than individuals must socialize themselves into an unknown future,[1] and this form of socialization must itself be unstable, since the normative and empirical touchstones of social action of all sorts have become decreasingly reliable. This can be seen especially in the way that governments are forced to conduct their foreign policies. Confronting situations that are without historical analog or precedent, governments nonetheless tend to plan for the future in terms of "lessons of the past." Each government has its own particular lessons which have tended to overwhelm its foreign policy. Just as the Munich experience gave rise in American foreign policy to the dictum "Never appease an aggressor,"[2] so the experience of two world wars led to a Soviet policy of control over the regimes in Eastern Europe and to the prevention of the development of a strong power in central Europe. These lessons of the past have turned the attention of both superpowers away from central problems of contemporary international society and in many ways still prevent the negotiation of forceful measures of arms control—which may be more in their common interests than are policies dictated by false lessons of the past and irrelevant to immediate security concerns.

Indeed, the whole terminology of international affairs is still permeated by past ideas and especially by the political and legal concepts of the Westphalia system. This is the terminology of power politics, of a world in which the principal units of international society are states and where force still plays an essential and instrumental role. A survey of the problems of contemporary international society would readily demonstrate the inadequacy of the Westphalian vocabulary and the Westphalian normative and empirical conceptualization of international society. But an examination of the norms of statecraft and of the moral values associated with international affairs would also show that in spite of the pervasive salience of the Westphalian heritage, there are important normative manifestations of the effects of moderniza-

[1] See the discussion of this in Marion J. Levy, Jr., *Modernization: Latecomers and Survivors* (New York: Basic Books, 1972), pp. 42–51.

[2] See Ernest R. May, *"Lessons" of the Past: The Use and Misuse of History in American Foreign Policy* (New York: Oxford University Press, 1963).

tion in current usage. If at one time the survival and security of the nation-state were the central values of international society and of national statecraft, these norms have vastly changed under the impetus of modernization.

In this chapter we will review some of the more salient effects of modernization on international values as well as on the organization of international life. An examination of these changes will be useful for our discussion for several reasons. First, it will serve as an additional set of empirical indices to support the general argument I have presented concerning the effects of modernization on international politics. Second, the discussion of values and normative standards is too frequently omitted as irrelevant in the analysis of international politics. Yet new normative standards have become a central force in modern international politics. They not only reflect other, perhaps more fundamental changes but also constrain governments in the selection of actions vis-à-vis others. Finally, and of central importance, is the gap between the requisites of international order and the actions governments are willing to take to provide both order and decent standards of life around the globe. This gap reflects several of the dilemmas that we have already reviewed, including those stemming from the growing interdependence of national societies, on the one hand, and the continued decentralized organization of the international arena, on the other hand. This dilemma also reflects the coexistence of different and frequently antithetic notions about how international society *should* be organized and about how international values *ought* to be distributed.

In order to confront these issues directly, we will first review the Westphalian conception of international law and the nature of international normative standards within the Westphalia system as well as in a more general context. Then we will turn to an examination of substantive changes in these normative standards.

THE WESTPHALIA SYSTEM OF
INTERNATIONAL VALUES

If modernization has had a revolutionary impact on international normative standards, changes that have occurred in international values can be examined through a review of changes in the legal order.

Modern international law begins with the Peace of Westphalia itself and the codification of prevailing assumptions in the seventeenth century of how international society ought to be organized. I outlined the basic codification of Westphalia in Chapter 2. Before reviewing and expanding upon this earlier discussion, it will be helpful if I now briefly expound upon how international law will be treated in the remainder of this chapter.

International law will be regarded principally as a codified reflection of the norms of international conduct that prevail at any point in time or in any era. This sociological conception of international law is rather recent.[3] Traditionally international law has been approached from one of two perspectives. On the one hand, the positivist tradition in law places emphasis on the growth of codified regulations governing official and private behavior at the international level. Applicable law in this tradition has been explicitly and officially agreed upon by appropriate authorities. Obligations for the subjects of international law are thus explicitly defined in codified texts. On the other hand, there has also been a hortatory tradition in international law, beginning with Hugo Grotius in the seventeenth century, which places emphasis on a future ideal order in international society according to which governments, smaller social groups, and individuals ought to govern their behavior in order to facilitate the growth of justice, peace, and stability in the international system.

The Westphalia system of international law can be examined from each of these perspectives. From the positivist point of view, the Treaties of Westphalia represented the codification of certain principles and concepts which had been stressed by earlier writers on law who worked in the hortatory tradition. In particular, they represented the codification of two doctrines that had been expostulated by writers who have been called naturalists: the doctrine of sovereignty and the doctrine of the law of nature.[4] Both these doctrines can also be ex-

[3]For examples of this type of treatment of international law, see William D. Coplin, "International Law and Assumptions about the State System," *World Politics,* XVII (July 1964), pp. 615–635; Richard Falk, "Introduction," in Richard A. Falk and Wolfram Hanrieder, eds., *International Law and Organization* (Philadelphia: Lippincott, 1968), pp. 1–11; and Stanley Hoffmann, "International Systems and International Law," in Klaus Knorr and Sidney Verba, eds., *The International System,* (Princeton, N.J.: Princeton University Press, 1961), pp. 205–237.

[4]The naturalists take their name from their rejection of law as a manifestation of a divine order and from their stress on a state of nature whose origins need not

amined from a sociological perspective, in that they reflected the growth of European political systems in the sixteenth and seventeenth centuries from the feudalistic order of the Middle Ages and an earlier ideal hierarchy which, rather than being secular, reflected the norms of Christendom.

The doctrine of sovereignty, as we have seen in Chapter 2, relates to conditions believed to be universally valid in political society. All rulers were believed to be the principal lawmakers and law enforcers within societies. In this respect they were all equal and owed no allegiance to others in any presumed international hierarchy. Neither secular nor religious fealty was owed to other political elites. Each ruler was bound only by certain laws, which, like "sovereignty," limited the exercise of power. Otherwise masterless man was free to create his own political realm. As noted earlier in this book, this notion of sovereignty was perfectly reflective of political conditions in Europe in the late sixteenth century. The feudal hierarchy had distintegrated gradually. This disintegration was then accelerated by the Thirty Years' War. The major political problem of the time was the definition of political order for the creation of stable social conditions as well as for the development of monarchic power. The doctrine of sovereignty thus reflected the conditions and requisites of secular political order.

The doctrine of the law of nature developed into its modern form at the same time that the doctrine of sovereignty gained acceptability. An earlier version of the law of nature had existed and reflected notions of international hierarchy under medieval Christian philosophy. The law of nature in medieval law was based on the notion of "right reason," according to which proper conduct could be discerned by appeals to rationality and clarity, which reflected divine will. In the transformation of the law of nature under Westphalia, it was argued that all legal and political systems confront situations which fall outside the conditions included in explicit rules.[5] One could confront such situations by resorting to principles that lay outside formulated law. According to naturalists of the time there was a set of fundamental rights that all states possessed. These were not necessarily codified. Rather they were

---

have been divine. Their emphasis therefore is tied to the secularization of politics that is symbolically represented by the Peace of Westphalia. See J. L. Brierly, *The Law of Nations,* 6th ed. (New York: Oxford University Press, 1963), pp. 1–25.

[5] See, for example, Carl J. Friedrich, *The Philosophy of Law in Historical Perspective,* 2d ed. (Chicago: University of Chicago Press, 1963), pp. 27–66.

derived from the state of nature itself and from what appeals to reasonable conduct would likely dictate. These given rights of all states were self-preservation, independence, equality, due respect, and peaceful intercourse with others.[6]

The rights derived from the law of nature or from the doctrine of sovereignty can all be deduced from the Westphalia system as outlined earlier. From a sociological point of view, the prevailing conditions in international society in the sixteenth and seventeenth centuries supported the view that the most significant feature of the international system was the absence of order.

This posed a striking contrast to domestic or civil society where order, imposed from above, prevailed. In the state of nature within international society all actors were equal in terms of their exercise of sovereignty in domestic affairs. From this viewpoint certain premises were postulated as the basis of normative principles of international law. Coplin summarized these principles under three headings.[7] First, the state was viewed as an ultimate and absolute institutional value. The independence of the state was therefore an unchanging goal of statecraft. The security of civil society could be provided and maximized only by guarding the state's independence. Since individuals gained rights only by living in civil society, the state came to be regarded as the source of basic moral values of secular society. Second, given the fundamentally anarchic conditions prevailing in international society, all states had to seek to maximize their power in order to maintain their own independence. Since the international system was also believed to contain zero-sum conditions, where one state's gain was another's loss, international politics was essentially a struggle for power. In concrete terms, this meant that international politics was conditioned by a struggle between states for territory, population, and resources. Third, there was the premise that state survival required the maintenance of a minimal system of order among state actors. This order went beyond the simple maintenance of a balance of power that could counter the prevailing tendency of the state system toward anarchy and thereby enhance state survival. It also included the mutual recognition by all the states of the rights of each, including those rights noted above (the right to self-preservation and independence, the

[6]See Brierly, Part I.
[7]See Coplin, "International Law and Assumptions about the State System."

equality of state units in the international system, the respect due each, and the right to intercourse). This third premise certainly contained several contradictions when juxtaposed to the other premises of law in the Westphalian framework. The need to preserve a minimal system of international order might well, for example, involve the curtailment of one or more states' independence. Furthermore, the role of the great powers in a balance of power creates a de facto international hierarchy between them and lesser states, which contradicts the presumption of state equality. Nevertheless, these premises of international law fairly well represented empirical conditions prevalent at the time as well as the normative standards which governed state behavior.

The assumptions noted above could be found in the writings of both naturalist and positivist writers, who would differ in their interpretations of the origins of law. Rather than place emphasis on the doctrine of sovereignty or the laws of nature, positivists would argue that the origin of law, even at the international level, can be found only in voluntary agreements and not in doctrine. For positivists, international law is nothing more than the sum of rules that state actors have contracted among themselves. Thus legal rights can be deduced only from a legal system and not from a state of nature. They would also argue that only a positivist view of law permits an evolutionary view of law's development. The naturalist perspective would be far too static, and, at least implicitly, it would deny the possibility of change.[8] Contemporary views of law, however, would go beyond both positivism and naturalism, arguing that neither contains an adequate explanation of why international law is binding on its subjects. The naturalist viewpoint argues that law can be deduced from the state of international society, while positivists would argue that law can be understood only by an empirical examination of treaties and other international contracts. Yet it can be argued that most law is not observed by consent and that it cannot be deduced from an examination of international society. Rather, it can be argued that law is observed for other reasons, including the belief in binding obligation itself.

Contemporary writers tend to stress a sociological view of binding obligation or of authority in the international system. Brierly, for example, stresses that the ultimate explanation of the binding force of

---

[8]See Louis Henkin, *How Nations Behave: Law and Foreign Policy* (New York: Praeger, 1968), pp. 13–28.

law in international as well as domestic society is that man is constrained to believe that order is the governing principle of a world whose reality is never questioned.[9] It is a quick step from this to the historical-sociological view of Raymond Aron or Stanley Hoffmann. Hoffmann, for example, has examined international law in three discrete historical periods and has argued that the nature of law is a function of the number and kind of state units involved in an international system that may be predominantly conservative or revolutionary, hierarchical or egalitarian.[10] Henkin goes beyond both and bases his theory of legal obligation on an economic notion of opportunity costs. Accordingly, when the costs of adhering to some normative standard are lower than the gains that are derived, that standard is recognized as having authoritative force governing the behavior of states.[11]

This does not imply a skeptical view of law based on narrow positivism. The positivist position is usually based on a contrast that presumably exists between conditions in domestic and in international society. In the former, it has been argued, law is authoritative because it is backed by a government, which possesses a monopoly of the instruments of violence. In the latter no such center of political authority exists; or at best it could be argued that in the international system only a primitive center of political authority is evolving. In this sense positivists have tended to regard international law as a primitive stage in the evolution of an international legal system, which parallels a primitive stage in the development of domestic law. Insofar as the distinction between domestic and international society based on the nature of political authority in each holds, this analogy appears to be correct. However, it has also been frequently emphasized that this positivist viewpoint represents a distortion of the way law operates in both domestic and international society.[12] It is not true that law is seen as binding in domestic society because it is backed up by a state which possesses a monopoly of the instruments of political violence. In the American political system, for example, the Supreme Court can rule and indeed has ruled against the President or the army and its rulings have been obeyed. Law, in short, is binding more because it is

[9] Brierly, pp. 54–56.

[10] Hoffmann, "International Systems and International Law."

[11] Henkin, *How Nations Behave,* pp. 45–64.

[12] See Richard A. Falk, *The Status of Law in International Society* (Princeton, N.J.: Princeton University Press, 1970), pp. 7–83.

viewed as authoritative than because it is backed by the power of centralized government. If this is so, then the distinction between domestic society, with its highly centralized structures of political authority, and international society, with its highly decentralized political milieu, cannot wholly explain the differences between domestic and international law.

Governments exist in an international society which is replete with a set of norms, only some of which are codified. And despite what positivists may argue, nation-states cannot themselves determine whether they will be subject to those norms or to the laws which codify them. Customs and traditions of behavior together with norms derived from both domestic and international society and the opportunity costs of not abiding by international rules together create a powerful set of constraints on national behavior. Neither the goals of governments nor the means they select to achieve them in international society are completely arbitrary. Rather, they are molded by a complex set of normative standards which both rule out certain courses of action and warrant others. These have changed rather dramatically since Westphalia, if one looks at the norms which actually govern international behavior rather than simply at the codification of law from a narrow positivist perspective. In order to understand these changes, we will now look both at the substance of major international normative standards in the contemporary international system and at the processes which have brought them about.

THE REVOLUTION IN INTERNATIONAL VALUES

Changes in international values, normative standards, and law have been as fundamental as the other changes we have reviewed in earlier chapters. Like those other changes, these also result from the processes of modernization as they have affected the Westphalia system of international order. These changes, however, have not been complete. Nor have they resulted in a system which is wholly different from the Westphalian framework. In fact, the bases of international law still reflect the rhetoric of seventeenth-century diplomacy and norms. Additional values and norms have been amalgamated with those of the earlier system, and the result is not only a complex set of overlapping value systems but is also an increased likelihood that in contemporary international affairs conflicts are likely to prevail whose origins are competing value systems.

The Westphalia system was based on a set of assumptions concerning international behavior. Sovereign state units were regarded as the sole actors in international society and therefore the only subjects of international law. Neither international organizations nor subnational units (social groups or individuals) had an official role in the evolution of international society. They were neither active participants in the "legislation" of new international law nor the direct subjects of its application. These sovereign nation-state units were, moreover, regarded as equal, at least ideally. None could legislate for other sovereign units, nor did any have a right to curtail the autonomy and independence of others. The domestic activities and processes in any one state were outside the jurisdiction of any other state. As international law emerged, it was based on bilateral or multilateral treaties in which each participating government exercised what might be called a unilateral right of veto. In the absence of any overarching structure of political authority at the international level, only an individual government could say what it would or would not commit itself to do, and each was equal to others in this right. The assumption of masterless man also originally existed in the Westphalian structure of international law, although this was the first of the assumptions of that system to undergo change. Sovereign rights were possessed by individual monarchs. As monarchic systems gave way to other structures of political authority, the whole government bore the heritage in law of earlier individual rulers, in terms of both rights and obligations. The rights of diplomatic immunity in foreign countries, the sanctity of embassies, and diplomatic precedence at official diplomatic gatherings all bear testimony to this. Finally, the notion of a certain minimal international order based upon the equality of states also persists.

The bases of contemporary international law depend greatly on the assumptions of the Westphalia system. The stress placed by international law on the independence and autonomy of state units, the emphasis on law of territorial rights and sovereign jurisdiction, problems of recognition, and rights of participants and of neutrals in war all go back to the origins of the international legal order. Similarly law is still regarded as originating in conventions, in general practice, in the writings and decisions of international courts (and of domestic courts in cases involving international diputes), and via recourse to the general principles according to which "civilized" nations conduct their affairs.

Contemporary international law and normative standards cannot, however, be understood only with reference to their bases in the Westphalia system. Nor should this be surprising. The Westphalia system, after all, was based on a system of interaction of European states, none of which were industrialized. The nations of Europe shared the same civilization, cultural traditions, and history, which allowed them to develop a sort of psychological interdependence that also formed the basis of the notion that Europe was itself an independent system. The development of a global international system as a result of technological changes associated with the processes of modernization undermined this notion in several respects, which we will call the first major change in international law. This change represents what Wolfgang Friedmann calls the horizontal extension of international law, which itself has been responsible for major changes in the substance of international norms and values.[13]

The horizontal extension of international law refers to the incorporation of new actors into the international system. While this expansion in the number of subjects referred to in international legal processes began over a century ago, it was most dramatic after World War II. With the processes of decolonization which marked the end of European empires, the international system expanded dramatically in terms of the number of sovereign units that it incorporated. This can be seen in the astonishing growth in the membership of the United Nations, which originally had 51 members and now includes nearly 140 states. Of greater importance than the simple numerical multiplication of the number of state units in international society is the substantive change in international normative standards that took place as a result. While most of the new members of the international system themselves have a European heritage based on a history of colonialism or imperialism, they have also brought to international society a set of non-Western values that has undermined the original Westphalian notion of a shared set of cultural values and a common civilization. Obviously, recourse to the principles of "civilized" nations has a wholly different substan-

[13]Wolfgang Friedmann, *The Changing Structure of International Law* (New York: Columbia University Press, 1964), pp. 213-249.

tive content in a world of heterogeneity than it did in the far more homogeneous European order.

The horizontal extension of international law also refers to the incorporation of nonsovereign, nonstate units as both subjects of law and participants in its evolution. This aspect of the horizontal extension of international law obviously reflects changing values in the international system. Most obvious among these new units are international organizations, which have proliferated at regional, functional, and universal levels, in private as well as public life. Some notion of the growth in intergovernmental organizations (IGOs) and in nongovernmental organizations (NGOs) can be seen in Figure 3. Some of these organizations, including the United Nations and its predecessor the League of Nations, reflect new norms in international society associated with the depreciation of the use of force and violence as legitimate instruments of diplomacy. Others, like the International Postal Union, are designed to facilitate the control and standardization required for communication in a highly interdependent and global society. Still others, including the Organization of African Unity, the Arab League, and the European Communities, reflect growing regional self-consciousness or the perceived need to create markets that transcend the shrinking national community for economic as well as political rewards. These new organizations almost invariably provide mechanisms for adjusting international disputes and are significant additions, therefore, to both the processes by which private and public international law is created and the subjects to which such law applies.

It is surely no accident that the growth in the number of international institutions parallels the modernization process itself. Growing networks of communication and transportation have facilitated international intercourse at private as well as public levels and made possible the growth in these organizations. The destabilizing effects of modernization have also significantly motivated governments to form organizations to control these processes. Whether one looks to international economic organizations, reflecting growing economic interdependence across national boundaries, to international groups of political parties, or to forums for the expression of regional-cultural bonds, the modernization process surely lurks behind as a primary set of explanatory factors.[14]

[14]For a rather complete overview of the growth in all sorts of public and private international organizations, see Werner Feld, *Non-governmental Forces and World Politics* (New York: Praeger, 1972).

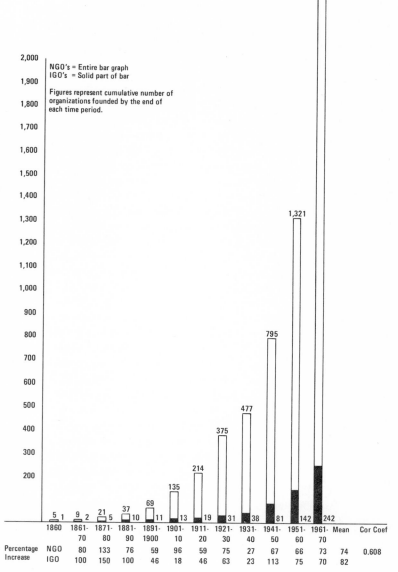

FIGURE 3. **Growth Pattern of International NGOs Compared with IGOs, 1860–1968**

From *Nongovernmental Forces and World Politics: A Study of Business, Labor, and Political Groups,* by Werner Feld, 1972, p. 177. Copyright © 1972 by Praeger Publishers, Inc., New York. Excerpted and reprinted by permission.

Subnational or cross-national groups as well as individuals have also entered the arena of international law and are an additional element in its horizontal extension. In fact, the extension of international normative standards to these levels in many respects preceded the growth in international organizations. The French Revolution with its Declaration of the Rights of Man and Citizen and the American Revolution with its emphasis on individual liberty were explicit attacks on the Westphalian notion that the nation-state was the sole proper unit of a just international order. The notion that human rights might prevail over national security concerns and that they ought not be violated by any government has a dual significance for the evolution of international norms. On the one hand, it establishes a new set of value standards and a notion of international justice which is quite different from that contained in the Westphalia system. In the latter, the state was the sole legitimate organization in international affairs as well as the main source of moral (political) values. With emphasis on the individual, a new standard of justice is established which points to an ideal international order in which individual rights can be secured, and in most instances also in which nation-states can be transcended and replaced by other forms of political authority. In the case of national groups, the notion that states may not interfere with rights to self-determination of substate or cross-state groups also interferes significantly with the notion that the state is the sole source of moral value. On the other hand, the establishment of these additional units as subjects of international law also represents a new source of international conflict and tension; for it creates conditions under which competing claims, some based on nation-state values and others based on individual or group values, can both be viewed as legitimate. When these conflicting claims become highly exacerbated, as they are when national groups claiming self-determination resort to violence to stake their claims, international tensions are obviously increased.

The extension of international norms to the level of groups or individuals has been codified and has thereby also in many cases provided forums for adjudicating disputes. The United Nations Universal Declaration of Human Rights is one such effort at setting normative standards but it has become too highly politicized to be useful. It has offered, for example, minority groups in some countries a legitimate basis for staking claims against foreign states, which can only be viewed by those states as a form of political interference or intervention. Thus Israeli claims concerning the rights of Jewish groups in the Soviet

Union to emigration may be eminently justified on new principles of international law, but are viewed by the Soviet government, which bases its claims on sovereign jurisdiction, as a form of political meddling. In some cases, however, new claims have in fact been justified. The Council of Europe has for example enacted its Covenant of Human Rights, concerning the rights of individuals and minority groups within member countries. This has allowed German-speaking groups in northern Italy successfully to bring claims before the European Court. It has also resulted in appeals by Greek citizens against the military regime which came to power in 1967, although in the latter case the Greek government decided to withdraw from the Council rather than to abide by the Court's decision. In the European Communities, both individuals and corporations are able to make appeals against the authorities of the Common Market as well as against member countries, albeit on a limited set of issues.

The extension of the scope of international law to individuals has also meant that individuals are coming to be viewed as having responsibilities to international normative standards that transcend their obligation to their own state. The Nuremburg trials after World War II and the Universal Declaration on Nuremburg affirmed this responsibility when the state orders an individual to commit crimes against humanity or other principles of civilized societies. The force of the Nuremburg judgments is, however, highly contentious. They were applied by the victors in World War II and were hailed by many jurists as recognition that the Westphalian view of international morality had developed into a wider normative system. Individual values could now take their place alongside state values as individuals became subjects of international law. Yet, as the war in Vietnam indicated, appeals to individual conscience which contradict governmental claims on the individual are not likely to find suitable forums for presentation. In the United States the court system has been highly reluctant to hear or affirm such claims, and at best the extension of international law to cover a new set of subjects remains confused, reflecting the inevitable contraditions of overlapping sets of moral standards in international society. At the same time, the question of under what circumstances an individual ought to resolve conflicting claims of obligation has become a subject of lively philosophical debate.[15]

---

[15] See, for example, Michael Walzer, *Obligations: Essays on Disobedience, War and Citizenship* (New York: Simon & Schuster, 1971).

Finally, international law has seen a rather highly developed extension not only in the private sector but also in the shadow area of multinational enterprises, which represents a combination of private and public actors. The rise of multinational corporations and banks as significant actors in the international system has been one of the most frequently examined subjects in international politics since World War II. The sales of many of these enterprises often surpass the GNP of all but a handful of states. Governments, whose primary goals have come to be associated with economic growth, have also become dependent upon external sources of capital, including direct investments by private multinational corporations and portfolio investments by banks. As we have already seen, these investments also represent increased control by foreigners over one's economy and so create a dilemma for governments, which wish both to increase investment via recourse to foreign capital and to increase their own control over their economies. Outright nationalization of foreign investment has thus become an attractive course of action, but it also results in claims for compensation whose resolution affects a government's ability to gain additional capital in the future. Here the proliferation of new actors in international society directly relates to other evolving norms of statecraft, including those pertaining to a presumed right of all societies to a just distribution of the world's wealth, as we will see below. The most just means to adjudicate conflicting claims of multinational corporations, host countries, and the countries in which the corporations are based is by no means clear. It does appear, however, that an empirical solution is now evolving, at least in the case of less developed societies, whereby host countries and foreign corporations work out on a contract basis increasing the host country's participation and its control over investments. Such contracts assure both a minimum level of profits for the foreign corporations that supply the capital and eventual control by the host countries.

In summary, the horizontal extension of international law reflects not only the increase in number of significant actors in international affairs, including both sovereign and nonsovereign units, but also the growing international consciousness concerning rights of nonstate groups to achieve their objectives. The Westphalia system, with its sole emphasis on the state as a fount of international morality, has not thus been replaced. But it has been highly modified by the incorporation of new units representing alternative sets of normative standards, which as frequently as not contradict the values represented in the state.

A second change in international values, which is also in many ways derivative of the horizontal extension of international morality, has to do with the use of force. With the state as sole unit of international society and the basis of civil society, the maintenance of its integrity became the primary value of statecraft under the Westphalian conceptualization. This gave rise to a hierarchy of values which placed a primacy on foreign over domestic concerns, since the preservation of the state and its autonomy was requisite to the achievement of domestic social order and other domestic values. Once new units arose as proper subjects of international society, it was inevitable that the legitimacy of the use of force in international affairs would be questioned. As we have seen, the rise of liberalism and Marxism as ideological responses to the modernization process questioned the values associated with the nation-state. In liberalism, the individual and his self-development were stressed as being of greater importance than the state. In fact liberal ideology argued that the existence of the state automatically placed an improper emphasis on foreign rather than domestic affairs. A new form of domestic order would enable civil society to transcend the state and eventually to eliminate the use of force as a legitimate form of governmental behavior for any reason except self-defense. In Marxism the state was an instrument of class oppression and class conflict. There too the use of force by a state was viewed as an illegitimate form of behavior and illegitimate instrument of government. The revolution of the proletariat would eventually eliminate the state, usher in classless society, and create a world in which the use of force would be unnecessary and impossible.

If the universalistic ethics stressed by liberalism and Marxism contradicted the emphasis of the Westphalia system on the legitimacy of the use of force by placing emphasis on individualistic and humanitarian values as opposed to state values, technological change associated with modernization reinforced universalism. This reinforcement was twofold. On the one hand, as weapons of increasingly greater destructive capability were developed and as warfare in the twentieth century became more violent and horrible, populations especially in modernized societies came to view the use of force as an unwarranted if not an illegitimate instrument of diplomacy. Appeasement was an acceptable policy for the British government to pursue on the eve of World War II, since it was a plausible alternative to the use of force. On the other hand, nuclear weapons, as we have seen, highly depreciated the utility of force even as a means of self-preservation, and forced governments to seek measures to control international violence in order to preserve the state's integrity.

Technological change has not served to eliminate warfare, but it has brought about a rebirth of the doctrine of just war. Governments are no longer likely to have recourse to the use of force without some justifiable explanation that goes far beyond the enhancement of state power. Anticolonialism and national self-development have assumed equal status with self-preservation as legitimate justifications of the use of force in the contemporary world. And as territorial stakes have declined in significance, the occasions for the use of force for self-preservation have decreased in frequency.

The growth in humanitarian and global values alongside those of the state has placed priorities on disarmament proposals, beginning in the aftermath of the French Revolution, when in 1816 the Russian Czar proposed a simultaneous reduction of all armed forces. Most nineteenth-century proposals for disarmament were, however, utopian and reflected the growth of ideological positions associated with the depreciation of violence. The new antiwarfare ethic was eventually brought into official international discourse around the turn of the twentieth century when at the Hague peace conferences of 1899 and 1907 the limitation of armaments and limitation of military budgets were first placed on the agenda of international conferences.[16] Disarmament, however, has become less a real goal of statecraft than an instrument of international propaganda designed to mobilize popular consent at home or abroad. It has also been pursued by status quo powers as a means of preventing revisionist states from increasing their power, as in the case of efforts after World War I to prevent German rearmament. It has also been an instrument of governments seeking to enhance their power by attempting to induce those with greater military capacity to reduce the level of their armaments. This has been the way the Soviet government has approached disarmament since World War II.

If disarmament has had few practical results, it has reflected a set of international norms that represent a turning away from the legitimacy of the use of force in international affairs. Like such efforts as the Kellogg-Briand Pact in 1928 or the more recent declarations of the

[16]See Inis L. Claude, *Swords into Plowshares,* 3d ed. (New York: Random House, 1964), pp. 261–283.

Soviet-American Summit Conference in 1973, it demonstrates how for international values have shifted away from those originally incorporated in the Westphalia system. Some critics of disarmament might argue that efforts to reduce or to eliminate armaments are either unrealistic or dangerous in that they create an illusion that warfare can be eliminated in a world that remains fundamentally anarchic and without an overarching structure of political authority. For them such documents as the United Nations Charter, which points to the illegitimacy of warfare or otherwise urges limitations on the use of force, turn the minds of governments as well as citizens away from the fundamental problems of international society.[17] Others have criticized disarmament efforts for having been so limited. Efforts to eliminate armaments are viewed by these critics as requisites of a just and stable international order, and real efforts in this direction, it is held, have been irresponsibly avoided by all governments.[18]

If changes in international normative standards have oriented governments to pay at least lip service to disarmament efforts, changing technology has provided a basis for measures of arms control and for the limitation of violence. Unlike disarmament, which aims at the elimination of all armaments, arms control measures are designed to enhance the control that governments have over their instruments of violence. In this sense modern arms control is part of a general policy of deterrence and is more often than not designed to enhance its stability. Arms control measures have been taken to prevent accidental war or to prevent situations from arising which could lead to wholesale use of nuclear weapons by the two nuclear superpowers. The Limited Test Ban treaty (1963), the Nonproliferation of Nuclear Weapons Treaty (1968), and the achievements of the Strategic Arms Limitation Talks each represent an effort in the direction of controlling armaments in order to enhance international stability. Unlike disarmament, these efforts specifically exclude the elimination of armaments and even view disarmament as potentially destabilizing. Rather they are designed to enhance the efforts of the major nuclear powers to assure the stability of an international system based on deterrent relationships.

[17]See the discussion in Hedley Bull, *The Control of the Arms Race* (New York: Praeger, 1965).

[18]See Harold Feiveson, "Arms Control and Disarmament," in Cyril E. Black and Richard A. Falk, eds., *The Future of the International Legal Order,* Vol. III (Princeton, N.J.: Princeton University Press, 1971), pp. 336–369.

Other forms of arms limitation agreements, concerning the seabeds, outer space and specific regions, like Antarctica, have also been ratified as means of controlling the use of violence in the world.

In summary, a second change in international values has related to the legitimacy of the use of force in international society. While recourse to violence remains legitimate for purposes of self-defense and while many regard it as legitimate for purposes of national self-development, the prevailing universal philosophies of the modern world and the decline in the utility of force in the nuclear era have severely constrained governmental options concerning when force may be used. The radical change that has occurred in international normative standards in this respect is that no longer do governments or societies regard violence as a necessary and legitimate instrument of diplomacy and practically all societies are normatively oriented to a world in which force ought to be eradicated. This is a far different world from one in which the use of force in international affairs was regarded as both a natural right and part of the dispensation of fate.[19]

In addition to the horizontal growth in the subjects of international law and the changes in the normative standards associated with the use of force, a third set of changes in normative values is associated with what Wolfgang Friedmann calls the vertical extension of international law.[20] By this is meant the growth in issues that are relevant to statecraft. In addition to the Westphalian problem of state sovereignty which forms the basis of contemporary international law and morality, a new set of issues has entered international treaties which reflects the domestic and international concerns of the twentieth century. These concerns are based also on another transformation in international concepts that has taken place. In the Westphalia system, the emphasis on state sovereignty required that states be regarded as equal in the

---

[19]Many observers have noted that the decline in the use of force as a legitimate form of statecraft has been paralleled by an increase in the use of instruments of violence in domestic society, either as a means of social control on the part of governments or as a means of social change on the part of dissident social groups lying outside a domestic consensus. As Hoffmann has argued, "there is the new prevalence of what I would call internalized world politics: the migration of force from, say, conquest to subversion and the mutation of war into a legitimate adjunct of revolution are one part of this phenomenon; another part is the resort to a variety of nonviolent techniques of 'informal penetration.' ..." Stanley Hoffmann. *Gulliver's Troubles, or the Setting of American Foreign Policy* (New York: McGraw-Hill, 1968), p. 59.

[20]See Friedmann, *The Changing Structure of International Law*, pp. 152–187.

international system. Each had an equal stake in self-preservation, and each was regarded, at least ideally, as sovereign, so that no outside parties could claim a legitimate voice in the domestic affairs of any one. The myth of state equality no longer prevails in the contemporary international system, marked as it is by fundamental inequalities in state power and, more importantly, in social equality and wealth. The recognition that societies do not have equal access to resources and are rather unequally developed economically has been coupled with the growth of a set of new normative standards. According to these standards, all governments have a responsibility to reduce international inequalities wherever they exist. In order to achieve goals associated with the redistribution of world income and wealth, international treaties and new international organizations have been ratified or created to deal with concerns of economic development and social, labor, economic, and welfare issues.

The vertical extension of international law, which incorporates the empirical acceptance of a de facto inequality among nations, has also involved the adoption of what Friedmann calls two new principles of international law. On the one hand, public contract law involving both international concessions and economic development has been developed in such a way as to clarify the interests of both host countries and foreign private and public investors. This new public contract law reflects the development of new goals of statecraft associated with national economic growth, internal income distribution, and economic autonomy. On the other hand, what Friedmann calls the "principle of unjust enrichment"[21] has achieved increased acceptability as a criterion for adjusting both private and public claims at the international level. It has been used, therefore, as a criterion for adjusting the claims of host countries on the issue of nationalizing foreign direct investment. It has also been used as a criterion for directing the efforts of aid donors toward recipients and for creating special preferential trade arrangements for less developed countries.

Just as norms oriented toward an egalitarian distribution of income have become increasingly fundamental within domestic society, so too have they become part of the prevailing ethic of international society. This can be seen in recent international negotiations on trade issues.[22]

[21] Ibid., pp. 206–210.

[22] Robert L. Friedheim, "The 'Satisfied' and 'Dissatisfied' States Negotiate International Law," *World Politics,* XVIII (October 1965), pp. 20–42.

The principle of unjust enrichment has become the fundamental normative standard underlying the actions and rhetoric of the United Nations Conference on Trade and Development (UNCTAD), which has seemed to pit rich countries against poor on this issue. Even if the industrialized societies and the relatively less developed societies seem at odds in UNCTAD and other forums, it is clear that virtually all governments now pay at least lip service to the notion that there is a global interest in achieving a more just distribution of justice in the world (defined in terms of an egaliatarian distribution of global wealth). The same set of notions underlies some aspects of negotiation on reform of the international monetary system, especially those involving the concept of a linkage between the creation of some new international credit facility or asset (like Special Drawing Rights) and development assistance.[23] Moreover, the United Nations and other international organizations, including the Organization for Economic Cooperation and Development in Paris and the International Bank for Reconstruction and Development, have as one of their principal aims the elimination of global poverty and discrepancies between rich and poor societies through the fostering of aid and other development efforts.

The vertical extension of international law, finally, also includes the development of legal principles associated with new requisites for creating stability in international society. There has been a manifest expansion of international law covering the host of transnational activities examined in Chapter 5,[24] as well as those involving claims against or by the increasing numbers of international organizations. International constitutional law, in short, has become an independent subject along with international administrative law, labor law, commercial law, and other areas toward which international law has extended.

SUMMARY

In summary, there is a sharp discrepancy between the major international normative standards and global goals in the Westphalia system

[23] See the debate "SDR's and Development: $10 Billion for Whom?" *Foreign Policy,* No. 8 (Fall 1972), pp. 102–128.

[24] See Wolfgang Friedmann, Louis Henkin, and Oliver Lissitzyn, eds., *Trans-*

and those found in contemporary diplomacy.[25] Virtually the whole of international morality centered around the preservation of sovereignty and the integrity of the state in the seventeenth century. To be sure, other values coexisted with that of the state, including the preservation of international order, the adherence to a set of Judeo-Christian standards of human behavior, the principles of civilized society, and natural law. But the nation-state was the major focus of international justice, since its viability was thought to be the basis of civil society. Now national and state values continue to play a role in international society, but that role is quite different from the one upon which international law was originally premised. No longer is the nation-state viewed as the major source of morality or a requisite to civil society. Rather, the nation-state is a major international value insofar as it represents a framework for the self-expression of national groupings.

Of equal importance is the set of other values which overlays that of the nation-state in contemporary international society. With the declining legitimacy of the use of force in international society, virtually all governments are now concerned with standards that will prevent its outbreak. In spite of the rebirth of strategic thought that occurred in the United States and the Soviet Union with the development of nuclear weapons, violence is not generally regarded as an acceptable instrument of state diplomacy. This is true whether war is viewed from a Clausewitzian perspective, as an instrument of power, or from an eschatological perspective, as a means of waging total war to create a world in which war would no longer occur.[26] Rather, war has come to be viewed as a perversion of other human values. It has simultaneously become a universal human value not simply to prevent nuclear war, but to reduce or prohibit the use of violence both among states and within them.

Additionally, in place of other of the Westphalian values, there has developed a new concern for global or regional economic management to cope with a world of increased interdependence. Economic manage-

---

national Law in a Changing Society: Essays in Honor of Philip C. Jessup (New York: Columbia University Press, 1972).

[25] For an overview see Cyril E. Black, "Challenges to an Evolving Legal Order," in Cyril E. Black and Richard A. Falk, eds., *The Future of the International Legal Order,* Vol. I (Princeton, N.J.: Princeton University Press, 1969), pp. 3–31.

[26] See Anatol Rapaport, "Editor's Introduction," in *Clausewitz on War* (Baltimore: Penguin, 1968), pp. 11–80.

ment and control now have three principal objectives. They are designed first of all to create a stable economic environment in which economic crises and depressions on a global scale can be prevented. Second, they are thought to be a requisite to global economic growth. Third, they are a sine qua non for facilitating the redistribution of global income. They are thus focused not only upon the problems of coping with global economic interdependence but also upon other values associated with the elimination of global poverty and famine and controlling global population growth according to the new international norms of unjust enrichment.

With the emergence of a truly global society for the first time in human history and the recognition of national and social interdependences, other international norms have also developed. These have to do with what might be termed the common fate of mankind. If international society is to survive in a form in which decent standards of life can be preserved for a maximum number of people, then actions must be taken to deal with activities both *within* and *among* states that affect a large number—if not all—of the members of international society. Thus there has been a concern in recent years with the conservation as well as with the allocation of the resources of the globe, under the recognition that these resources are limited and that their proper management is of interest to all. Similarly there has been a new concern with the management of the global commons.[27] From the seabeds to outer space, from the atmosphere to regions like Antarctica, there is a recognition that a global commons does exist and that no individual state has the right to contaminate it so that it will be of less use to others. This concern with the global commons is only partially reflected in international approaches to environmental protection as represented by such forums as the United Nations Conference on the Human Environment.[28] It is more fundamentally reflected in new attitudes toward state sovereignty and the recognition that limitations upon sovereign action are going to be required if international society is to be

[27]Miriam C. Camps, *The Management of Interdependence* (New York: Council on Foreign Relations, Council Papers on International Affairs, No. 4, 1974), pp. 81–89.

[28]See the special issue on "International Organizations and the Environmental Crisis" of *International Organization,* XXVI (Spring 1972).

preserved in a form in which a good many contemporary international values may be enhanced.[29]

Finally, as I have noted, there has developed a global concern for human rights, which is no less valid because of its rather different interpretation in liberal societies and in Communist societies. No group is regarded as having the right to commit genocide or to use uncivilized weapons like bacteriological warfare or gas. Increasingly the rights are recognized of individual humans to self-expression and self-satisfaction, to immigrate into societies where they would prefer to live (or at least to emigrate from those where they would prefer not to live), and even to disobey the state under certain circumstances where individual values conflict with state values. This last has been especially evident in Western societies where pacifist and antimilitarist sets of values have been recognized through the end of conscription and the increased use of the right to refuse to enter the armed forces by reason of conscientious objection.

In outlining these new international normative standards and values, I do not wish to leave the impression that they have all been recognized as universally valid or that they have been codified. Rather, my concern has been with the depiction of trends in international values. There are noteworthy constraints upon the achievement of all of them, including the problem which arises in any attempt to achieve all of them simultaneously, since some may contradict others and since global resources simply may be too limited for their simultaneous achievement. Other constraints exist insofar as the claims of governments to maintain nation-state values are still valid and clash with attempts to foster universal recognition of human rights or the development of a global commons. Moreover, any time an international conference may be held on any one of these new values, the opportunity arises for short-term governmental policies and international conflicts of interests to impede the articulation or achievement of a global interest. Thus in the United Nations Conference on the Human Environment in 1972 some less industrialized societies were more interested in accusing the industrialized societies of being the major polluters of the planet or of using the conference as a means of stifling development than they were

---

[29]Many of these themes are discussed forcefully in Harold and Margaret Sprout, *Toward a Politics of the Planet Earth* (New York: Van Nostrand Reinhold, 1971).

concerned with dealing with common global interest. And at any forum at which both China and the Soviet Union are represented, ideological disputes tend to constrain the development of a common approach.

International society, in short, is replete with a set of overlapping moral and ethical standards which conflict with one another and which can be the basis of conflict as much as a guide to the resolution of conflict. While in general the values which I have outlined have gained increased acceptability, it is important to note that the standards upon which they are based are by no means common. For most socieites, teleological standards exist, according to which the standard for evaluation is a function of the consequences of action. But even here major differences exist. Human rights tend to be valued in terms of hedonistic standards at the individual level, where the achievement of individual human goals is more important. Nationalistic values are also teleological, but may conflict with hedonistic values. Nationalistic values are largely a function of the degree to which national groups rather than individuals are enabled to achieve self-expression and autonomy. Human or global survival, which also depends upon teleological standards, can also, as we have seen, stand in stark contradiction to national self-development or a world in which all national groups achieve an autonomous governmental form. Overlapping these teleological standards is a set of deontological standards according to which actions are judged not according to their consequence, but rather according to standards that are otherwise perceived—either because they are directly perceptible to a set of individuals, as was thought to be the case in natural-law doctrine in the Middle Ages, or because they conform to a set of doctrinal principles like Marxism or those of Judeo-Christianity.

The growth of a globally acceptable set of standards of action has thus not been a result of the processes of modernization, even if a growing consensus seems to exist according to which a new set of values has emerged in the international system. As noteworthy as the changes in values since Westphalia has been the rate at which values have undergone flux and change. Change itself seems to impede the growth of a fully coherent set of values at the international level and creates problems of trade-off for all governments, when some highly valued goals can be achieved only at the expense of others and when different governments still have different heirarchies of values. Here as in our examination of other aspects of the effects of modernization on international society, we find that the growth in international values offers new hopes and new instabilities. The achievement of many of the new international values certainly could create a more decent standard of life around the world. But it is far less certain that these new goals can be achieved than it was that the more limited goals in the early modern state system could create an ambience of international stability. Paradoxically, then, the articulation of these new goals creates new tensions, as the goals themselves lie outside of human reach, and these new tensions are capable of erupting into forms of instability that might surpass those which existed when the Westphalia system was first created in the seventeenth century.

7

Paradoxes in Contemporary International Society

The effects of modernization on international society appear to be momentous whether one looks at the structures of interdependence in international society, the ways governments conduct foreign policy, or the multiple and often contradictory norms of statecraft. This is true for modernized societies, where interdependence has attained high levels, as well as relatively nonmodernized societies, where hopes for economic growth, prestige, and enhanced political autonomy are likely to be frustrated. The changes we have examined in this essay make it clear that international politics no longer conforms to the rhetoric and vocabulary of Westphalia, even though our capacity to describe and explain international events remains burdened by its outdated concepts. At the same time it could well be argued that the failure of the international system to become more centralized and the continued existence of the nation-state—indeed its multiplication in numbers—make it plausible to assert that the Westphalia system remains dominant. This is perhaps best seen in terms of the functions that national political organizations continue to perform.

Whether one looks at the security of the world as a whole, the growth in the global economy, the spread of ecological and environmental problems, the requirements of governments for resources and technology, or general social problems, national autonomy is everywhere on the decline and the need to rely on actions taken by others virtually universal. Yet the nation-state remains the major form of legitimate political organization capable of allocating resources within societies and of providing international order. It has been reaffirmed by the process of decolonization after World War II, by the growth of nationalism, and, certainly not least of all, by the emergence of nuclear deterrence. Here we find a basic paradox which seems to lie at the heart of contemporary international politics, where, at a time when the nation-state has appeared to be functionally obsolete, it has been reaffirmed by the same processes which would call for its transcendence. As Pierre Hassner has argued,

> To think about the fate of the nation-state today, even if one abstracts from its formation and disintegration, from the numerous cases of nations in search of a state and states devoid of a national basis, leads us immediately to a series of diverging trends and of contradictory conclusions: obviously in some respects the nation-state is flourishing and in others it is dying; it can no longer fulfill some of the most important traditional functions, yet it constantly assumes new ones which it alone seems able to fulfill. What is significant is that the relative importance of these features and the balance between them varies from case to case.[1]

This central paradox concerning the position of the nation-state is but one of a set of paradoxes that describe the central features of international society today. By way of summary and conclusion we will examine a further set of paradoxes in this chapter, which should facilitate a recapitulation of the major themes of this essay.

Another paradox stems from efforts to conduct foreign policy in a world that is undergoing persistent and transformatory change. This paradox is one of illusion and refers to the quixotic qualities of foreign policy in the contemporary international arena. Foreign policy today, whether it is conducted by a great or lesser power, in a highly industrialized or relatively non-industrialized society, tends to reflect an almost inevitable gap between perceptions of what the world is and the actual structures of international relationships. Reality changes so quickly that the reflexes for action typical of governments tend always to lag behind. This disjunction between reality and perceptions of it is, of course, endemic in policy; policy tends to be based upon past

[1] Pierre Hassner, "The Nation State in the Nuclear Age," *Survey*, LXVII (April 1968), p. 3.

experiences rather than guided by some notion of what the future may hold. As has often been noted, generals are constantly preparing for future wars based on lessons learned from the past, while in the meantime new technology has rendered obsolescent the strategic lessons of former military engagements. In a world in which change has become the norm, it is especially inevitable that this gap will widen.

It may well be the case that short of some breakthrough in theorizing about international politics which would enable statesmen to take actions on a calculus guided by a well-validated notion of their actual consequences, foreign policy will always be guided by lessons of the past. But unless statesmen are sensitive to the fact that these lessons were drawn from a past world which differs from the present, foreign policy actions may worsen rather than ameliorate immediate dilemmas that confront all governments. When a government takes action based upon analogies from the past which are no longer (if they ever were) relevant to the present or future, they may seriously jeopardize national security and prosperity. Indeed, in a world in which interdependences magnify the consequences of social action, policies based on past analogies are likely to have such deleterious consequences.

There may in fact be no escape from this dilemma in contemporary statecraft. All governments, even the most pragmatic, tend to invoke a set of principles to guide foreign policy. The generally accepted maxim that foreign policy ought to be prudential seems inevitably to lead to the searching for formulas that are derived from history or from notions of necessity associated with the doctrine of reason of state. Foremost among these, of course, is the principle of the balance of power, which was said to hold either in terms of a universal law of history or in terms of a primitive rationality model.[2] But the balance of power was a doctrine appropriate for an era in which international relations were both decentralized and territorially based. As Richard A. Falk has argued, "At the present stage of world history, as a result of increasing *interdependence* and of a rediscovery of resource *scarcity* and *limits to growth,* we are beginning to experience the early stages of a

<hr/>

[2] For discussions of the various meanings of balance of power, including the balance as policy, see Ernst B. Haas, "The Balance of Power: Prescription, Concept, or Propaganda," *World Politics,* V (1953), pp. 442–477; and Inis L. Claude, Jr., *Power and International Relations* (New York: Random House, 1962), pp. 11–39.

new transition process that is moving the world political system toward some form of non-territorial central guidance."[3] The requisites of order in contemporary and future international society are, in short, increasingly based on issues for which territoriality is irrelevant and where centralized governance is required. Prudential statecraft which relies on the permanence of the state either will not maximize domestic welfare or will be counterproductive.

Policies which are directed under some general set of principles or rules tend to be axiomatic, as Ernest R. May has argued. As noted in earlier chapters, one such policy that was influential throughout the post-World War II period in American diplomacy has been based on the "lessons of Munich," and consisted in the principle that "armed aggression anywhere was a threat to nations everywhere."[4] The adoption of this axiomatic policy guideline has been of momentous consequence to U.S. foreign policy. It has led each postwar administration to follow an essentially conservative policy and to seek in a variety of incidents of international violence the designs of aggressive forces abroad. Perhaps the most traumatic example of policy pursued under this guideline was American participation in the Indochinese war. Convinced that warfare in Vietnam was inspired either in Moscow or in Hanoi, successive American governments failed to analyze other causes of violence, including civil war and revolutionary warfare associated with the breakdown in older social norms in Vietnamese society as a consequence of decolonization and nation building. Anxious to contain what were perceived to be expansionist tendencies in communism or in either of the major Communist powers, these American governments were unable to come to grips with the underlying nature of social change in Vietnam and pursued a policy based on misperceptions that were of momentous consequence both within the United States and in Vietnam.

There are a number of general difficulties encountered whenever foreign policies are based on lessons of the past. Such policies tend to

---

[3] Richard A. Falk, *What's Wrong With Henry Kissinger's Foreign Policy* (Princeton, N.J.: Princeton University, Center of International Studies, Policy Memorandum No. 39, July 1974), p. 34. Emphasis is his.

[4] Ernest R. May, "The Nature of Foreign Policy: The Calculated versus the Axiomatic," *Daedalus*, XVI:4 (Fall 1962), p. 662. See also May's more extensive essay, *"Lessons" of the Past: The Use and Misuse of History in American Foreign Policy* (New York: Oxford University Press, 1973).

assume that the principles of action are efficacious and clear. Yet such principles are bound to be reflective of ideal-typical patterns of thought which need not necessarily be related to the actual patterns of action. In this sense, policies based on past lessons tend to suffer from confusions between what is and what ought to be. Moreover, no set of axiomatic principles can by itself suggest criteria for evaluating policy responses. This is because lessons of the past tend to be accepted without a great deal of critical attention. There is no guarantee that any situation confronted by a government will belong to the same universe of cases as the incident or event upon which the lesson is based. Ernest May himself argues that this problem may be rectified by bringing into government critically able historians who can guide the political leadership in the determination of appropriate historical precedents for current dilemmas. But May's prescription itself underestimates the degree to which lessons of the past must be based on validated theory if they are to be reliable. It also overstates the degree to which historians employed in government may compensate for the abuses of history. Political and social research into perceptions would indicate that "when expectations and desires clash, expectations seem to be more important,"[5] and that these expectations are almost inevitably based upon cognitive distortions that stem from the uncritical and almost automatic reflexes of decision makers, which filter new information through existing images and desires. Even if historians could help to rectify the abuse of historical lessons, however, they would be unable to deal with the major problem associated with the paradox of illusion: namely, that the real world has been changing so rapidly that policy is virtually never oriented to the world for which it is designed. And even when efforts to deal with policy issues approximate real world conditions, the lag between goal formation and implementation is such that current policy tends to be oriented toward last year's problems.

The paradox of illusion is itself based in part on the ideological orientation of foreign policy in the contemporary world. Just as reliance upon liberal ideology underlies many policy illusions in the United States, so too the claims of Marxist rhetoric lie behind illusions in Soviet diplomacy. Both of these contemporary ideologies were, as we saw earlier, designed to transcend a world of politics and to create

[5]Robert Jervis, "Hypotheses on Misperception," *World Politics,* XX (April 1968), p. 461.

a just order based on a harmony of interests among people. Their radical designs for the transcendence of political impediments were in both cases predicated upon the notion that political and economic phenomena could be separated from one another. For liberalism, the implementation of a laissez-faire economy both domestically and internationally would eliminate those special interests that perverted the true interests of the members of society. In Marxism the revolution of the proletariat would lead to the elimination of class conflict by eliminating social classes and would thereby usher in an era in which humanity's dream could be satisfied. In the case of the United States, acceptance of the liberal assumption has led to the goal of making economic policy a technical matter and to the discouragement of using economic policy—especially in foreign affairs—for political goals. In Soviet diplomacy, the rhetoric of revolution has tended to orient Soviet interests toward a policy that has isolated the Soviet Union from much of the industrialized world of the West.

The world is such that regardless of the imperatives of ideology, politics cannot be transcended. So long as individual people and collectivities exist with divergent and contradictory preferences and objectives and so long as resources remain relatively scarce, political conflicts will continue to exist. Different governments will attempt to bargain with one another in the achievement of their similar or divergent goals, and they will continue to compete for scarce resources. This is an inherent aspect of mankind which has never been and is not likely ever to be transcended in this world. The paradox is that in spite of this continuing impediment to the realization of ideological goals, ideologies continue to exist and in variant forms infuse governments with their legitimate authority.

The same dilemma confronts liberalism and Marxism in terms of their aim to separate economic from political goals. As we have seen in earlier chapters, the imperative of liberalism that governments pursue economic goals for their own sake and that they avoid the political manipulation of economic processes was institutionalized in the international economic arena after World War II. Cordell Hull's dream of placing economics and politics on their separate tracks was embodied in the Bretton Woods system. Trade and monetary institutions were established for the Western countries under the belief that neither should be manipulated for particularistic and narrow foreign policy purposes. With the exception of East-West economic issues, where boycotts remained in force, the liberal goal certainly seemed to have been approached. Yet just as the liberal nirvana was apparently being attained, it broke down through the force of an inner contradiction: economic and political affairs cannot really be separated from one another. In the contemporary world economic and political processes have become different facets or aspects of the same sort of phenomena. This repoliticization of economic affairs, especially in the international arena, came vividly to light in the international monetary crises of the later 1960s and early 1970s. Even if they had not erupted, however, it would have inevitably been realized that the two are inseparable. This is the case for a number of reasons.

First, the policy-making elites in the superpowers, having been socialized into a world of nuclear weaponry and strategy, have virtually accepted their political stalemate at the nuclear level. Crises once anticipated in the nuclear realm either have not emerged or, when they have erupted (as in Cuba in 1962), have seemed only to reinforce the stalemate. As a result, the nuclear powers have accepted the decline in the utility of the use of force and turned increasingly to economic diplomacy to achieve even their high policy objectives. The diplomacy of aid toward less developed countries, the priorities of intracamp trade and monetary issues, and the handling of investment and technology transfers between East and West all reflect this new use of economics for high politics.

Second, it might well be argued that the politicization of economic affairs would have occurred even in the absence of nuclear deterrence. Welfare-type policy objectives developed under the influence of domestic industrialization have now gained a nearly equal footing with the classical foreign policy goal of military security. As the energy crisis of recent years has also demonstrated, economic security seems to have replaced military security as the major foreign policy objective now pursued by industrialized societies. Welfare, defined in terms of increases in the material well-being of the citizens of industrialized and nonindustrialized societies alike, became attached to the phenomenal growth in world trade after World War II, and consequently attention to the politics of economic affairs became increasingly important to governments. Recently fearful of scarcities in a variety of raw materials, these same governments have begun to pursue policies designed at a minimum to maintain and not diminish the levels of material well-being they have already achieved.

This latter factor is, in itself, a third element in the politicization of economic affairs. Scarcities in some vital raw materials may result from (1) governmental manipulation of supplies, as in the case of OPEC oil in the 1970s, or (2) generalized growth in demand, which spurts suddenly ahead of available supplies, or (3) the natural decline in resources available under existing technology. This sort of politicization is inevitable in periods of scarcity, whatever its source. In the post-World War II period it has existed at the peak of periods of world economic boom, e.g., in the early 1950s during the Korean War and in the early 1970s. There is much debate concerning the permanence of scarcity whenever scarcities occur, but such debates usually are forgotten as new technolgoy becomes available to harness resources more efficiently or as new resource supplies are discovered. The world economic system has been capable of defusing political questions associated with access to foreign markets but has thus far not been able to handle questions of just global distribution of resources in short supply. In the latter type of situation, major obstacles exist which have prevented the implementation of short-run efforts to defuse politicized issues. When a few governments have de facto control over some vital resources, as in the case of oil, efforts to use the resources as an "economic weapon" seem inevitable. Thus we have found the oil weapon used for general Middle Eastern diplomacy after the OPEC cartel became institutionalized. An equally intractable situation is found when a government withholds resources or commodities from foreign markets in order to satisfy domestic demands first. Thus when the U.S. government withheld soybeans from its foreign customers in 1974, it injected bitterness among its foreign buyers.

Fourth, the need to create a highly integrated and centrally controlled international financial system is a direct result of structural transformations in national economies that took place in this century. Yet such a system has not been created, and as a result, crises have become inevitable in international economic affairs and have had a political cast. As Fred Hirsch has argued, "To a real degree, the pre-1914 [gold] standard avoided external financial crises at the expense of international financial and economic instability. Of the modern triangle of conflicting economic objectives, stable exchange rates stable prices—domestic growth at full employment, the pre-1914 system aimed only at the first."[6] Now, all three are goals of nearly equal prior-

---

[6]Fred Hirsch, *Money International: Economics and Politics of World Money* (Garden City, N.Y.: Doubleday, 1966), p. 56.

ity, as governments have expanded their responsibilities for maintaining minimum standards of welfare and for increasing domestic wealth. So long as the level of integration in the international monetary system remains low, and so long as the achievement of domestic growth at full employment remains a political necessity for all governments, internal financial and economic stability and growth will necessarily have destabilizing consequences of a highly politicized nature in diplomacy.

Fifth, the politicization of economic affairs has taken place in most governments because economic diplomacy became a substitute for military diplomacy, with most governments increasingly unable to expend money on the maintenance of armed forces and the development of useful weapons systems. If diplomacy is less effective in terms of the classical alliance politics of coalition building, given the asymmetries internal to NATO and Warsaw Pact as well as the nature of control over nuclear weapons systems, then diplomatic action in economic affairs will remain an attractive substitute for the use of force and capable of bearing significant political payoffs.

Finally, economic relations have become a focus of politics, especially but not only in times of economic crisis, because of another paradox of liberalism: the achievement of a world of high levels of interdependence. The basic aim of liberalism was the establishment of an interdependent network of relations that would knit together the diverse societies of the world, mainly through the agency of economic activity and especially of trade. Indeed, the major purpose of attempting to separate out economic from political activities was precisely to create the foundation of a global network of interdependence unhampered by political forces. The interdependence was itself also instrumental. It was viewed as the means by which a natural harmony of interests could emerge that would herald an era of permanent peace. Yet it is a paradox of liberalism that while the goal of interdependence has been achieved, the result has been instability rather than stability, and the emergence of new forms of political conflict rather than the transcendence of conflict. As societies have become more interdependent through the phenomenal and unprecedented growth in world trade since World War II, the objectives of various societies have apparently also become increasingly incompatible, and a whole set of new tensions has developed that seems to deny the ultimate achievement of the liberal goal of world harmony.

A final paradox applicable to both ideologies has to do with their primary emphasis on domestic priorities and their predictions that they each herald an era in which foreign policy can be eliminated and social welfare increased. Yet each superpower has increased greatly throughout most of this century its expenditures on weapons, weapons-related technology, and large-scale standing armies. If almost everywhere else in the world military expenditures have been declining in terms of their share of national wealth, in the two superpowers, the major spokesmen of a new age of diplomacy, the older diplomacy seems to have found one of its last refuges. To be sure, the exigencies of nuclear deterrence are in many ways responsible, as is the fact that both superpowers did not directly participate in the classical European balance of power. It is nonetheless ironic to find in them the impulse to transcend the older diplomacy coupled with the major impediments to the fulfillment of ideological objectives.

If these ideological paradoxes portray some of the major ironies of diplomacy in the twentieth century, perhaps the most trenchant paradoxes stem from rather unanticipated developments in nuclear technology. The paradoxes of deterrence and of strategy seem most vividly to depict some of the major structural characteristics of diplomacy in our era. I reviewed these paradoxes in an earlier chapter, but it would be useful to recapitulate them at this point. Hans J. Morgenthau has argued that there is a major

> contradiction between our modes of thought and action, belonging to an age that has passed, and the objective conditions of our existence [which] has engendered four paradoxes in our nuclear strategy: the commitment to the use of force, nuclear or otherwise, paralyzed by the fear of having to use it; the search for a nuclear strategy which would avoid the predictable consequences of nuclear war; the pursuit of a nuclear arms race joined with attempts to stop it; the pursuit of an alliance policy which the availability of nuclear weapons has rendered obsolete.[7]

The first of these paradoxes stems from the decrease in the utility of force as weapons have become increasingly powerful. Nuclear weapons transcend to such a degree former levels of destructive power that they also transcend the more finite and restrictive objectives to which force

---

[7]Hans J. Morgenthau, "The Four Paradoxes of Nuclear Strategy," *American Political Science Review*, LVIII:1 (March 1964), p. 23.

has generaly been applied. As a result, threats to use nuclear force are generally not credible, since they upset traditional ends-means calculations associated with negotiation and strategy.

The second paradox reflects the imposition of rationality upon interstate behavior in the nuclear age. Nuclear weapons were developed in what Raymond Aron has called "the century of total war."[8] The lessons of two world wars seemed to be that in a period of mass political participation and ideologically based foreign policies, wars would no longer be limited to well-depicted and finite objectives. Rather they would be fought in order to destroy one's adversaries' social and political bases and also to form the bases of a new international system. With nuclear weapons, wars to end all warfare could also no longer be credibly fought, since they would reap the destruction not simply of one's adversary but also of oneself and of the material basis of civilization. As a result, the most powerful instruments of force ushered in a new age of strategic thinking, which forced nuclear powers to formulate limited objectives and to contemplate precise conditions under which nuclear weapons might or might not be used. Nuclear weapons also were of consequence to the ideological basis of governmental legitimacy in the two superpowers. Since nuclear deterrence virtually stalemated a variety of changes in the international system, it also raised the question of whether the major goals of liberalism or of Marxism could ever be fully implemented. This has served to call into question the ultimate goals portrayed in the rhetoric of both the United States and the Soviet Union and thus also to undermine from within the legitimacy of both governments, but especially that of the Soviet Union.

The third nuclear paradox concerns the simultaneous pursuit of an arms race and of arms control. The arms race continues in part as an inexorable result of new developments in technology and the fear that if one does not implement new weapons systems, one's adversary will. It also continues as a result of the remnants of older thinking concerning warfare. In a decentralized and relatively anarchic milieu such as one finds in international society, suspicions concerning the motivations of other governments are omnipresent and the impulse to gain "superiority" on a permanent basis creates an additional motivation to

---

[8] Raymond Aron, *The Century of Total War* (Garden City, N.Y.: Doubleday, 1954).

expend resources on armaments. At the same time, however, the rationality imposed upon state behavior increases the marginal utility of negotiation and inspires governments to stabilize an adversary relationship in order to prevent nuclear warfare. Increased communication concerning intentions and capabilities together with efforts to dampen the costs of arms races is thus as much a part of the nuclear relationship as is competition in armaments. The two major superpowers today remain each other's most formidable potential enemies, but they are also each other's major partners in stabilizing and molding the system's major security relationship. As Raymond Aron has argued, however,

> The idea that the two great powers of an international system are brothers at the same time as being enemies should be accepted as banal rather than paradoxical. By definition each would reign alone if the other did not exist. And candidates for the same throne always have something in common. The units of an international system belong to a single zone of civilization. Inevitably they both claim, to some extent, the same principles and conduct a debate at the same time that they carry on a combat.[9]

The fourth of Morgenthau's nuclear paradoxes concerns the pursuit of an increasingly obsolescent policy of alliance. Both the Soviet Union and the United States have pursued a policy of alliance integration and have made utterances concerning collective decision making among a set of ideally equal and sovereign alliance partners. But the rhetoric of alliance—and indeed the necessity of alliance—for major nuclear partners and nonnuclear partners alike is contradicted by the requirements of control over the major system of deterrence. As Henry Kissinger has argued,

> Nuclear war requires tight command of all weapons, which is to some degree inconsistent with a coalition of sovereign states. Moreover, the enormous risks of nuclear warfare affect the credibility of traditional pledges of mutual assistance. In the past, alliances held together because it was believed that the *immediate* risk of conflict was less than the *ultimate* danger of facing a preponderant enemy alone. But when nuclear war hazards the lives of tens of

[9] Raymond Aron, *Peace and War: A Theory of International Relations,* Translated by Richard Howard and Annette Baker Fox (Garden City, N.Y: Doubleday, 1966), p. 536.

millions, some aliens may consider the outbreak of a war the worst contingency and, in times of crisis, act accordingly.[10]

It may well be debatable that "all of these paradoxes result from the contrast between traditional attitudes and the possibility of nuclear war and from the fruitless attempts to reconcile the two," as Morgenthau argued.[11] Certainly, some of these paradoxes result in part from the lag between perceptions of reality that are rooted in an older system of diplomatic relations and the newer requirements of strategy and policy brought about by industrial and technological change. But some of these paradoxical circumstances would exist whether or not there was a problem of perception or the lingering of outmoded ways of thinking. This is most obviously the case with regard to the paradox of nuclear and economic interdependence, summarized in detail in Chapter 5: that the greater the amount of available force beyond the nuclear threshhold, or the greater the amount of economic capacity, the less useful is national potential for the achievement of positive goals. This paradox and a set of others stemming from interdependence have been noted by Thomas L. Hughes as some of the major causes of political malaise in governance today. Hughes notes the following general paradoxes that are pervasive within government:

> the paradox that most nations consider us [the United States] to be the most powerful state on earth, but do not feel obliged to do our bidding—the audio-visual paradox that others see us but they do not hear;
> the paradox that our political influence has effectively lessened at the same time that the primacy of our power is being reconfirmed;
> the paradox that the revolution of rising expectations is now being accompanied by the counterrevolution of falling prospects engendered by the technological gap and the population explosion;
> the paradoxes of interdependence and the new nationalism—the independence of the dependent, the limits of the U.N. peacekeeping, the recalcitrance of cultures;
> the paradox of the escalating volume of communications and their declining meaning and significance;

[10] Henry A. Kissinger, *The Troubled Partnership: A Re-appraisal of the Atlantic Alliance* (New York: McGraw-Hill, 1965), pp. 11–12. Emphasis is his.

[11] Morgenthau, "The Four Paradoxes of Nuclear Strategy," p. 23.

the paradox that where governments are for us, their people are against us; and that where governments are against us, the people may still be on our side.[12]

A final paradox that I will note and that is characteristic of contemporary international society may be called the paradox of revolution. Revolution seems to be one of the political bywords of international society in the twentieth century. Communist societies proclaim revolution in an increasingly obsolescent and contradictory bourgeois order in the West. The governments of relatively nonmodernized societies seek to revolutionize international society in order to make it more just, by which they apparently mean more equitable in terms of the distribution of global wealth and income as well as more egalitarian in terms of the distribution of world power (thus enabling them to throw off the yoke of hegemony and to achieve a degree of political and economic autonomy). Still others seek in revolutionary change the dissolution of the nation-state as the major unit of global society and the forging of transnational linkages which would provide both elements of central control, or guidance, and the means of achieving the elimination of poverty, the redistribution of wealth, and the freedom of individuals to express themselves without the hindrance and obstruction of national or state oppression. According to most of these arguments a major obstacle to change, and especially to revolutionary change, is found in the West, where industrialized societies are thought to be the major upholders of a conservative status quo. The stake of these societies in orderly transition and in maintaining the structure of international society, which will enable them to continue their relatively uninterrupted postwar prosperity, has forced them to adopt relatively conservative postures oriented toward international stability if not toward a refusal to accept international change.

Yet if we review the major sources of instability and of transformation in the international system, from the growth of multinational corporations to the flow of private transactions on an interpersonal basis, it would not be misleading to argue that they stem largely from the dynamism of these very conservative political systems. In short, revolution in the international system stems from dynamic changes related to industrialization and technological change. The roots of

---

[12]Thomas L. Hughes, "On the Causes of Our Discontents," *Foreign Affairs,* Vol. 47, No. 4 (July 1969), pp. 657–658.

revolution and of transformation in the international system are thus in the industrialized societies of the world, and in particular in the United States. These industrialized societies are the really revolutionary ones; and a general overview of international change in this century would support this claim. It is in these industrialized societies that we find social relationships undergoing persistent transformation in this century. It is also there that we find what are perhaps the most significant efforts to grapple with new ways to understand the fundamental meaning of the set of transformations that I have been discussing throughout this essay.

It could also be argued, moreover, that changes within the industrialized societies of the world have been highly destabilizing for societies elsewhere. Together with the impulse toward stability and the status quo which can be found in the foreign policies pursued by governments in the industrialized world has come social and technological change that has upset traditional patterns elsewhere. This seems to be the case whether one looks at the new norms that emerge from these societies concerning the mobility of people, the role of women in society, the effects of education on social and technological change, or even, paradoxically, the role of resources as an element of national capability. The value of resource-rich countries containing oil, bauxite, manganese, or other natural resources that have become requisites of continued industrial growth is in large measure due to changes within the industrialized world. Had this not been the case, the relatively recent change in the importance of Iran or Saudi Arabia would certainly not have occurred. Moreover, just as these natural resources have increased in value as a result of industrialization in the northern hemisphere, so too technological change which will make industrialized societies less dependent on these particular natural resources will in the future likely depreciate the power recently achieved by resource-rich societies to blackmail them.

The paradoxes of international society that we have reviewed briefly are major characteristics of contemporary international society, whether they stem from a lag between outmoded concepts and new problems, as Morgenthau would claim, or are fundamental to these changes themselves, as in the case of the effects of nuclear weapons and of transnational economic forces on the adequacy of the nation-state to fulfill its traditional functions. They all point out what I earlier argued: that contemporary international society is a transitional one, in the two senses of the term "transitional." It is transitional in the sense that it is undergoing continuous and persistent change; it is also transitional insofar as it represents a more general movement from the Westphalia system of relationships to something new and unprecedented.

Although this is a transitional system, it is by no means clear what its next stage will be. Change in international society is now generally accepted, but what would constitute a just international order is subject to dispute. There are what appear to be inexorable tendencies toward centralization in the mechanisms of international control. Certainly a global society that has achieved increasing levels of interdependence would require centralized mechanisms of control if it is to be subject to rationalized direction. But even here two major obstacles to prediction emerge in any effort to discern the movement of "historical forces" in the contemporary system.

On the one hand, the very fact that modernization has brought with it new forms of instability implies that the breakdown of the system may well be as likely as its evolution to a new form of centralized control that would transcend the nation-state system, just as the Roman Empire collapsed into a highly decentralized milieu. The outbreak of nuclear warfare, the spread of endemic famine, the breakdown of the societies of the industrialized world under the impetus of a revolt against centralized authority, or the inability to accept the exigencies of interdependence would lead to greater decentralization and lower levels of wealth, and nothing can rule out the occurrence of any of these situations.

On the other hand, if one accepts as inevitable the growth of centralized forms of international control, it is by no means clear what the organizational nature of the controls will be. Neither traditional forms of control nor new ones seem to be ruled out. Incipient breakdown, for example, could well lead to the imposition of some order from above, including forms of organizational control that resemble historical empires. Nor is some form of world or regional federalism implausible which would preserve the institutions of the nation-state while permitting them to coordinate their policies toward transnational and common problems, in spite of the depreciation of this normative vision in current political and academic debates. The once fashionable functionalist viewpoints, common to the Saint-Simonians of the nineteenth century and the followers of David Mitrany in this century, which predict the growth of international infrastructure that transcends traditional national boundaries and which are organized around particular issue areas, are also plausible. In spite of the rejection of these frameworks by recent proponents of various alternative models of world order, neither these forms of global organization nor those propounded by such schemes as the World Order Models Project are likely to be implemented in the future.[13]

It is, indeed, characteristic of contemporary international politics as well as of the study of international behavior that the Westphalia system or paradigm upon which international norms and behavior have been based for three hundred years no longer works in the way that was formerly accepted. It is also clear that the breakdown in that system is largely attributable to the characteristics and consequences of the revolution of modernization in human affairs. While the current international system contains obvious roots of instability which will impel it to some radical form of evolution over the course of the next few decades, no one now has the knowledge that would facilitate prediction of the forms that this evolution will take. Nor does the theoretical knowledge now exist that would ease the task of statecraft to mold a desirable system of world order, and that would also take cognizance of the detrimental and unwanted consequences of any particular form of action. Modernization has, indeed, served to transform international affairs. But the nature of the transformation and the system which will take root in the future remain enigmas that scholars and statesmen alike will puzzle over for a long time to come.

---

[13] See Saul H. Mendlovitz, ed., *On the Creation of a Just World Order: Preferred Worlds for the 1990's* (New York: Free Press, 1975).

Index

A

Actual patterns, 49
Aid for development, 95
Alliance policy, 189–190
Allison, G. T., 101, 102n
Allocation of resources, 97–100
Ambrose, S. E., 125n
Antimilitarism, 79
Appeasement, 152
Arms control, 169, 188–189
Aron, R., xiii, 15, 75n, 78n, 79n, 158, 188, 189n
Arrow, K. J., 121n
Asymmetrical relations, 132–149
Autonomy, 3, 10, 31, 45, 74, 97, 104–106, 108–113, 118, 121

B

Balance of power, 28, 38–42, 45–46, 52, 74, 180
Barraclough, G., 13
Barthélemy, J., 55n
Bergmann, G., 49n

Bergsten, C. F., 144n, 148n
Black, C. E., 4n, 7n, 9, 15n, 173n
Bodin, J., 32n, 33
Boulenger, J., 26n
Brandt, W., 130
Bretton Woods system, 183
Brezhnev, L., 82
Brierly, J. L., 33n, 155n, 156n, 158n
Brodie, B., 5n, 90n
Brown, L., 144n
Brown, S., 3n, 130n
Brzezinski, Z., 11, 46n
Bull, H., 169n
Bureaucratic politics, 101–102

C

Cabinet diplomacy, 101
Calleo, D. P., 116n
Camps, M., 144n, 174n
Capitalism, 60
Carr, E. H., 31, 42n
Chace, J., 46n
Change, 15, 179, 182